THE JOURNAL OF
CORPORATE CITIZENSHIP

Issue 58 June 2015

Theme Issue: **Large Systems Change: An Emerging Field of Transformation and Transitions**

Guest Editors:

Steve Waddell, NetworkingAction, USA
Sandra Waddock, Boston College, USA
Sarah Cornell, Stockholm University, Sweden
Domenico Dentoni, Wageningen University, The Netherlands
Milla McLachlan, Stellenbosch University, South Africa
Greta Meszoely, Center for Business Complexity and Global Leadership, USA

ISBN: 978-1-78353-436-4

T0361081

print ISSN 1470-5001   *online* ISSN 2051-4700

Greenleaf
PUBLISHING

THE JOURNAL OF CORPORATE CITIZENSHIP

General Editor Professor Malcolm McIntosh

Regional Editor *North America*: Professor Sandra Waddock, Boston College, Carroll School of Management, USA

Publisher Rebecca Macklin, Greenleaf Publishing, UK   *Publisher* Anna Comerford, Greenleaf Publishing, UK

Production Editor Sadie Gornall-Jones, Greenleaf Publishing, UK

EDITORIAL BOARD

CORRESPONDENCE

The Journal of Corporate Citizenship encourages response from its readers to any of the issues raised in the journal. All correspondence is welcomed and should be sent to the General Editor c/o Greenleaf Publishing, Aizlewood's Mill, Nursery St, Sheffield S3 8GG, UK; jcc@greenleaf-publishing.com.

All content should be submitted via **online submission**. For more information see the journal homepage at www.greenleaf-publishing.com/jcc.

Books to be considered for review should be marked for the attention of the Book Review Editor c/o Greenleaf Publishing, Aizlewood's Mill, Nursery St, Sheffield S3 8GG, UK; jcc@greenleaf-publishing.com.

• All articles published in *The Journal of Corporate Citizenship* are assessed by an external panel of business professionals, consultants and academics.

• *The Journal of Corporate Citizenship* is indexed with and included in: **Cabells, EBSCO, ProQuest**, the **Association of Business Schools Academic Journal Guide, ABDC** and **Journalseek.net**. It is monitored by 'Political Science and Government Abstracts' and 'Sociological Abstracts'.

SUBSCRIPTION RATES

The Journal of Corporate Citizenship is a quarterly journal, appearing in March, June, September and December of each year. Cheques should be made payable to Greenleaf Publishing and sent to the address below.

Annual online subscription
Individuals: £80.00/€112.50/US$150.00
Organizations: £540.00/€650.00/US$850.00

Annual print and online subscription
Individuals: £90.00/€120.00/US$160.00
Organizations: £550.00/€672.50/US$860.00

Annual print subscription
Individuals: £80.00/€112.50/US$150.00
Organizations: £180.00/€240.00/US$320.00

The Journal of Corporate Citizenship
Greenleaf Publishing Ltd, Aizlewood Business Centre, Aizlewood's Mill, Nursery Street, Sheffield S3 8GG, UK
Tel: +44 (0)114 282 3475   Fax: +44 (0)114 282 3476   Email: jcc@greenleaf-publishing.com.
Or order from our website: www.greenleaf-publishing.com/jcc.

ADVERTISING

FSC
www.fsc.org
MIX
Paper from responsible sources
FSC® C013604

Printed in the UK on environmentally friendly, acid-free paper from managed forests by CPI Group (UK) Ltd, Croydon

DOI: [10.9774/GLEAF.4700.2015.ju.00002]

Editorial

Issue 58 *June 2015*

Malcolm McIntosh

General Editor, Journal of Corporate Citizenship

"I have stopped finding fault with creation and have learned to accept it. We have some power in us that knows its own ends. It is that which drives us on to what we must finally become... This is the true meaning of transformation. This is the real metamorphosis."
— David Malouf, *An Imaginary Life* (1978)

Change comes anyway, even if we like to think we can nudge it along. Large systems change is always emergent. Working within and as part of, not separate from, the inevitability of systems change the key features from a longitudinal perspective of change are concerned with evolution, adaptation and the ability of humans to learn.

In the history of the *Journal of Corporate Citizenship* this special issue is one of the most important because it does what *JCC* has always said it is aiming to do: it makes links, joins dots, and it takes a systems approach. I was part of this group's work and the energy and commitment of these people with diverse backgrounds and from all over the world, led by Steve Waddell in Boston, has been wonderful.

Handover

JCC is now fifteen years young and growing with every issue. In this time we have been grateful to a number of distinguished editors. In between each I have run the journal for two-year periods. The next incumbent from 2016–2018 is to be an old contributor to the journal who will be well known to the progressive community that reads *JCC*. David Murphy is now based at the Institute for Leadership and Sustainability (IFLAS) at the University of Cumbria in the English Lake District—Peter Rabbit and wandering daffodil country for many of you. You may remember some of his signature books such as *In the Company of Partners,* written with Jem Bendell in 1997. With David's experience working across the range of issues that are involved in the field of corporate citizenship and in academia, business and various UN agencies I know that the journal will buzz over the next few years. I am delighted and grateful that David has agreed to take up this role and we can look forward to a host of interesting issues.

Readers in Corporate Citizenship

In May and September 2015 we will be publishing a unique experiment. We chose some forty papers from the last fifteen years of the *Journal of Corporate Citizenship* and then asked the authors to write brief updates based on the questions: What did you get wrong? What would you write now? What has changed? What did you get right?

Almost everyone we contacted agreed to this project (and it may lead to a whole new way of conducting research: reflective thinking). Many said that this was the first time in some lengthy careers that they had carried out this exercise. So, insight has occurred on their and our part—and

there is also some humour. The first volume, *Business, Capitalism and Corporate Citizenship* will be out in June and the second, *Globalization and Corporate Citizenship: The Alternative Gaze*, in September. The aim is to provide essential readers in corporate citizenship for people old and new to the subject area—and to provide interesting insights into reflective thinking.

Best wishes,

Malcolm

Professor Malcolm McIntosh, BEd MA DipTEFL PhD FRSA
Founding Editor, *Journal of Corporate Citizenship* (1999–2015)

Thinking The Twenty-First Century: Ideas for the New Political Economy by Malcolm McIntosh was published by Greenleaf Publishing in 2015.

DOI: [10.9774/GLEAF.4700.2015.ju.00003]

Large Systems Change

An Emerging Field of Transformation and Transitions[*]

Issue 58 *June 2015*

Steve Waddell
NetworkingAction, USA

Sandra Waddock
Boston College, USA

Sarah Cornell
Stockholm University, Sweden

Domenico Dentoni
Wageningen University, The Netherlands

Milla McLachlan
Stellenbosch University, South Africa

Greta Meszoely
Center for Business Complexity and Global Leadership, USA

In this paper we put forward a theory of large systems change (LSC), where large systems are defined as having breadth (i.e. engaging large numbers of people, institutions, and geographies) and depth (i.e. changing the complex relationships among elements of power and structural relationships simultaneously). We focus primarily on transformational LSC, recognising that such systems are complex adaptive systems in which change is continuous and emergent, but directions can be supported. A typology of change actions with two core dimensions—'confrontation' and 'collaboration' on the horizontal axis and 'generative' and 'ungenerative' change on the vertical—suggests that change strategies can be classified into four broad archetypes: forcing change, supporting change, paternalistic change, or co-creating change. LSC theory development focuses on three core questions: what is the foundation of LSC concepts and methods, what needs to change, and how does LSC occur? We conclude by reviewing how papers in the Special Issue fit into these questions.

---

* This Special Issue is the product of the GOLDEN Ecosystems Labs.

The need for large systems change

OURS IS AN HISTORICALLY UNPRECEDENTED era of human, technological and natural systems transformational change. Their increasing intensely interconnected and interdependent qualities are creating both tremendous challenges and opportunities. Traditional tools and methodologies are inadequate for understanding and addressing today's pressing complex issues, advances in science, technology, and computing power and capacity. New understanding, tools and methodologies demonstrate the potential for greatly enhancing action to steward emergence of a flourishing future.

This 'new' is coming from several directions. The study of complex adaptive systems (CAS) is not new, but the foundational principles of complexity science now are being broadly used to reveal new ways of processing empirical data at increasing rates and scale. Poverty, economic crises, conflict, corruption, natural disasters, food insecurity, and epidemics are not new, but our limited success at addressing them is provoking significant innovations. Our recent world financial crisis, terrorism, natural disasters, climate change, health epidemics, and other pressing challenges suggest now is a good time to take stock with the aim of developing an integrating new framework for understanding and acting.

The scale of these 'wicked' problems is unprecedented (Churchman, 1967; Rittel & Webber, 1973). They require action across social, political, technical, economic and environmental domains. While some might believe that business-as-usual will resolve or at least contain some of these problems, others—and we are among them—believe that rather massive systemic change we refer to as large systems change (LSC) is central to addressing them and creating a thriving future. We take the position that although LSC may be experienced as positive or negative, purposive LSC is both desirable and possible: while recognising many controversies about what desirable futures look like, we believe that the widespread public identification of challenges such as those mentioned above suggests a broad sense of desired direction. Though some might associate this direction with 'sustainability', we prefer the term 'flourishing futures' (Ehrenfeld, 2005). However the desired future is characterised, we believe that new paradigms for action are required to effect LSC.

We believe that advancing our purposive action capacity can be greatly enhanced by thinking of LSC as a field. To support the emergence and identity of LSC as a field, we build on the knowledge and experience of the editors and authors of this Special Issue to propose a holistic framework for conceptualising large systems, how they are changed, and who can influence these changes.

The need for a theory of large systems change

We all know how hard change can be. Just think of how hard it is to make changes at the individual level, altering yourself or your habits in any significant way. For example, losing weight, changing eating habits, or breaking a bad habit like biting your nails can be challenging. It takes time, energy, commitment, resolve, and a willingness to do things differently. Perhaps most of all, it takes a belief that the ability to envision and realise change is both needed and possible.

Imagine the scaling of that individual level change to a whole organisation, and you arrive at a vast organisational development literature. This literature consistently demonstrates how intractable established patterns of behaviour are and how difficult it is to make change when the multiple interacting systems of an individual organisation are involved (e.g. Buchanan, 2011; Weick & Quinn, 1999; Beer & Walton, 1987). Systems change of the sort needed to deal with issues as big as poverty, climate change, sustainability, or inequity is obviously even more complex as it involves numerous different types of organisations, numerous policies and norms, numerous sets of beliefs and practices, and a complexity of other interacting elements including numerous change initiatives.

The term 'theory of change' has been popularised as a way to guide action and develop strategies to address change challenges (e.g. Klein, 2014). An operationally oriented definition of the term characterises a theory of change as a coherent set of ideas about how change processes develop, can be managed, and evolve throughout the change process. Making the assumptions about relationships between actions and outcomes explicit is central to a 'theory of change' approach. Used in a broader sense, theories of change are associated with geological eras (ICS, 2013), paradigm shifts (Kuhn, 1962), tipping points (Gladwell, 2002), revolution (Malia, 2008),

evolution (Darwin & Bynum, 2009; Gersick, 1991; Malia, 2008) and social movements (Della Porta et al., 2009; McAdam et al., 1996; Tilly, 2005). We see value in developing a theory of LSC that builds on this diverse foundation, while recognising that others might offer complementary theories.

Definitions

By large systems change (LSC), we mean change with two characteristics. One we refer to as breadth: change that engages a very large number of individuals, organisations and geographies across a wide range of systems. Indeed, given the interconnectedness of humanity, we see the need to think about global systems change engaging local-to-global (glocal) dimensions. The second characteristic we refer to as depth: LSC is not simply adding more of what exists or making rearrangements within existing power structures and relationships, but rather changes the complex relationships among these elements at multiple levels simultaneously. LSC means fundamental revisioning of what is possible and ways of sense-making that lead to previously unimaginable outcomes.

There are three main types of change: incremental, reform, and transformation.

▶ **Incremental change** focuses on reinforcing or reducing systems, while allowing it to gradually shift in a more or less continuous way, such as when a retail company expands by opening stores in new locations, and when wind turbine technology is replicated as an emerging innovation

▶ **Reform** happens when there is a shift of power or dominance among linked system components, again within a given system, such as when laws move regulation from government to business (self-regulation)

▶ **Transformational change** occurs when there is fundamental systemic change resulting from new ways of understanding what is possible and acting on them, such as South Africa's movement from pre- to post-apartheid, or the reconfiguration of physical and ecological processes in the natural environment resulting from human-driven climate change (Waddell, 2011)

Although incremental change (more of the same) and reform (changing rules) may lead to LSC and are part of its dissemination, transformation provides our over-arching change framework.

The 'systems', we refer to in LSC are complex adaptive systems (CAS), which describes both human systems and natural ecosystems. These are dynamic systems, with multiple interacting and interrelated parts. Change is continuous and emergent at all levels of the system and its paths are unpredictable. In these complex systems, there is really no such thing as stasis (or what in economics is called equilibrium) because of the dynamic and interactive nature of the system. However, there are periods of greater and lesser turbulence; the former is associated with 'revolution' and the latter with stability. The tenets of complexity theory (e.g. Prigogine & Stengers, 1984; Nicolis & Prigogine, 1989; Stacey, 1997; Kauffman, 1995) help us to consider some of the characteristics of LSC with which any change agent—or, better, change systems agent(s)—must contend. Complex

challenges are without obvious beginning or end points, interdependent, and lack agreed solutions.

In LSC the change agents themselves are embedded within the system that is to be changed; that is, they are part of, rather than separate from, the relevant complex problem (Waddell *et al.*, forthcoming). Hence bringing in an outside consultant (or group) to foster the change is not feasible; LSC happens from within the relevant system, even when change is deliberate and intended.

A typology of change actions

Can we propose a framework that provides a basis for comprehensively mapping the enormous range of change actions? This will greatly facilitate development of strategies that draw from understanding about the range of choices, implications behind strategic choices, when one choice might be better than another, and sequencing of choices. It will help deepen conversations between advocates of different strategies to hopeful evolve more effective action.

Figure 1 is one possible such framing typology. It draws from several sources, most notably from a common call to more explicitly include power issues in change processes, Scharmer's Theory U (Scharmer, 2009), Isaac's work on dialogue (Isaacs, 1999), and Kahane's book *Power and Love* (Kahane, 2010). Kahane explains his book as reflection on Martin Luther King, Jr's statement that 'power without love is reckless and abusive and love without power is sentimental and anemic'. Love is action based in connection and relationship with others, and power is the driver of people and entities to realise and grow their own interests.

Both power and love can be either generative or degenerative. The former is a creative force and the latter is experienced by many as destructive, although Kahane conceives it as "decay". 'Generative' relates to 'generative dialogue' (Isaacs, 1999; Scharmer, 2009), which is associated with empathy and concern for the whole to produce action and transformation with a drive towards highest aspirations. 'Degenerative' is seen as its opposite: action and transformation produced by narrow concerns and shutting down, with a focus on personal power and rewards. The degenerative side of 'love' approaches is that they can smother and oppress individuals and groups. Power, Kahane describes, is experienced at the extreme as:

> An individual or group that exercises power to achieve its desires and ambitions, but pays no attention to the desires or ambitions of others, will end up steamrolling the others. This degenerative power shows up disturbingly as greed or arrogance and catastrophically as rapaciousness or violence (Kahane, 2013).

Figure 1 A typology of change actions

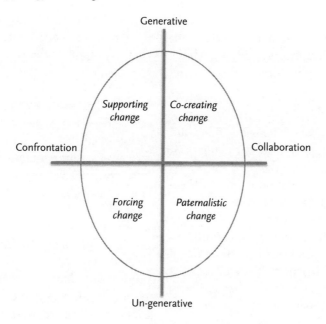

These ideas led us to develop Figure 1, with a vertical axis of generative to un-generative. The horizontal axis is confrontation to collaboration, to get at the underlying dynamics of extremes of how power and love can be experienced. 'Positive' or 'negative' evaluations will be different for different actors depending on their goals and power concerns. They are described archetypally as follows:

▶ **Supporting change** occurs when power-holders use their resources to realise change, convinced it is for the broader good. However, they use unilateral action as is associated with 'lifting up' and *noblesse oblige*. Doing this can be the objective of government legislation, philanthropy, and community organising, although these actions can figure in other types of change as well. In the US, this strategy fits with the 'what's good for business is good for America' (or vice versa) mindset

▶ **Forcing change** occurs when a stakeholder group(s) acts to grow power in relation to others, often through confrontational tactics and strategies, perceiving that resistance to change in their desired direction (or moves to change the status quo) make this necessary. As a strategy, forcing change is often associated with such things as capital and labour strikes, government legal sanctions, armed insurrections, and occupations

▶ **Paternalistic change** actions are associated with power being used in ways that maintain the status quo. Consultation by power holders with the marginalised is a common activity in this when the power holders do so without opening up and responding to questions about power dynamics. They take actions in the name of others and with identifiable benefit, but with the paired objective of maintaining or reinforcing the status quo. Much lobbying of government fits in this strategy, as well as top-down government consultative approaches to regulation and being 'in control' of responses to challenges

▶ **Co-creating change** represents collaborative strategies to develop LSC such as with multi-stakeholder mass movements; processes to develop statements of principles for business and activities to implement them; public–private partnerships; and education and outreach programmes. A common underlying strategy is to bring together diverse stakeholders with early adopter insiders as a way to transform issues of joint concern

This typology aims to get at underlying dynamics of change that are behind a popular name for a strategy that can confuse these dynamics. For example, 'codes' can be a strategy applied in any of these four types of change strategies (see Table 1) depending on the intent and composition of the strategies' participants. This is a demonstration of the value of such a typology.

Much of the most impactful change effort arises from a drive for power and self-serving goals. However, most people working on complex change issues focus on generative collaboration strategies we would place in the co-creating change quadrant. Such change strategies are reflected in approaches like Theory U (Scharmer, 2009), appreciative inquiry (Cooperrider & Whitney, 2005), most social innovation labs (Hassan, 2014; Westley *et al.*, 2012) and work in the transformation management tradition. The assumption is that by getting people together to create shared visions of the future, collaborative efforts at change will emerge. People will open their hearts, minds, policies, and institutions to realise a larger emerging collective need and potential. They will change, relate better to each other, learn to collaborate around issues important to all, and thus begin the change process each in their own ways, moving the change initiatives so that change effort participants' 'power' in the traditional sense is simply another 'resource' and factor available for the change effort rather than one that determines outcomes. This is the highest integration of power and love.

The suggestion we make here is that the co-creating change strategy should be placed in the context of other types of change actions to both understand and develop powerful change approaches. The forcing and supporting change actions are almost always important for transformational change advocates as well; paternalistic change strategies can actually hinder transformation. They must be approached skilfully. The interplay between these strategies can be seen in big historic shifts. For example, referring to Martin Luther King, Jr again

and the 1960s struggle of American blacks for their voting rights: King and his contemporary Malcolm X were coming from a minority position which each organised into a power block. Co-production was not proving a successful strategy. With a generative base, King emphasised a non-violent supporting change response, and he was supported by some with power such as white religious groups in his efforts. Malcolm X took a more violent and revolutionary position with a forcing change strategy. They were always facing dangers of being 'bought off' with incremental change when they were working for transformational change. The latter finally began with empowering government legislation which then led to many co-creating change activities to 'give life' to the legislation. Table 1 lists a few examples illustrating the use of all four archetypal strategies in several major efforts to accomplish LSC.

Table 1 Examples of strategic-tactical change actions

Name	Supporting change	Forcing change	Co-creating change	Paternalistic change
Components	Generative confrontation	Un-generative confrontation	Generative collaboration	Un-generative collaboration
Dynamic	Empowering Raising up	Confronting Violence (physical, verbal, etc.)	Collaborating Co-evolving	Suppressing Maintaining status quo
	Willingness to share power	Willingness to ignore harm	Willingness of everyone to change	Willingness of disempowered for marginal improvement
Popular terms	*Noblesse oblige* Upliftment	Forcing	Co-production	Paternalism Obstructionism

Continued

Name	Supporting change	Forcing change	Co-creating change	Paternalistic change
Archetypal strategies	Community organizing Philanthropy Human rights legislation Opening up legal cases Education	State force Strikes (capital, labor) Demonstrations	Multi-stakeholder fora Public engagement Social labs	Reinforcing legal cases Financial pay-offs Consultation
Example 1: Black American voting rights	King and non-violent action	Police violence	Inter-racial faith coalitions	Eliminating poll taxes (while maintaining other barriers to voting)
Example 2: Codes of conduct	Rainforest Alliance (NGO controlled)	Opposing gvt standards	Forest Stewardship Council (multi-stakeholder)	Sustainable Forestry Initiative (industry controlled)

Key questions for LSC

We approach development of large systems theory of change through three questions. In this section we investigate them with the goal of suggesting some boundaries for the field of LSC in terms of knowledge and action. In the following section the questions are used to review the contributions of the papers in this Special Issue.

Question 1: What is the foundation of LSC concepts and methods?

The field of LSC has evolved from a strong foundation of a vast body of research and action from disparate disciplines, genres, and sectors. Each of these approaches provides an important lens with which to view social, political, economic, technological, and physical systems and their corresponding issues. While each has made significant contributions, many of today's problems intersect numerous fields and disciplines requiring an approach that reflects this reality. LSC emerged out of an appreciation of the depth and scale of the complex issues we face and need for multidisciplinary action and insights. It builds on these trans-disciplinary change strategies to effect unimagined possibilities.

Figure 2 aims to provide an initial, illustrative sketch of the relevant knowledge domains that support and remain critical to the development of theoretical and practical knowledge about LSC. Rather than proposing a comprehensive depiction, this descriptive figure is simply illustrative of the wide range of approaches that contribute to and support our understanding of complex adaptive systems and LSC. This figure was developed in consultation with numerous experts working on LSC challenges and issues.

The figure depicts a range of traditions that emerged to address complex change challenges, i.e. those problems for which LSC is needed.

The figure proposes a range of traditions and workstreams that have been deployed by the authors or others in LSC. The figure illustrates several[1] major streams of work or traditions in which LSC is being addressed in some ways, albeit not considered as LSC in quite the holistic way we conceive of it. The streams are represented by the 'arms' coming out of the centre of the figure: governance, learning and evaluation, cultural change, business in society, environment, complexity science, spiritual/psychological, peace and conflict resolution, and socio-economic development. The next level depicts various streams of work that derive from the major traditions. There are, of course, many ways the traditions could be represented and parsed; the main point of the figure is to emphasise that there is a rich, but fragmented, LSC knowledge base that provides the foundation for active multi-, inter-, and trans-disciplinary action to effect sustainable and structural change resulting in unimagined possibilities.

Figure 2 Mapping of large systems change approaches currently in use
Source: Waddell (2014)

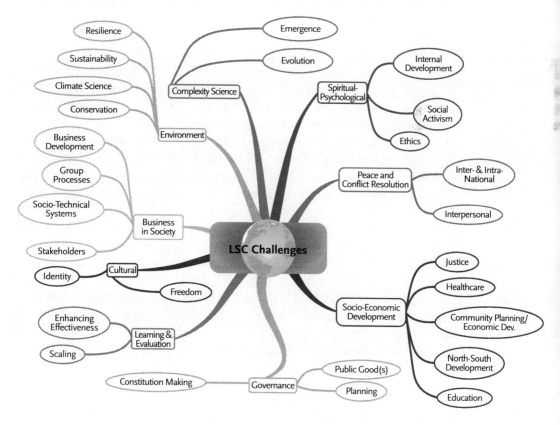

1 Of course there are many ways to divide up these traditions, and Gersick (1991) identified six. This figure is simply illustrative.

Complexity science provides for understanding the structure and dynamics of interconnected and co-evolving systems and the context to develop strategies for change at multiple levels within the complex network. A false causality is not assumed—instead one works with the system's dispositions (Snowden, this issue). By expanding the framework of reference for action in each field to incorporate their understanding of CAS, practitioners are likely more inclined to appreciate the broader impact of their actions on actions of others. This will likely result in more effective and comprehensive strategy to effect sustainable change.

As Figure 2 suggests, the **business in society** (BiS) and **socio-economic development** (SED) traditions have developed particularly rich sets of approaches ranging from normative ideas about what is the right way to operate businesses, to corporate (social) responsibility approaches to stakeholder relationships, and numerous approaches to social and economic development with a wide range of methodologies (see Tandon this issue) that could stimulate systems change. Historically, the BiS tradition is focused on questions about the responsibilities of the corporation as the core stakeholder, with emphases in the literature on socio-technical systems, stakeholders, group processes, and business development. The SED tradition focuses on broader societal stakeholder concerns, including justice, healthcare, education, economic and community development, and North–South development as major substreams of work. Many of the SED literature and approaches, however, are technocratic, linear, and not systemic.

Over time these BiS and stakeholder perspectives have increasingly intersected as the perspective of corporations has broadened and the SED traditions have recognised the importance of the contribution of corporations to addressing their concerns. Both traditions have historically shared what might be described as an institutional-structural focus in their efforts to conceive change. Individuals' roles have often been framed, particularly in the BiS tradition, around the concept of 'leadership', typically in a hierarchical heroic model. Group processes, as 'teams' in BiS and 'communities' in SED, have spurred a rich tradition that has grown into the shared concept of 'multi-stakeholder convenings', and the socio-technical systems tradition has major roots in the vast literature on planned change and organisational development.

Approaches that start with reflexivity, learning and enhancing individual and group awareness have developed within what is here termed the **spiritual-psychological** (SP) tradition. Individuals' inner states of awareness and insight (as opposed to heroic leadership) are emphasised as being central strategies to bringing change about (see Scharmer & Yukelson and Betit, this issue). These approaches are focused on raising awareness in groups of individuals so they can work together collaboratively on change. Historically, SP approaches have produced different types of intentional communities or communities of practice around ways of living or particular practices.

Both institutional and individual interactions are foci of the **peace and conflict resolution** traditions, which have received perhaps the most significant and concentrated attention as 'complex change challenges' because of their obvious life-and-death issues (see

Fitzduff, this issue). Again dialogue surfaces as a key method (e.g. Lederach, 2005; Saunders, 2003; Susskind et al., 1999). Conflicts such as those with the Apartheid regime in South Africa, the persistent Israel–Arab crisis, Northern Ireland's troubles, internecine guerrilla activity in Colombia, and violence in Central America, as examples, have produced an impressive array of methods relevant to complex change from interpersonal strategies to post-conflict reconciliation commissions. The potential for multi-disciplinary and cross-sector knowledge transfer to effect change in this and so many other areas is likely to have significant impact on the interacting systems and influence the CAS.

As the **governance** traditions suggest, the need for effective government/governance has produced in the political science field and beyond notable processes for national conversations around constitutional arrangements and strategies to advance agendas such as regional planning. Thinking of top-down government being 'in control' is giving way to concepts of collaborative and deliberative governance involving all organisational sectors, especially some initiatives at the global level (e.g. Biermann et al., 2012; Glasbergen and Schouten, this issue). Collaborative governance (Zadek & Radovich, 2006) approaches contrast with standard hierarchical government and the coercive power implied by mandate; 'experimentalist governance' (Sabel & Zeitlin, 2012) integrates flexible, recursive processes more democratically than traditional top-down approaches. At an even broader cultural level, other methodologies have developed to support shifts in popular insights

and values such as the wide range of media and specific methods, such as Theatre of the Oppressed. Political, cultural, and socio-economic complex change strategies have produced a range of methods associated with community organising, collaboration and purposeful conflict generation such as with strikes (Victoria & Albert Museum, 2014).

The most impressive growth in the traditions over the first decades of the 21st century is associated with the **environmental** tradition, with the concepts of 'resilience' (e.g. the Resilience Alliance) and 'transitions' (e.g. the Sustainability Transitions Research Network). Concerns about degradation of the natural environment originally brought biologists and natural scientists into the transformation fray, with a gradual realisation that addressing their concerns must categorically address socio-economic and political concerns not purely ecological ones. This tradition has led to holistic stakeholder strategies around natural resource issues ranging from fisheries to, increasingly, climate change.

Question 2: What needs to change?

A key question that change agents, who themselves are part of the system undergoing change, must ask is: What needs to change? Wicked problems are embedded in the complex system with different stakeholder perspectives on what the problem is, why it exists, and what should be done about it. Individuals, including 'experts', focus on particular aspects of the problem, reflecting the proverbial problem of blind people touching different parts of the elephant and imagining different animals. Can a comprehensive framework be developed?

Figure 3 provides one way of conceiving what needs to change in LSC as a series of related spheres or circles that are integrally linked to each other but represent different important facets of the change process. Each circle, called an LSC sphere, can be viewed as a set of systems that change over time. At the broadest level is the natural environment, which underpins and influences everything in the system. The next sphere consists of memes (Dawkins, 2006); that is, shared beliefs, values, and other cultural artefacts providing an idea- and information-based framework that aligns and creates identities within different subsystems. The socio-political structures are familiar informal (e.g. family) and formal (e.g. corporations, governments, NGOs) organisations and institutions that constitute societies, in which individuals, with their own beliefs and values, act on social and natural systems.

In fact, most theories of change focus on one of these perspectives, leaving the other layers weakly articulated, if at all. Following Wilber's developmental notions, the broader systems encompass and constrain in some ways the narrow systems in nested fashion (Wilber, 2000). LSC must deal with all of them holistically and appreciate their dynamic impact within a CAS to realise change. Collectively these perspectives represent the system of interest to us: a 'large system' in the sense of having multiple components of very different kinds, with many interactions playing out at various scales of time and space. The figure is loosely organised as a cascade of spheres, where changes in the outer systems play an interactive role in emerging the options for change in the inner systems (shown by the curved arrows). As you move towards the inner systems, change tends to be more specific and definable and takes place in shorter timeframes. In the outer systems, change is more likely to be more diffuse, broad ranging, and slower. Importantly, these interactions are dynamic and create feedback, thus the mindset and actions of an individual may affect technology or memes which influence the individual to potentially create or adopt a disruptive technology.

Figure 3 should not be interpreted as being a rigid hierarchy of systems, or even of approaches to understanding systems. Rather it is a dynamic and co-evolutionary model of a complex reality. There are many ways to define or theorise systems, in terms of deciding on their boundaries and the kinds of relationships between components that are deemed to matter. There are also other ways to theorise this framework for large systems change that go beyond our practice-oriented pragmatic approach.

Figure 3 What changes in large systems change?

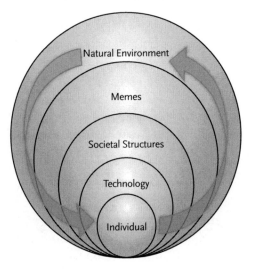

Natural environment

At the broadest level, change happens within the context of nature including human beings' relationship to and treatment of nature. Earth's weather, natural resources, flora and fauna are limiting and enabling factors in large systems change. At transformation's grandest scale, change is counted in 'geological ages'. Transitions from one age to another are defined by the International Commission on Stratigraphy based on geological evidence of global events, such as changes in Earth's orbit around the sun, planetary impact events, massive volcanic eruptions, and mass extinctions (ICS, 2013). The field of **Earth system science** seeks to understand these events, which are associated with shifts in the physical composition of land, oceans and the atmosphere, and the responses to these changes by living organisms. This large systems change concept has come into more common parlance with the proposition that we are now in the Anthropocene—an era arguably beginning with the Industrial Revolution, when human activity began to have a dramatically increasing level of influence on natural systems (Crutzen, 2006; Steffen *et al.*, 2007). As the predictive power of the field of Earth systems science reaches its limits in the light of human-caused changes, new ways of conceptualising linked social-ecological systems are being explored. The idea of **panarchy** (Holling *et al.*, 2002) and other forms of global governance, is important in this context, as it addresses evolving hierarchical systems that link biological, ecological, and various human elements across temporal and spatial scales.

Memes: shared values, beliefs, and cultural artefacts

The rise of the Anthropocene can be seen as the product of change in the other systems shown in Figure 3 and an example of the second circle: changes in memes, or values, beliefs, and cultural artefacts. Memes, following Dawkins (2006), are ideas with 'spreading power'. Memes, broadly defined to encompass the intangible ideas that shape how people in different settings view the world, are the core underpinnings of societies: for example, shaping ideologies of various sorts and the perspectives, such as about change itself, that come from those ideologies (see Waddock, 2015). The meme circle of large systems change is where work on scientific paradigm shifts (Kuhn, 1962), for example, is placed, as a way to describe such important changes in the perspectives of large swaths of people, such as pre- and post-Copernican, and pre- and post-Cartesian ways of understanding the world. Shifts in scientific paradigms involve change in definitions of *what* an analysis should observe, the kinds of questions that should be asked, how the questioning should be developed, and how the results should be interpreted.

This layer is also evident with belief systems of various labels, including a number of 'ies', such as monarchies, democracies, and theocracies; and political 'isms', such as imperialism, socialism, communism and capitalism; and religious ones such as polytheism, monotheism, atheism, and more particular denominations within them. Within each of these broad categories is a memeplex (complex set of memes) (Blackmore, 2000) or a range of ways of understanding the world, where the core dimensions to be understood are the functioning of the physical environment, the relationships among different cultures or groups of people, and the relationship between humanity and its environment. Memes are the cultural artefacts that constitute the belief sets on which societies are based, much as genes make up the DNA that determines the constitution of every living being and have an effect on the world beyond themselves.

Of course, such labels are given to the dominant organising imperative or dominant meme: any particular example contains various degrees of many of these memes, and conflicting memes can exist within a given culture such as a conservative versus a progressive perspective (see Lakoff, 2014). But moving from one social-political belief system to another is another form of large systems change, which can be associated with revolutions (e.g. the French and American revolutions in the 18th century, pre- to post-Apartheid South Africa, and the 'coloured' revolutions[2] at the turn of this millennium), as it can involve a basic realignment of power structures and ways of life.

Societal structures

The third circle is the formal and informal social, political and economic institutions and organizations in societies, including global structures. Here we find governance

mechanisms of various sorts, ranging from the family to organisational to national to global level. It includes the many networks that are part of our daily lives, and the ways that they are increasingly influenced by virtual communications. Many change initiatives focus explicitly on institutions within this circle, recognising that how our institutions are shaped, function, and perform, and the policies and practices that they generate, shape how people experience life within a given system. Many of the socio-economic development, governance, cultural, complexity, and business-in-society traditions noted in Figure 2 focus on this circle.

Technology

Large systems change is also associated with changes in physical technologies. Eras, for example, are named for core technologies, such as the bronze and iron prehistoric ages, and more recently the industrial era and the information age. Dominant (and sometimes emerging) technologies can have significant influences on the social-political and economic systems. For example, in some developing parts of the world, today's widespread access to cell phones in developing countries has shifted power in agricultural production to farmers, who now have ready access to market information, and away from middle-men whose power previously depended on their privileged access to that information. In the electricity industry power is shifting from utilities to 'prosumers': those who both consume and produce energy. Innovation theories address this layer of large system change, and learning and

---

2 e.g. the 'Rose Revolution' in Georgia in 2012, the 'Orange Revolution' in Ukraine in 2004, and the 'Tulip Revolution' that took place in Kyrgyzstan in 2005.

evaluation and complexity traditions of change often work with this circle.

Individual

Many current change traditions approach LSC as a challenge of individual awareness and capacities. Collaborative strategies in the spiritual-psychological, cultural, socio-economic development, and governance traditions often start with individual awareness and attempt to create collaborative strategies. They are, at one level, working with the memes or 'large systems' set of assumptions and beliefs held by individuals and attempting to change them through interaction, awareness-raising, and cooperation. In one important strand of theory, this layer of individual agency is interpreted in the traditional frame of leadership. In another strand, there is recognition that LSC is connected to an individual's sense-making about relationships between people and the natural environment, often associated with a sort of spiritual awareness (Weick *et al.*, 2005; Werkman, 2010).

Question 3: How does LSC occur?

From observing LSC, are there any general propositions to make about how it occurs? Certainly work to date suggests some. We would like to build on this to advance the understanding for taking purposive action. If we assume that LSC must occur in the context of a CAS, questions abound: for example, what are sets of interventions that can support movement in a desired direction? What types of processes and engagement of various stakeholders are needed to bring about LSC? Where does effective LSC begin and how?

How are others brought into an initial change effort so that they feel part of the change process? Here we provide some observations to contribute to propositions about the LSC process.

Observation 1: LSC seeds can be in any LSC sphere

There is a strong tendency of those working on LSC issues to assert a key beginning point. For example, Scharmer clearly advocates the beginning is with individual awareness. However, as noted in the discussion of the LSC spheres, we observe that different analysts and activists focus on different spheres with success; complexity or wicked problems thinking would indicate that it is next to impossible to determine an actual beginning point for any change.

Observation 2: LSC potential is constant with facilitating factors

Such factors include:

▶ **Opening up.** New insights and getting in touch with unrecognised limiting assumptions can lead to new ways of acting, new rules and new beliefs

▶ **Closing down.** Restricting actions, reducing knowledge and limiting resources can dramatically change the inertia in a system

▶ **Addressing contradictions.** Both Marx and Kuhn emphasised tensions between espoused practice, structures and beliefs, and those observed and arising

▶ **Hitting boundaries.** Existing systems contain enormous inertial pressures to adapt to change, rather than accept transformation. However, incremental adaptation changes can force LSC, as Malthus (2013), Diamond (2005) and analysts of the fall of the Roman Empire have theorised

Observation 3: LSC involves change throughout all of the LSC spheres

While recognising that the temporal horizons are of great variation, LSC appears to work across the spheres of Figure 3. LSC in one sphere produces changes in another. Without accommodation in other spheres, the change will remain a marginalised idiosyncrasy rather than a LSC.

Observation 4: LSC is evolutionary and revolutionary

Reviewing six knowledge domains, Gersick investigated theories of revolutionary change and found a commonality that warrants repeating: 'Systems evolve through the alternation of periods of equilibrium, in which persistent underlying structures permit only incremental change, and periods of revolution, in which these underlying structures are fundamentally altered' (Gersick, 1991: 13).

A core question for those interested in realising peaceful purposive change is how the period experienced as equilibrium can work with factors within the various spheres and develop important experimental-transformational responses in the desired direction.

Observation 5: LSC development occurs in stages

Development stages move from inducement to prototyping to dissemination where true LSC is experienced.

LSC can be rapid or slow; however, it must go through a period of testing to develop new DNA in the LSC spheres with protected spaces (skunk works) for transformation.

Observation 6: Transformation moments are always emerging, but unpredictable

These observations reflect the constant presence of inducing factors and an axiom of complexity science. The real question for LSC is: What do purposive change efforts look like, since emergence is a constant?' Chaos theory suggests that specific predictions cannot be made—but general patterns of change can be sensed. For purposive change efforts, the first may be debilitating, the second inspiring. The development stages will not lead to transformation at pre-determined points. This observation is reflected in both the lack of prediction of the Arab Spring, and its collapse. Tipping points are an attractive idea, but not only are they hard (impossible?) to define, but there are many examples of false positive declarations of transformation. The message for purposive change makers is that efforts must be persistent and include a healthy dose of reflection and humility!

Observation 7: Change initiatives can be undertaken from wherever a change agent sits within the system

Deliberate or purposive LSC requires acts of leadership or what Raelin (Raelin, 2003) calls 'leaderfulness' from anywhere in the system. But the outcomes of any given act of leaderfulness cannot be fully determined in advance given the complexity of the systems.

Observation 8: The role of memes is central in shaping behaviours, beliefs, practices, norms, and systems

Memes are the core ideas on which ideologies, ideas, and belief systems of all sorts are built, but far too little is understood about how they influence behaviours or the change process positively or negatively.

Observation 9: LSC itself has stakeholders who must work collaboratively for purposive transformation

Individuals who perceive a need for LSC usually strive to identify their role, or roles, in these processes of change. How is each of us contributing to LSC? In particular, using the language of organisation studies in LSC (Lawrence and Lorsch, 1967), how do roles in LSC differ from each other in achieving LSC? How do we integrate and catalyse our efforts towards complementary rather than conflicting outcomes? This question on how roles are defined and integrated is crucial: individuals, organisations and institutions seeking solutions to problems at large scale risk exacerbating problems when they collide rather than coordinate with the roles of others targeting the same end point.

We can think of differentiating and integrating roles for LSC along at least two different dimensions. The first dimension may lead to differentiation of our roles based on the initial resources that each individual brings to play: including financial, physical, intellectual and social resources. These resources could be thought of as an initial endowment that each of us receives. This may lead individuals to work in one specific sphere of change, or across different spheres

(Figure 3). Moreover, within or across different spheres, individuals may take one or more of these different roles that were identified through a World Bank-funded exploration (Waddell, 2014):

▶ **Complex issue owners** are those who are taking leadership to respond to complex change challenges. They are usually organisations, classically governments and inter-governmental organisations and their agencies and foundations; NGOs; occasionally businesses; and, in more mature issue fields, multi-stakeholder entities

▶ **Funders** provide financial support to address complex challenges. They include high net-worth individuals, foundations, research funders, and government agencies

▶ **Practitioners** are those who are supporting action through organising and application of methodologies to a particular complex challenge. Classically these are consultants or employees of a problem owner

▶ **Trainers and educators** are those who are building capacity of practitioners, complex issue owners and issue stakeholders to address their challenge

▶ **Action and conventional researchers** are those who engage in analysis of data of an issue to produce knowledge and methods to inform action. Action researchers, particularly important in LSC given the collaborative emergent learning imperative, work with stakeholders in an issue to support real-time co-production of knowledge and action. Conventional social scientists work in an issue expert mode with particular emphasis on controlled, quantitative and historic experiences

▶ **Change issue stakeholders** are those who are influenced by the topic of change

Papers in this Special Issue

As editors of this Special Issue, we are pleased to share four invited Turning Point pieces from leading academic practitioners and seven full article contributions that highlight the challenges and complexity of LSC. In this section, we briefly review those contributions.

The papers represent a great diversity in LSC forums: individual competencies, peace-making, government services, a private company, national issue arenas, global networks, glocal arenas, and fields of research and practice. They bring in a global complexity of actors, their roles and change approaches. They embrace the forms of complexity Kunkel notes as: dynamic, generative, social and institutional, and value. Of course, within the space constraints of a Special Issue, the variety of perspectives cannot be comprehensive. We note, for example, that a Western/Northern tradition is clearly dominant.

The contributions are notable for their action-based qualities. This is certainly not a simple coincidence. Loorbach *et al.* explain the purposive nature of transition management (TM) in ways most, if not all, contributors would agree as a basis of their

own work: '...to better understand the failure of policy and markets in delivering a fundamental reorientation of the development pathway of modern societies and an opportunity to explore new ways to achieve breakthroughs'. The contributors to this Special Issue share a commitment to active engagement in the betterment of the world through LSC, and eschew traditional positions about neutral objectiveness.

This is not to say that they do not value traditions of rigour and discipline, however. They are committed to reflective, analytic action, and practice using and advancing development of research tools in a most serious of ways applied to the world's most serious of issues. There is, however, a clear value basis for the future that they are supporting that goes beyond sustainability to realising participatory, flourishing futures. This is a hallmark foundation of what we mean when we refer to the field of large systems change.

Contribution to typology of change

In terms of the typology of change presented earlier, these papers are less diverse. They tend to focus on the co-creating generative-love quadrant with multi-stakeholder processes, while verging into the consultative, status-quo led quadrant of leading change with generative power. Holton, in her review of social movements, enters more categorically into forcing change degenerative power approaches: 'leaders', she says referring to Heifetz, 'can "ripen" issues through conflict'. Nevertheless a lesson she presents is that 'Leading from a social movements perspective requires courage to leave behind familiar power-vested responses...'.

Glasbergen and Schouten explore the interaction between the typology quadrants with three governance forms for large systems change: market-driven, state-driven, and public–private institutions. Market-driven and state-driven transformations would represent approaches for generative power leading change; yet the risk is that, without pressure from stakeholders in the system, these could turn into forms of degenerative forcing and paternalistic change. Public–private institutions have the potential to become forms for co-creating change, although the risk is that, without a continuous attempt to find coherence with other institutions towards large systems change, they could turn into forms of forcing change (yet masking by co-producing change). Thus, Glasbergen and Schouten conclude by mentioning that, most likely, only a coherent combination of these three typologies of governance would lead to co-producing change.

When Moore looks at issues of scaling, she emphasises a complex change dictum reflected in the Glasbergen and Schouten conclusion: develop multiple paths and experiment. Loorbach et al. describe this within the TM tradition as innovation, co-evolution and empowering front-runners, with an acceptance of a high likelihood that success will not follow immediately or directly or at all.

Contribution to defining the range of LSC knowledge and methods

The contributions to this Special Issue reflect the assertion that LSC as an emerging field of study draws from many sources. Some contributions themselves cite this quality, perhaps most notably Loorbach et al.'s categorical reference to complexity science, governance, sustainability science and social innovation as foundations for TM. Others are associated in particular with peacebuilding, business in society, social movements, systems analysis, and leadership.

Within this range one knowledge tradition stands out. Complexity science and complex adaptive systems references are perhaps most commonly referenced. Its most formal articulation is evidenced in the analysis by Moallemi et al. of Iran's fuel cell development, drawing heavily from systems analysis. Also, Snowden's Turning Point contribution highlights a complexity science approach.

With Holton's paper, we become immersed in social movements theory lessons for LSC. Loorbach et al. specifically look at TM from a governance perspective; Glasbergen and Schouten integrate this with a business-in-society tradition. Leadership is highlighted by Kuenkel. The Carris companies' transition to a fully employee-owned company (see Betit, this issue), has origins within a combination of the business-in-society, governance, and socio-technical systems approaches to change.

Three particular points arise from the contributions in terms of methodologies. One is that the LSC field is not simply about action within one tradition; it is very much inter- and transdisciplinary. The second point is that it is both quantitative and qualitative, but the former tradition such as reflected in the Moallemi paper appears poorly integrated, based on the editors' experience and the admittedly narrow representation of the papers. There are enormous potential contributions to LSC from, for example, emerging big data approaches. Snowden's SenseMaker methodology, not a feature in this issue, is a good example of this direction as well as work by MIT's Center for Collective Intelligence. This quantitative weakness is also reflected in the lack of clear ways impact measurement is addressed (recognising all the difficulties of time spans, counterfactuals, attribution, and problems in defining goals).

Of course there are traditions that have important roles in LSC that are at best weakly represented here. For example: the TM paper makes reference to social learning, and Holton approaches social movements not in a traditional rational-analytic problem-solving mode, but rather as an exercise in emergent creative thinking and flexible adaptation. However, there is also a gap with 'learning' as a tradition contributing to LSC. Emergent learning is stressed as key to LSC, but we lack contributions that reflect this.

Contribution to understanding what needs to change

One theme in the papers is the importance of thinking and acting in terms of the 'whole' rather than focusing simply on a part. This wholeness comes in many forms. At its most basic it involves broadening of awareness: Scharmer and Yukelson state 'that behaviours within systems cannot be transformed unless we also transform (deepen) the quality of *awareness* that people in these systems apply to their actions, both

individually and collectively'. This means understanding relationships between organisations, goals, and issues; from individual to societal; and in Glasbergen-Schouten's and Fitzduff's cases understanding the glocal, and Betit's in understanding change at the company level.

This awareness and how to develop it is, of course, a focus on the individual change sphere as the point of departure that is also reflected in Kuenkel's work. The papers actually present a nice array of approaches in terms of the earlier model of the spheres of change. TM focuses on technology; Betit with the Carris example focuses on an organisation while emphasising employee awareness; Tandon with mining in India looks at government as an institution; with social movements Holton looks at memes in the context of specific institutions—a combination also apparent in the Glasbergen-Schouten look at global networks, Moallemi with Iran's fuel cells and Moore's analysis of scaling processes. Fitzduff with peacebuilding provides the greatest focus on memes as a basis for LSC action.

The importance of interacting activity among the spheres of change is reflected in the contributions, although of course not with that language:

▶ TM is explicit about the levels of change (niche to landscape) and acknowledges diverse co-evolving processes (economy, technology, ecology) through cycles of destabilisation and reconfiguration

▶ Fitzduff writes that 'a systemic, integrated, and holistic approach to developing sustainably peaceful societies is more effective than the more usual one dimensional approach'

▶ Glasbergen and Schouten discuss the role of societal structures as starting point for change. Through institutions (e.g. global standards), multiple actors interact to develop shared beliefs and shape the natural environment. At the same time, institutions have the power of facilitating the development and outreach of technology with effects on all individuals involved in LSC

▶ Betit explores the 20-year transition of the Carris Companies from a traditional firm to a wholly employee-owned and managed ESOP (employee stock ownership plan) company, focusing explicitly on the role of leadership, on changing employee and management awareness, and on the numerous small changes that resulted in the overall system change of the company, as well as the ripple effects that the Carris transition had beyond the firm itself

▶ To realise scaling, Moore points to the importance of multi-level action

Contribution to explaining how purposive LSC occurs

There is a common rejection of traditional management practice as incompatible with, and even counter-productive to, LSC. The predefined outcome focus of management drives out the innovation that is at the heart of LSC: if the transformation can be so clearly articulated, it must have already been experienced and therefore not a transformation at all. Moreover, the solutions 'roll out' approach of traditional management is at fundamental odds with the sustainability emphasis on the need for contextual (environmental, social, political, cultural, economic) sensitivity. Snowden points to three core assumptions behind traditional decision making that are simply wrong for LSC challenges: order, rational choice and intentional capability.

This does not mean the papers are without operationalisable LSC pathways guidance as the very term 'transition management' suggests. Almost all the contributors propose some sort of stage development process. So it is not surprising that the contributors are strong advocates of an incremental evolutionary perspective. At first blush, this may seem at odds with the authors' desire to greatly speed up LSC in response to pressing issues such as climate change. However, deeper in the contributors' message is that they say 'evolution', but aim for an intensity that many would experience as 'revolution'.

In this LSC process the role of visioning the future remains a contentious issue. The most strident proponents of defining futures and then building them are associated with the Sante Fe Institute modelling tradition. This is reflected in the Moallemi et al. article on Iranian fuel cells. Rather than defining futures, Snowden emphasises the importance for LSC efforts of thinking in terms of propensities and dispositions. In one of her lessons in this issue, Holton cites Snowden (this issue): 'Sustainability and resilience are more likely to be achieved if we enable change rather than trying to determine what that change would be in advance'.

However, creating visions of the future—exploring potential future realities—is emphasised among many in this issue as a key ingredient in developing forward energy. Kuenkel refers to taking responsibility to consciously shape reality towards a sustainable future; Scharmer and Yukelson refer to activating the power of intention; Betit holds the vision of the Carris company owner as instrumental in realising transformation.

There might be agreement that the real issue is about how visioning and modelling are used: in a deterministic, goal setting way or in a way to generate conversations and action in a certain direction. Certainly the Moallemi *et al.* article offers an opportunity to greatly deepen understanding of dynamics and roles within a system that seems valuable input for action.

There is an emphasis on change through prototyping and experiments as core to the development process. This is where the 'incremental' change comes in. 'Successes' collectively lead to a new dominant meme, to mix TM and our thinking. However, the world is replete with prototypes and experiments, and a core question is how to move beyond them. How to scale transformation is a core question for TM. Betit uses the image of enlarging ripples from a pebble tossed into a pool as the impact of transformation of the company. Happily, scaling is the focus of Moore's paper as she distinguishes between three strategies: scaling up and out focuses on the legal environment; scaling out on numbers impacted; scaling deep is a hearts and minds (and memes) experience. In her description of development of the field of peacebuilding, Fitzduff very much reflects this scaling activity.

The geographic scales of Glasbergen and Schouten range from local to global. Although institutions play a prominent role in LSC, they recognise that institutions alone cannot achieve their transformative potential without a different source of change linking them. To find coherence across institutions, a broader sphere of change is needed and, at the same time, individuals within the system have the power to influence the transformative power of institutions.

The question of what are the key roles in LSC produces diverse answers from the contributions, as reflected in their diverse spheres of change foci. Individual leadership is particularly important in the view of several. Moore explores the roles necessary to realise LSC and identifies shielding, nurturing, and empowering. Similar to shielding, TM emphasises the importance of protecting front runners. The common concern is both for protecting emerging transformations from the incumbent memes and actors and for growing clarity about what possible alternatives are most powerful.

Conclusion

LSC is a field of study and action that is characterised by its focus on transformational pathways towards a participative, flourishing future through inter- and trans-disciplinary approaches that value engagement with practitioners and those aspiring for such futures. Its emergence holds great promise for addressing critical issues. Advancing its development requires aggressiveness to cross the many disciplinary, institutional and other boundaries and build the necessary scale of effort; however, humbleness is also required to recognise that although we have substantial knowledge and methodologies for approaching LSC, we are still at early stages of their development.

To apply the question of how to scale to the field of LSC, the contributors and editors reflect it happening at the three levels identified by Moore (this issue): broadening by increasing the numbers of people and organisations identified with it; going up and out with a more receptive environment arising with failures of traditional management approaches; and deepening of knowledge and methods for supporting LSC. We hope that you, the reader, will find this Special Issue makes a valuable contribution in this direction.

References

Beer, M., & Walton, A. E. (1987). Organization change and development. *Annual review of psychology, 38*(1), 339-367.

Biermann, F., Abbott, K., Andresen, S., Bäckstrand, K., Bernstein, S., Betsill, M. M., ... Zondervan, R. (2012). Navigating the anthropocene: Improving earth system governance. *Science, 335*(6074), 1306-1307. doi: 10.1126/science.1217255.

Blackmore, S. (2000). *The meme machine.* Oxford, UK: Oxford University Press

Buchanan, D. A. (2011). Reflections: good practice, not rocket science–understanding failures to change after extreme events. *Journal of Change Management, 11*(3), 273-288.

Burnes, B. (2009). Reflections: Ethics and organizational change–Time for a return to Lewinian values. *Journal of Change Management, 9*(4), 359-381.

By, R. T., Burnes, B., & Oswick, C. (2012). Change management: Leadership, values and ethics. *Journal of Change Management, 12*, 1–5.

Churchman, C. West. (1967). Guest editorial: Wicked problems. *Management Science, 14*(4), B141-B142.

Cooperrider, David L., & Whitney, Diana. (2005). *Appreciative inquiry: A positive revolution in change.* San Francisco, CA, USA: Berrett-Koehler.

Cornell S. and Parker J. Critical realist interdisciplinarity: a research agenda to support action on global warming. In: Bhaskar R. et al. (eds) *Interdisciplinarity and Climate Change.* Routledge. pp. 25-34.

Crutzen, Paul J. (2006). The 'anthropocene' *Earth system science in the anthropocene* (pp. 13-18): Springer.

Darwin, Charles, & Bynum, William F. (2009). *The origin of species by means of natural selection: Or, the preservation of favored races in the struggle for life*: AL Burt.

Dawkins R. (1976, 3rd edition 2006) *The Selfish Gene*, Oxford University Press.

Della Porta, Donatella, Kriesi, Hanspeter, & Rucht, Dieter. (2009). *Social movements in a globalizing world (second expanded edition)*: Palgrave Macmillan.

Diamond, J. (2005). *Collapse: How societies choose to fail or succeed*, Penguin.

Ehrenfeld, John R. (2005). The roots of sustainability. *MIT Sloan Management Review, 46*(2), 23-25.

Gersick, Connie. (1991). Revolutionary change theories: A multilevel exploration of the punctuated equilibrium paradigm. *Academy of Management Review, 16*, 10-36.

Gladwell, Malcolm. (2002). *The tipping point: How little things can make a big difference.* Boston, MA, USA: Little, Brown and Company.

Gunderson L. and Holling C.S. (2001) *Panarchy: Understanding Transformations in Systems of Humans and Nature*, Island Press.

Hassan, Zaid. (2014). *The social labs revolution: A new approach to solving our most complex challenges.* San Francisco, CA, USA: Berrett-Koehler.

Holling, C. S., Gunderson, L., & Ludwig, D. (2002). In quest of a theory of adaptive change. In L. H. Gunderson & C. S. Holling (Eds.), *Panarchy: Understanding transformations in human and natural systems.* Washington, DC: Island Press.

ICS. (2013). Http://www.Stratigraphy.Org/ Retrieved Oct. 28, 2013, from http://www.stratigraphy.org

Isaacs, William. (1999). *Dialogue and the art of thinking together.* New York, NY: Currency Doubleday.

Kahane, Adam. (2010). *Power and Love: A theory and practice of social change.* San Francisco, CA, USA: Berrett-Koehler.

Kahane, Adam. (2013). Love and power: When are they generative, instead of destructive? *Yes! magazine,* Summer, http://www.yesmagazine.org/issues/love-and-the-apocalypse/a-critical-balance.

Kauffman, S. (1995). *At Home in the Universe: The Search for the Laws of Self-Organization and Complexity.* NY: Oxford University Press.

Klein, Naomi (2014). *This changes everything: Capitalism vs. the climate.* San Francisco: Berrett-Koehler.

Kuhn, Thomas. (1962). *The structure of scientific revolutions.* Chicago, IL: The University of Chicago Press.

Lawrence, P.R., and Lorsch, J.W. (1969). *Developing organizations: Diagnosis and action.* Reading, MA: Addison-Wesley.

Lederach, John Paul. (2005). *The moral imagination: The art and soul of building peace.* New York, NY, USA: Oxford University Press.

Malia, Martin. (2008). *History's locomotives: Revolutions and the making of the modern world.* New Haven, CT, USA: Yale University Press.

Malthus, T. R. (2013). *An essay on the principle of population,* Cosimo, Inc.

Nicolis, Grégoire, and Ilya Prigogine (1989). *Exploring Complexity: An Introduction.* New York: W.H. Freeman.

Prigogine, I. and Stengers, I. (1984). *Order Out of Chaos: Man's New Dialogue with Nature.* Boulder, CO: New Science Library.

Raelin, Joseph. (2003). *Creating leaderful organizations: How to bring out leadership in everyone.* San Francisco, CA, USA: Berrett-Koehler.

Rittel, Horst W. J., & Webber, Melvin M. (1973). Dilemmas in a general theory of planning. *Policy sciences,* 4(2), 155-169.

Sabel, Charles F, & Zeitlin, Jonathan. (2012). Experimentalist governance.

Saunders, Harold H. (2003). Sustained dialogue in managing intractable conflict. *Negotiation Journal,* 19(1), 85-95.

Scharmer, C Otto. (2009). *Theory u: Learning from the future as it emerges:* Berrett-Koehler Publishers.

Stacey, R.D. (1991). *The Chaos Frontier: Creative Strategic Control for Business.* Oxford: Butterworth-Heinemann.

Steffen, Will, Crutzen, Paul J., & McNeill, John R. (2007). The anthropocene: Are humans now overwhelming the great forces of nature. *Ambio: A Journal of the Human Environment,* 36(8), 614-621.

Susskind, Lawrence E., McKearnen, Sarah, & Thomas-Lamar, Jennifer. (1999). *The consensus building handbook: A comprehensive guide to reaching agreement:* Sage.

Tilly, Charles. (2005). *Social movements, 1768 - 2004:* Paradigm Publishers.

Victoria & Albert Museum. (2014). *Disobedient objects.* London: V&A Publishing.

Waddell, S. (2011). *Global action networks: Creating our future together.* Bocconi University of Management. Hampshire, UK: Palgrave-Macmillan.

Waddell, Steve. (2014). Addressing the world's critical issues as complex change challenges: The state-of-the-field. http://goldenforsustainability.com/what-golden-does/eco-system-industry-lab/: World Bank and GOLDEN Ecosystems Labs.

Waddell, Steve, McLachlan, Milla, Meszoely, Greta, & Waddock, Sandra. (Forthcoming). Large scale change action research. In H. Bradbury (Ed.), *Action research handbook:* Sage.

Waddock, S. (2015). Reflections: Intellectual Shamans, Sensemaking, and Memes in Large System Change. *Journal of Change Management,* http://www.tandfonline.com/doi/full/10.1080/14697017.2015.1031954#.VWiD-kbwDfc.

Weick, K. E., & Quinn, R. E. (1999). Organizational change and development. *Annual review of psychology,* 50(1), 361-386.

Weick, Karl E, Sutcliffe, Kathleen M, & Obstfeld, David. (2005). Organizing and the process of sensemaking. *Organization science, 16*(4), 409-421.

Werkman, Renate. (2010). Reinventing organization development: How a sensemaking perspective can enrich OD theories and interventions. *Journal of Change Management, 10*(4), 421-438.

Westley, Frances, Goebey, Sean, & Robinson, Kirsten. (2012). *Change lab/design lab for social innovation* (Vol. January). Waterloo Ontario, Canada: Waterloo Institute of Social Innovation and Resilience.

Wilber, Ken. (2000). *A theory of everything: An integral vision for business, politics, science and spirituality.* Boston, MA, USA: Shambhala Publications.

Zadek, Simon, & Radovich, Sasha. (2006). Governing collaborative governance: Enhancing development outcomes by improving partnership governance and accountability. Cambridge, MA, USA: Corporate Social Responsibility Initiative - Harvard University.

Steve Waddell is Principal of NetworkingAction. Responding to the 21st century's enormous global challenges and realising its unsurpassed opportunities require new ways of acting and organising. For 30 years Steve has been supporting this with organisational, network, and societal change and development. He does this through NetworkingAction with collaborative consultations, education, research, and personal leadership. For the last 10 years he's focused largely on multi-stakeholder global change networks (Global Action Networks) as a large systems change strategy. Currently he is deeply engaged with development of the Potsdam Initiative as a network of LSC stakeholders.

✉ 14 Upton St., Boston, MA 02118, USA
🖥 swaddell@networkingaction.net

Sandra Waddock is the Galligan Chair of Strategy, Carroll School Scholar of Corporate Responsibility, and Professor of Management at Boston College's Carroll School of Management. Author of more than 100 papers, she has published 11 books, the latest of which is *Intellectual Shamans* (Cambridge, 2015). Her current research interests are large system change, intellectual shamans, wisdom, and memes.

✉ Carroll School of Management, Boston College, Chestnut Hill, MA 02467
🖥 waddock@bc.edu

Sarah Cornell is an environmental scientist at the Stockholm Resilience Centre, Stockholm University. Her research is on global environmental change, and the place of people in driving change, and understanding and responding to it. In this transdisciplinary area, she works with climate modellers, resource economists, policy analysts, ecologists—and with regular people in businesses and her local community, helping to build the knowledge, dialogues and action that are needed for sustainability.

✉ Stockholm University, 10691 Stockholm
🖥 sarah.cornell@su.se

Dr. **Domenico Dentoni** is Assistant Professor in Agribusiness Management and Strategy at Wageningen University (Netherlands), and Principal Investigator at the Global Center for Food Systems Innovation, funded by US Agency for International Development. With support from the Governments of Ecuador, Malaysia, Poland, Australia and US, he leads research projects on designing, managing, bridging and evaluating multi-stakeholder partnerships that stimulate systems innovation in agribusiness. He was awarded with Best PhD thesis award in Agricultural Economics in 2009 at Michigan State University. His publications are available on his blog: <http://domenicodentoni.blogspot.nl/p/publications_3.html> and at Google Scholar: <https://scholar.google.it/citations?user=QLjjVw8AAAAJ&hl=en>.

💻 domenico.dentoni@wur.nl

Milla McLachlan is an independent consultant on food systems change, and part-time Professor in Human Nutrition at Stellenbosch University. Milla is the Co-founder of the Southern Africa Food Lab, a multi-stakeholder initiative to facilitate transformation towards social and environmental sustainability in the regional food system. Previously, she served as Nutrition Advisor at the World Bank in Washington, DC, and as senior policy analyst at the Development Bank of Southern Africa. She holds a PhD and MA from Michigan State University, has published several peer-reviewed journal articles, book chapters and review papers, and co-edited *Combating Malnutrition: Time to Act*, a World Bank publication on the need for innovation in nutrition change strategies.

✉ 5411 SE 66th Ave, Portland, OR, 97206 USA

💻 millam@sun.ac.za

Greta Meszoely, Ph.D. is Founder and Executive Director of the Center for Business Complexity and Global Leadership. Working in business and academia, Greta leverages her expertise in complex systems and governance to enable sustainable large system change, innovation, and develop fundamental management competencies to support effective governance.
For two decades she has leveraged her research to support economic development, integrated resources management, and human rights in the US, Africa and the Middle East. Greta continues to advise corporations in the US and Europe to achieve sustainable change. Dr Meszoely holds a PhD in Law and Public Policy, an MA in International Relations and Comparative Politics, and a BS in International Business from Northeastern University.

✉ 80 Chandler St, Boston MA 02116

💻 greta@businesscomplexity.com

DOI: [10.9774/GLEAF.4700.2015.ju.00004]

Turning Point

Building Peace in a Complex World

Mari Fitzduff
Brandeis University, USA

T USED TO BE THAT a peace agreement was enough—the mediators relaxed, congratulated themselves, maybe moved on to the next project—until they looked back and started to notice how few of the agreements lasted. Hence the need for the peacebuilding field to reassess their approaches to resolving conflicts and recognise that they need to be much more comprehensive than existing conflict resolution approaches sometimes imply. It is all too easy to assume that the prime requirement for solving a conflict is to work with those people who are apparently key to any peace process, such as the politicians, military or paramilitary leaders. To prioritise these groups for attention is the strategic temptation for those wishing to see a speedy end to a conflict. However such political agreements will often prove to be insufficient unless they contain, and are complemented by, a wide variety of interrelated social and economic development processes, many of which are connected. Without economic development, redressing inequality will be seen as a win/lose situation, particularly for those who currently have most resources. Without increasing employment possibilities young men can be more easily seduced into engaging with ethnic or religious ideologies. Without developing new community leadership, it is often impossible to shift a detrimental political system to a more amenable one. Where military and paramilitary violence has reigned, it is often difficult to lessen it without security sector reform. To be effective, decommissioning and demobilisation need trusted security institutions, as well as the provision of alternative employment, which needs better economic development, etc. etc.

It is also increasingly clear that most of our conflicts are now glocal and interlinked not just internally but externally. While the tensions of the cold war, which were the bane of many conflicts, have abated, the link between conflicts and our Western lifestyle is clearer than ever. The desire for resources such as timber, opium and cocaine, coltan (vital for mobile telephones), diamonds, and oil, and the frightening merry-go-rounds of a highly profitable weapons industry are often significant contributors to the continuance of wars around the world.

It is also now increasingly recognised that climate change will increase the risks of violent conflict (IPCC 2014).

Hence the growing understanding that the conflicts of today are never one-dimensional, their causes are often many, and the result of a complex interplay of many different factors that influence each other on a continuing basis. Accordingly the response to them needs to be strategic and multi-pronged, and often both domestic and international. The recognition of the fact that any conflict is a complex dynamic, and one that is rarely as linear as is suggested by the normal frames for conflict analysis, has become increasingly the norm (Korrpen *et al.* 2008).

A growing number of institutions and individuals working in the peace-building field have now recognised the truly complex nature of conflicts. They have come to the conclusion that a systemic, integrated, and holistic approach to developing sustainably peaceful societies is more effective than the more usual one-dimensional approach (Coleman 2012; Fitzduff 2013; Ricigliano 2012; Zelizar 2013). This means that the strategies for preventing and resolving conflicts require complementary efforts across many relevant fields, between levels of society (i.e. grassroots to elite) and between institutions, domestic, international, and transnational. Working across such fields, and levels, allows the many facets of a conflict to be addressed more satisfactorily.

Thus systems thinking, which examines the dynamics between the principal actors, structural causes, proximate causes and the triggers of a conflict, and takes their agendas, behaviours and connections into account, is more likely to succeed in effecting sustainable peace (Chigas *et al.* 2011) Such systems think-ing is becoming the norm in the peacebuilding field. It does not necessarily replace the traditional tools and methods of conflict analysis, but rather sup-plements traditional conflict analysis methods. Such thinking helps to identify the dynamic relationships among different factors, rather than just the factors themselves. It therefore has the potential to help bridge the gap between analysis and programming by ascertaining gaps in the programming, and possible extra points of leverage and approaches for interrupting or changing the conflict.

Such thinking also leads to an understanding that there are no one-off solu-tions, but rather a requirement to develop the capacity on the part of actors and institutions to generate their own solutions on a continuing basis rather than curtailing their efforts to end a particular cycle of violence. It is particularly helpful for understanding long-standing or recurrent conflicts about which multiple, and often contrasting, analyses exist.

Such thinking about the complexity of most conflicts of today has multiplied. Within the United Nations family, the UNDP, UNDESA and others have been working to ensure that the development dimensions of crisis situations can lead to long-term development agendas that are integrated with conflict manage-ment and conflict prevention measures. This approach has been institutional-ised in the UN Interagency Framework for Preventive Action which supports the development of integrated, multi-dimensional strategies for understanding, responding to and resolving potentially destructive conflicts. In theory, it helps the relevant UN departments and agencies to 'Deliver as One' in conflict areas, although delivering on consensus and partnerships has not been easy.

An integrated form of complementarity has also become more important in the approaches to development by many of the United States government agencies, such as the US State Department's Office of the Coordinator for Reconstruction and Stabilization. Their strategic document focuses on the myriad of essential tasks for post-conflict reconstruction including the necessity for security, governance, humanitarian assistance, economic stabilisation and justice and reconciliation to work in a complementary fashion (Office of the Coordinator for Reconstruction and Stabilization, 2005). In the 2011 Quadrennial Diplomacy and Development Review, the State Department, the Department of Defense, and the development agency, USAID endorsed the concept of '3D Security' (Schirch *et al.* 2006), which seeks to integrate defence, diplomatic, and development approaches to the resolution of conflicts into a coherent initiative. The EU has similarly adopted such an approach (Gross 2013). Other international actors are now also advocating systems analysis of conflicts, and promoting the idea of 'whole of government' or 'whole of community' integrated approaches to the mitigation of conflicts (OECD DAC 2008) in the hope that conflicts can be more effectively prevented, mitigated and transformed by adopting a more systemic approach.

References

Chigas, Diana and Woodrow, Peter (2013) Systems Thinking in Peacebuilding Evaluations: Applications in Ghana, Guinea-Bissau and Kosovo, in: Ole Winckler Andersen, Beate Bull and Megan Kennedy-Chouane (eds.: Evaluation Methodologies for Aid in Conflict. Routledge Taylor and Francis Group.

Coleman, P., Vallacher, R., Bartoli, A., Nowak, A. & Bui-Wrzosinska, L. 2011. 'Navigating the Landscape of Conflict: Applications of Dynamical Systems Theory for Addressing Protracted Conflict.' In Korppen, D., Ropers, N. & Giessmann, H. The Non-Linearity of Peace Processes: Theory and Practice of Systemic Conflict Transformation. Opladen & Farmington Hills, MI: Barbara Budrich Publishers.

Fitzduff, M. (2004). Meta-conflict resolution. http://www.beyondintractability.org/bi-essay/meta-conflict-resolution.

Fitzduff (2013) Public Policies in Shared Societies: A Comparative Approach. Routledge London.

Gross, Eva: (2013) Peacebuilding in 3D: EU and US CHAILLOT PAPER No 130 European Union Institute for Security.

Intergovernmental Panel on Climate Change (IPCC) Climate Change 2014 Synthesis Report

Körppen, Daniela, Schmelzle, Beatrix and Wils, Oliver: (2008) A Systemic Approach to Conflict Transformation: Exploring Strengths and Weaknesses Berghof Handbook Dialogue Series.

Organization for Economic Cooperation and Development, Development Assistance Committee, (2008) Guidance on Evaluating Conflict Prevention and Peacebuilding, Paris.

Ricigliano, Robert (2003) 'Networks of effective action: implementing an integrated approach to peacebuilding' Security dialogue Vol. 34 No. 4: 445-462.

Ricigliano, R. (2011) Making Peace Last: A toolbox for sustainable peacebuilding. Boulder, CO: Paradigm Publishers.

Schirch, Lisa, Kishbaugh, Aaron, Pemberton, Miriam (2006) Leveraging '3D' Security: From Rhetoric to Reality: Knitting defense, development, and diplomacy together—the ups and the downsides of a real work in progress. http://fpif.org/leveraging_3d_security_from_rhetoric_to_reality/

United States Joint Forces Command (2005) Draft Planning Framework for Reconstruction, Stabilization, and Conflict Transformation J7 Pamphlet US Government http://www.dtic.mil/doctrine/doctrine/jwfc/jwfcpam_draft.pdf

Woodrow, Peter and Chigas, Diana (2011): Connecting the Dots: Evaluating Whether and How Programs Address Conflict Systems, in: The Non-Linearity of Peace Processes: Theory and Practice of Systemic Conflict Transformation, Ropers, N. et al. (eds.), Berghof Foundation.

Zelizer, Craig: (2013) Integrated Peacebuilding: Innovative Approaches to Transforming Conflict Westview Press.

Mari Fitzduff is Professor and founding Director of the Master's professional programmes in Coexistence and Conflict at Brandeis University, USA. Previously (1997–2003) she was Chair of Conflict Studies at Ulster University in Northern Ireland where she directed UNU/INCORE. In 1990, she was the founding Chief Executive of the Northern Ireland Community Relations Council. She has worked extensively with international and national organisations on issues of conflict in Africa, Asia, Europe and the Americas. Her publications have included a three-volume series on *The Psychology of Resolving Global Conflicts: From War to Peace* with co-editor Chris Stout and *Public Policies for Shared Societies*. Her latest publication is *An Introduction to Neuroscience for the Peacebuilder*.

✉ Master's Program in Coexistence and Conflict, Brandeis University, Mailstop 035, Waltham, MA 02454-9110, USA

🖥 fitzduff@brandeis.edu

DOI: [10.9774/GLEAF.4700.2015.ju.00005]

Turning Point

Theory U

From Ego-system to Eco-system Economies

Otto Scharmer
Massachusetts Institute of Technology, USA

Adam Yukelson
Presencing Institute, USA

N WORKING WITH LEADERS, TEAMS and organisations we noticed that the tools and processes we developed with our colleagues at the Presencing Institute and the Society for Organizational Learning (SoL) worked with some leaders and teams, but did not work at all with others. We began to explore why that was so.

What we found is summarised in a quote from an interview Otto did with Bill O'Brien, the late CEO of Hanover Insurance: 'The success of an intervention depends on the interior condition of the intervenor' (Scharmer, 2009: 27). In his experience with change and development processes, Bill noticed that the awareness or intention that people brought to a situation had a profound impact on the quality of the results they achieved.

The recognition of the deeper *source* level of social reality creation set us on a path of inquiry into the recent findings in leadership, management, economics, neuroscience, contemplative practice, and complexity research. In essence, we found that behaviours within systems cannot be transformed unless we also transform (deepen) the quality of *awareness* that people in these systems apply to their actions, both individually and collectively.

The process of accessing these deeper levels of knowing is what we came to call Theory U (Scharmer 2009). The premise of Theory U is $r = f(a_i)$; that is, the reality and results (r) that a system of players enacts is a function of the awareness (a) that these players operate from. The *quality of results* within a system depends on the *quality of awareness* from which the players in that system operate.

Theory U differentiates between four states of awareness ('field structures of attention') that individuals, groups, institutions, and larger systems use as they operate. By 'field' we mean a set of interdependent connections. Each field state of awareness originates in a different inner place:

► Habitual awareness

► Ego-system awareness

► Stakeholder awareness

► Eco-system awareness

Table 1 depicts a matrix of social evolution in which these four different states of awareness are applied to all levels of social systems: individual (micro), team or group (meso), organisational (macro), and large systems (mundo).

Columns 1–4 of Table 1 identify four primary processes that players in complex social systems use to collectively bring forth social reality: attending, conversing, organising, and coordinating. In the development of social systems, participants and stakeholders evolve through four stages and structures of engaging with the social field: as a habitual pattern (level 1), as a transactional frame (level 2), as a relational web of connections (level 3), and as a landing strip that allows the emerging future to become present (level 4: presencing). As complexity increases, it becomes possible for systems to move from levels 1 and 2 to levels 3 and 4—if the actors in the system can tune their awareness to these emerging possibilities. There are also instances in which the movement happens in reverse (regression). Table 1 shows how these four states of awareness play out on each level.

Table 1 Matrix of social evolution: four fields of awareness; four system levels

Field: Structure of Attention	Micro: ATTENDING (individual)	Meso: CONVERSING (group)	Macro: ORGANIZING (institutions)	Mundo: COORDINATING (global systems)
1.0: habitual awareness *suspending*	Listening 1: Downloading habits of thought	Downloading: Speaking from conforming	Centralized control: Organizing around hierarchy	Hierarchy: commanding
2.0: ego-system awareness *redirecting*	Listening 2: Factual, open-minded	Debate: Speaking from differentiating	Divisionalized: Organizing around differentiation	Market: competing
3.0: stakeholder awareness *letting-go*	Listening 3: Empathic, open-hearted	Dialogue: Speaking from inquiring others, self	Distributed/networked: Organizing around interest groups	Negotiated Dialogue: cooperating
4.0: eco-system awareness	Listening 4: Generative, open-presence	Collective Creativity: Speaking from what is moving through	Eco-system: Organizing around what emerges	Awareness Based Collective Action co-creating

Practices

Accessing these different levels of awareness requires a process that allows individuals, groups and systems to transform and shift the level of awareness they are operating from. This process unfolds simultaneously at different levels: at an individual level through the art and practice of deep listening, and at a group level through shifting conversational fields. In our work, we found that the process with organisations and larger systems is a journey through the following stages:

1. **Co-initiating**. Bringing together a diverse microcosm of the key players in a system in order to form a core group that can uncover their common intention

2. **Co-sensing**. Diverse stakeholder groups are equipped with methods and tools for suspending habitual ways of paying attention, and are taken to the edges of their system in order to experience it from a new perspective

3. **Co-inspiring**. Connecting to the deeper sources of knowing, using contemplative practices, solo experiences, dialogue, intentional stillness, journaling, and a new method called social presencing theatre[1]

4. **Co-creating**. Exploring the future by doing, using rapid-cycle prototyping and a seven-step case clinic process[2]

5. **Co-shaping**. Evolving, sustaining and scaling the new across an ecosystem; an iterative process requires the participants to repeatedly assess changes across all three aspects of the journey: the personal, the relational, and the institutional

Principles

In working with groups and organisations we identified a set of principles that guide the process of shifting the awareness of a field. The following 10 points are a summary:

▶ **Engage the whole system at all levels.** In any change process, all levels of the system need to be integrated, the micro (individual), the meso (team), the macro (institutional), and the mundo (eco-system)

▶ **Engage the whole human being at all levels of intelligence.** The U-process integrates three levels of intelligence: the open mind (IQ: intellectual

---

1 www.presencing.com/social-presencing-theater
2 www.presencing.com/tools/case-clinics

knowledge), the open heart (EQ: emotional and relational knowledge), and the open will (SQ: self-knowledge)

▶ **Use systems thinking in order to reintegrate matter and mind.** Traditional social science and systems theories in the West are based on a split between matter and mind in the social field—that is, a split between the results that we collectively enact and the awareness from which we operate. Closing that feedback loop is the essence of all deep systems thinking (Senge 1996; Scharmer 2009). Theory U takes systems thinking beyond the realm of just thinking and into the realm of systems *sensing*

▶ **Use deep immersion journeys.** Step out of existing patterns, go to hotspots of disruptive change and connect to the reality that is outside of established mental models (see Scharmer 2009; www.Presencing.com)

▶ **Integrate first-, second-, and third-person knowledge.** All action science is based on 'letting the data talk to you'. The challenges of this century, however, require extending the territory of scientific observation from merely exterior data (the third-person view) to the deeper (more subtle) levels of human experience —that is, adding first-person and second-person knowledge to the traditional third-person knowledge view (Chandler and Torbert 2003: 133–52; Scharmer and Kaufer 2013)

▶ **Connect to the source of the self.** Presencing practices and moments of mindfulness allow leaders to connect to their deeper sources of knowing and to ask the two questions at the root of all great leadership and creativity Who is my Self? What is my Work?

▶ **Activate the power of intention.** Leadership is grounded in the capacity to connect with the deeper intentions that underlie the human journey. This journey, if attended to, connects us more deeply with ourselves, with one another, and with the living world around us. The power of intention is about the capacity to activate the deeper levels of human will

▶ **Prototype in order to explore the future by doing.** Most current practices of action research and organisational learning are bounded by reflecting on and modifying the experience of the past. Yet, all major disruptive challenges in our systems today require us to move beyond modifying the past. They invite us to sense and actualise emerging future possibilities. This practice, learning from the emerging future, makes it possible to translate a sense of possibility into intention and intention into action by creating small living examples to explore the future by doing, and by integrating the intelligence of the head, heart, and hand

▶ **Cultivate the power of place.** Social movements, great innovations, and sustainable change are born and developed in places. Today's global challenges and movement-building dynamics require a blended infrastructure of online communities and a global network of vibrant entrepreneurial hubs

▶ **Build platforms for global awareness-based action research.** Use massive open online courses (MOOCs) to combine teaching with interactive, personal, and small-group dialogue spaces, in which a global community of change makers can collaborate around common aspirations and challenges (see Scharmer 2014)

References

Chandler, Dawn, & Torbert, Bill. (2003). Transforming inquiry and action interweaving 27 flavors of action research. *Action Research, 1*(2), 133-152.

Scharmer, C. Otto. (2009). *Theory u: Leading from the future as it emerges* (First Edition). San Francisco, CA, USA: Berrett-Koehler.

Scharmer, Otto, & Kaufer, Katrin. (2013). *Leading from the emerging future: From ego-system to eco-system economies*. San Francisco, CA, USA: Berrett-Koehler Publishers.

Senge, Peter M. (1996). Leading learning organizations. In T. P. F. D. F. Goldsmith and F. Hesselbein (Ed.), *The leader of the future*. San Francisco: Jossey Bass, Inc.

Otto Scharmer is a Senior Lecturer at MIT, and founding chair of the Presencing Institute. He co-founded the Global Wellbeing Lab and is founding chair of the MIT IDEAS program. He introduced the concept of "presencing" — learning from the emerging future — in his books *Theory U* and *Presence* (the latter co-authored with Senge, Jaworski, and Flowers). His new book *Leading From the Emerging Future: From Ego-system to Eco-system Economies* (with Katrin Kaufer) focuses on transforming business, society, and self. He holds a Ph.D. in economics and management from Witten-Herdecke University in Germany and in 2015 received the Jamieson Prize for Excellence in Teaching.

✉ Senior Lecturer,
Sloan School of Management, MIT,
77 Massachusetts Ave., E62-419,
Cambridge MA 02139, USA

🖥 Scharmer@mit.edu

🌐 www.ottoscharmer.com;
www.presencing.com

Adam Yukelson is an action researcher, writer, and educator based in Cambridge, MA. In his work with the Presencing Institute he equips change-makers with a framework and methods to reinvent the larger eco-systems in which they operate, and helps them reflect on, capture, and share what they learn with others. He is currently a co-facilitator and designer of the edX course U.Lab: Transforming Business, Society, and Self (with Otto Scharmer).

✉ 20 Waldo Ave #3, Somerville, MA 02143, USA

🖥 Yukelson@presencing.com

A leading wellbeing festival in the Lake District

A fusion of academic conference, business fair and music festival, with outdoor activities on the shores of England's largest lake, at Brathay Hall, Ambleside

16-18 JULY 2015

AT BRATHAY HALL

The festival will include:

- Plenary keynotes, panels and paper presentations
- Interactive facilitation, creative activities, boat trips, tai chi, music, dancing and festivities
- A side programme of events run by sustainability advisors Futerra
- The launch of an ongoing interdisciplinary network on leadership, sustainability and wellbeing.

Featured speakers include:

- Charles Eisenstein, philosopher and de-growth activist
- Nandita Das, Indian film actress and director, and activist on race and gender
- Funmi Iyanda, recently named one of Forbes 20 Youngest Power Women in Africa who helped launch the #BringBackOurGirls campaign
- Jo Confino, an executive editor of the Guardian newspaper and chairman and editorial director of Guardian Sustainable Business, now the world's leading source of news for sustainability professionals
- Lynne Franks, celebrity business woman, author, broadcaster and speaker. Famous for her leadership in public relations, she is thefounder of SEED – Sustainable Enterprise and Empowerment Dynamics.

For more information visit: **www.leadingwell.org**

Proudly sponsored by:

DOI: [10.9774/GLEAF.4700.2015.ju.00006]

Turning Point

Propensities and Dispositions

David Snowden
Cognitive Edge, UK

A NEW AWARENESS OF THE ANCIENT counterpart to order began over a century ago with Poincaré and several others, and has surged in recent decades. In fact there is a fascinating kind of order in which no director or designer is in control but which emerges through the interaction of many entities. Emergent order has been found in many natural phenomena: bird-flocking behavior can be simulated on a computer through three simple rules; termites produce elegant nests through the operation of simple behaviors triggered by chemical traces; each snowflake is a unique pattern arising from the interactions of water particles during freezing. The patterns that form are not controlled by a directing intelligence; they are self-organizing. The new science of complexity spawned by these findings is interdisciplinary, touching fields from mathematics to evolution to economics to meteorology to telecommunications (Kurtz & Snowden 'The new dynamics of strategy: Sensemaking in a complex and complicated world' *IBM Systems Journal*, Vol 42, No 3, 2003 pp 462-483).

In the above-referenced article, written over a decade ago, Kurtz and I questioned the universality of three basic assumptions that pervade decision making and policy formulation:

▶ **The assumption of order.**
That there are underlying relationships between cause and effect in human interactions and markets, which are capable of discovery and empirical verification

▶ **The assumption of rational choice.**
That faced with a choice between one or more alternatives, human actors will make a 'rational' decision based only on minimising pain or maximising pleasure

▶ **The assumption of intentional capability.**
That the acquisition of capability indicates an intention to use that capability, and that actions from competitors, populations, nation states, communities,

or whatever collective identity is under consideration are the result of intentional behaviour

We argued, from a base in complex adaptive systems theory, that those assumptions were only true for highly constrained systems; ones in which tight coupling enables predictability of outcome. What has been interesting since then, is the attempt by many manifestations of systems thinking, to assume the language of complexity without fully understanding the implications. We see this in techniques such as Backcasting and the whole movement to define an ideal future state and argue for their achievement. More fundamentally it is wrong to believe that thinking that problems in large systems are solved by dealing with the system as a whole from a planning or design perspective. Paradoxically, to create a whole system impact requires a focus on the present not on the future; on exploring the evolutionary potential of the present.

One of the best ways to understand the nature of a complex adaptive system is to imagine a flat surface surrounded by magnets that can change in polarity and strength. On the table are cast iron discs. If one of the magnets changes strength then the position of the discs will change in a repeatable and predictable way. That, in the popular forms of organisational theory is called a *driver*, or sometimes (mistakenly) an archetype. The problem is that in a complex system all of the magnets can change in parallel, both in strength and polarity so the same thing will only happen again at the same way twice by accident. The magnets are better understood as *modulators*. In effect the current state of the system represents its *dispositions*, the nature of the definable elements in the system and its propensities. In a complex adaptive system we do not see linear material cause; that is the big conceptual switch that too many thinkers and practitioners miss in the engineering-dominated metaphors and models of systems dynamics.

So what do we do differently? How do we achieve change? Indeed what can be changed?

First, if we are to manage the emergent possibilities of the present, then describing that state from divergent perspectives is a vital starting point. In day to day life attitudes and beliefs are determined by the micro-narratives of data related to daily existence; the stories of the water cooler, the school gate and the checkout queue. Micro-narrative maps allow us to see what is possible and where natural attitudinal maps can act as enablers or blockers. In addition we need to describe the system in terms of what can be changed. What boundaries exist? What constraints are sustainable or changeable? What identity structures attract behaviour? Ultimately we will ask three questions: (i) what can I change? (ii) Of those things that I can change, where can I monitor the impact of that change? (iii) Of those things where I can monitor the impact, where can I amplify success or dampen failure?

Second, we need to shift from *fail-safe* design of interventions with defined outcomes to multiple parallel *safe-to-fail* interventions designed to test those evolutionary possibilities. Ideally some of those interventions should be oblique in nature, some naive. This also allows for conflict resolution; it is easier to agree that someone's idea of how to change things is coherent without having to agree it's right. So if the idea is coherent we run an experiment.

Finally, the way we engage people needs to work at all levels within an organisation or society (or both). One way to do that, which works with the narrative mapping described earlier, is to simply ask *how would we get people to tell more stories like this, fewer like that*. Abstractions and ideal statements about how things should be are less engaging, less pragmatic.

The danger with too much current *whole systems* thinking is that it commits exactly the errors identified at the start. It assumes we live in a causal universe where we can engineer an outcome; that if people are presented with an idealised future they will rationally select it; and worst of all that behaviour can be intentional in all circumstances.

Ironically it means we also shift to allowing new patterns to emerge that are not determined in advance. In childhood we are told stories of what hasn't worked (think fairy stories) but we create our own pathways to unknowable futures. Sustainability and resilience are more likely to be achieved if we enable change rather than trying to determine what that change would be in advance.

References

Dreborg K.H. (1996) 'Essence of backcasting', *Futures* 28(9): 813-828

Snowden D (2010) 'Naturalizing Sensemaking' in Mosier and Fischer *Informed by Knowledge: Expert Performance in Complex Situation* p 223-234

Prof. **Dave Snowden** is the Founder and Chief Scientific Officer of Cognitive Edge and Director of the Centre for Applied Complexity at the University of Bangor.

✉ 51 Lockeridge, Marlborough SN8 4EL, UK

🖥 snowded@me.com

Corporate Citizenship Readers

Edited by Malcolm McIntosh

- Seminal essays written by some of the leading thinkers and pioneers in the corporate sustainability and responsibility movement, including John Ruggie, Peter Senge, R. Edward Freeman and Chris Laszlo
- Featuring new analysis and up-to-date commentaries from original authors
- Essential 'Readers' for academics, NGOs, practitioners and policy-makers

This two-volume set is a collection of seminal and thought-provoking essays, drawn from the *Journal of Corporate Citizenship*'s archive, accompanied by new analysis and reflection from the original authors. Written by some of the most widely recognized academic and business pioneers of the corporate responsibility and global sustainability movement, the volumes make for essential reference texts for anyone interested in the radically awakening new global political economy.

The Journal of Corporate Citizenship *was launched in 2001 by Founding Editor Malcolm McIntosh and Greenleaf Publishing. Today, it continues to fulfil its mission to integrate theory and practice and provide a home for enlightened transdisciplinary thinking on the role of business and organizations in society.*

MALCOLM McINTOSH is former Director of the Asia Pacific Centre for Sustainable Enterprise at Griffith University and is now at Bath Spa University. He was previously Special Adviser to the UN Global Compact.

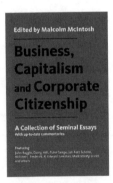

Business, Capitalism and Corporate Citizenship
A Collection of Seminal Essays

In the first decades of the twenty-first century, the theory and practice of corporate citizenship and responsibility adapted significantly. The pieces in this volume capture the essence of these changes, with illuminating reflections by their pre-eminent authors on success, failure, learning and progress. Featuring contributions from John Ruggie, Peter Senge, R. Edward Freeman, and Georg Kell, it charts the rise of corporate citizenship, sustainability and CSR.

June 2015 | ISBN 978-1-78353-499-9 | Available in all standard ebook formats. Single-user ebook price. | Prices: ebook/pb: £35.00 | €45.00 | $50.00 hb: £90.00 | €125.00 | $130.00

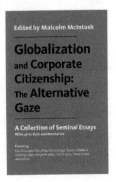

Globalization and Corporate Citizenship: The Alternative Gaze
A Collection of Seminal Essays

The theory and practice of corporate citizenship and responsibility has many alternative perspectives from the business-as-usual gaze. The essays in this volume encapsulate the essence of these alternative ideas and embrace the idea that the new methods of the next century may not lie in mainstream capitalist thinking. This volume features contributions and new analysis from Klaus M. Leisinger, Chris Laszlo, Simon Zadek, David Cooperrider, Marjorie Kelly and others.

Sept 2015 | ISBN 978-1-78353-496-8 | Available in all standard ebook formats. Single-user ebook price. | Prices: ebook/pb: £35.00 | €45.00 | $50.00 hb: £90.00 | €125.00 | $130.00

DOI: [10.9774/GLEAF.4700.2015.ju.00007]

Turning Point

Mining Resources

Driving Social Justice?

Rajesh Tandon

Participatory Research in Asia, India

N MANY PARTS OF THE world, extraction of resources by mining companies has got stuck in vicious circles. India is no exception. More than one hundred large projects for the extraction of coal, iron ore, oil/gas, uranium and other minerals are stagnating at different stages of building the infrastructure after contracts were signed with the government over the past decade. These companies are both Indian and multinational; the regions are spread around the country, though more intensively concentrated in the sites where indigenous (tribal) communities have lived for millennia.

As a consequence, billions of dollars' worth of investment is stuck without yielding returns; local communities are facing violence from police and other criminal gangs operating in these areas to grab land; production of vital raw material for power, steel and other industries is lagging, resulting in economic slow-down; and youth of these communities are becoming frustrated and restless, demanding 'quick-fixes' from the government.

Can such a scenario be averted? Yes, if we look at the complex web of causes underlying this malaise and explore solutions that take a whole-system approach to addressing large-scale challenges. A large part of the problem lies in key actors (government and business) taking a sectarian and partial approach. Provincial government leaders want to attract investment in their provinces; they are interested in rapid economic development so that millions of families can be lifted out of poverty. The officials at provincial capitals negotiate contracts (and 'deals') with companies (and their local agents in most cases). The CEOs of the companies visit for a half-day photo-shoot with the chief ministers, and the media splashes a 'good' story. The implementing arm of the government at the district level is then mobilised to enable mining and construction of industrial infrastructure at the sites. Securing land from thousands of families (mostly from tribal communities) becomes a headache.

The local tribal communities have been waiting for generations to secure government development programmes to improve their socio-economic standards, to get the schools and hospitals, and security of livelihood beyond subsistence agriculture. Suddenly, they hear some rumours about the government's plans to displace and dispossess them from their ancestral lands and sources of meagre livelihoods. Local elites begin to 'buy off' lands from individual families through inducement, seduction and/or coercion. A confusing and chaotic environment develops, leading to mass protests and occasional violence against police and local authorities.

A reading of the above typical scenario suggests that the over-arching purposes of government, business and communities are not too dissimilar—improvements in the living standards, employment and well-being of the communities. Both government and private investments are needed to make that happen. However, government and business leaders 'make deals' without bringing the other stakeholders, especially the leaders of local communities, around the table. Even when they are brought in at a later stage, it is more to 'bless the deal' already made between government and business. Methods deployed in ensuring such blessings—using threats, bribery and co-option—result in temporary 'agreements', cause divisions among local communities, and soon degenerate into vicious circles of blame and resistance.

The new Companies Act (2013) in India makes a number of critical provisions for ethical, transparent and accountable governance of companies for the first time. Much of corporate governance in India has been mired in secrecy, family intrigues, insider-trading and deal-making. The new Act requires that each company has at least one-third independent directors, including a woman director, on its board. It requires transparency in conduct of business and reporting, and that its functioning for public accountability be strengthened as per specific provisions.

In addition, the new Act also provides for each company to spend at least 2% of net annual profits on corporate social responsibility (CSR) activities. The Act lists a number of social and economic development areas for the use of such CSR funds, under the direction of a board sub-committee, with a board mandated policy in this regard.

These new provisions of the new Companies Act in India create an opportunity to develop roots of 'corporate citizenship' in the country. Despite economic liberalisation 25 years ago, large corporations are still not seen as a welcome and integral part of the fabric of Indian society. Recent scandals of crony capitalism have not helped their cause either. Much of the traditional CSR activities by companies have been mostly public relations exercises.

How can the provisions of the new Companies Act be deployed by companies to build the roots and foundations of corporate citizenship in India? In my view, the companies involved in the mining of resources in India, and stuck in a log-jam described above, can use ethical corporate governance and CSR to design whole-system approaches that include communities and other local stakeholders as a part of co-construction of solutions that are sustainable, durable and resilient. Mining of resources cannot be driven by short-term profits alone; responsible use of those resources is also critical in the long run.

In this approach, companies can deploy CSR funds to mainstream stakeholders' engagement, to become enablers of accountability of public services and champions of inclusive well-being. By mainstreaming CSR into supporting a whole-system approach, resource extraction companies can also contribute to the well-being of other stakeholders, especially local communities. It is in this approach to envisioning 'mining resources' as a complex system that companies can also contribute to social justice. Once the leadership of such companies realises that the contract for mining and industrial production is 'located' in a complex socio-economic reality of haves and have-nots, the excluded and marginalised, they may choose to 'run away' from the scene; or, they may determine to engage with the whole system and thereby contribute to social and economic well-being of local society, and to sustainable justice.

Dr **Rajesh Tandon** is an internationally acclaimed leader and practitioner of participatory research and development. He is President and Founder of PRIA (Participatory Research in Asia), established in 1982. In 2012, he was appointed Co-Chair of the UNESCO Chair in Community Based Research and Social Responsibility in Higher Education.

✉ Participatory Research in Asia,
42 Tughlakabad Institutional Area,
New Delhi 110062, India

🖥 rajesh.tandon@pria.org

DOI: [10.9774/GLEAF.4700.2015.ju.00008]

Transition Management

Taking Stock from Governance Experimentation[*]

Derk Loorbach, Niki Frantzeskaki and
Roebin Lijnis Huffenreuter

Dutch Research Institute For Transitions, Erasmus University Rotterdam,
The Netherlands

- Transitions
- Transformative governance
- Sustainability
- Energy
- Cities
- Resilience
- Liveability

In 2001, transition management was introduced into the science-policy debate around sustainable development and complex societal issues. Transition management (TM) at that time posed a number of generic principles derived from an understanding of complex societal sustainability challenges as persistent problems. These formed the basis for the experimental development of a range of new instruments, strategies and actions to influence the speed and development of sustainability transitions. Since its introduction, the field of transitions at large and the research and practices around the TM concept have evolved considerably, including a fundamental scientific debate, the build-up of an empirical basis and a grounded portfolio of TM instruments. In this paper we will take stock of and reflect on the advances in the field of TM based on our experiences with experimentally applying, refining and developing the basic premises, tenets and possible interventions.

Derk Loorbach is director of DRIFT and Professor of Socio-economic Transitions at the Faculty of Social Science, both at Erasmus University Rotterdam. Derk is one of the founders of the transition management approach as new form of governance for sustainable development. He has over one hundred publications in this area and has been involved as an action researcher in numerous transition processes with government, business, civil society and science. He is a frequently invited keynote speaker in and outside Europe.

Dutch Research Institute For Transitions, Erasmus University Rotterdam, Mandeville Building (former T-Building),16th floor, room 36, 3062 PA Rotterdam, Netherlands

loorbach@drift.eur.nl

Dr **Niki Frantzeskaki** was born in Chania, Crete, Greece in 1980 and graduated in Environmental Engineering at TU Crete (Greece) with honours in 2003. Her Master's studies were realised at TU Delft (The Netherlands) where she graduated with a Master of Science in Engineering and Policy Analysis with honours in 2005.

Dutch Research Institute For Transitions, Erasmus University Rotterdam, Mandeville Building (former T-Building),16th floor, room 36, 3062 PA Rotterdam, Netherlands

frantzeskaki@drift.eur.nl

Dr **Roebin Lijnis Huffenreuter** obtained a double research master at the Erasmus Institute for Philosophy and Economics and proceeded his academic career at the Dutch Research Institute For Transitions (DRIFT). His current research is focused on financial-economic transitions and sustainability; analyzing the possible tradeoffs between economic efficiency and ecological effectiveness in large scale financial-economic systems.

* We thank the editors of the special issue as well as the three anonymous reviewers for their valuable and constructive feedback.

RANSITION STUDIES IS AN EMERGING field of research that seeks to integrate insights from areas such as complexity science, innovation studies, sociology and environmental science to better understand large scale systemic change in societal systems and explore possibilities for influencing the speed and direction of change in these systems. It originated from a policy-science debate in the Netherlands around the fourth National Environmental Policy Plan. In this debate, the concept of transitions was proposed as an approach to better understand the failure of policy and markets in delivering a fundamental reorientation of the development pathway of modern societies and an opportunity to explore new ways to achieve breakthroughs. Since then, the field of transition studies has become an international research field comprising a multitude of core concepts, approaches and intervention methods. In this paper we take stock of one of these streams of research, namely transition management, and the experiences with some 15 years of action-oriented research in this area.

In essence, transition management studies complex adaptive societal systems (such as societal sectors, regions, or cities) that go through fundamental nonlinear changes in cultures (for example, attitudes, perceptions, and routines), structures (for example, institutions, ways of organising, hierarchical orderings), and practices (for example, behaviour, implementation procedures, and daily routines). Transitions are defined as the result of co-evolving processes in economy, society, ecology, and technology that progressively build up toward a revolutionary systemic change on the very long term (Rotmans *et al.* 2001; Frantzeskaki and de Haan 2009; Loorbach 2010). Because of this complexity, transitions are impossible to predict, fully comprehend, or steer directly, but they are seen as a pattern of change that can be anticipated. These processes can be adapted to in such a way that the inevitable nonlinear shifts and associated crises provide massive windows of opportunity for accelerated reorientation toward sustainability.

Core concepts in transition studies are regimes and persistent problems. The basic idea is that over time dominant and locked-in configurations emerge that are dynamically stable. Our current societal systems have emerged out of the era of industrial transformation and developed around central control mechanisms, fossil resources and linear models of innovation and knowledge production (Loorbach, 2014). They have brought welfare and growth but also our current sustainability challenges. From this perspective, the challenge to move towards sustainability is understood as the need to achieve fundamental systemic change, implying disruptive power shifts.

The hypothesis underlying transition management is that (collective) understandings of the origin, nature and dynamics of transitions in particular domains will enable actors to better anticipate and adapt to these dynamics so as to influence their speed and direction. In research practice, this has led to a multitude of practice-based governance experiments in which structured multi-actor processes have simultaneously informed science in terms of insight in transition dynamics, actor perceptions and strategies, as well as helping actors to develop visions, strategies and interventions in their respective transition contexts. This paper takes stock of the literature and experiences that were the result of this governance experimentation by reflecting on the literature and theoretical debates, as well as synthesising the experiences in applied projects in which the authors were involved.

The paper is structured as follows. We first synthesise the current theoretical understanding of the challenge of governance in the context of transitions. We briefly reflect on the debate around the basic ideas and principles for governance in transitions and touch on the more fundamental debate around issues of power, politics, manageability and normativity. We then synthesise the operational approach developed over the past years in terms of transition management: the action-based research approach around creating transition networks, visions, strategies and experiments. We illustrate the application through the experiences with transition management in a big area development process in Rotterdam, the Netherlands. Based on this we identify and highlight a number of challenges we see for further research.

Transition governance

Theoretical basis

The transition governance approach positions itself within the broader field of complexity science (Midgley, 2003; Gell-Mann, 1994), governance (Kooiman, 1993; Pierre, 2000), sustainability science (Kates 2001; O'Riordan 2013) and social innovation (Westley et al., 2011). A society, or the planet, is seen as a complex and adaptive system in which change is a result of processes of co-evolution. Co-evolution also takes place between system metabolic processes (for example, demographic processes), problem processes (for example, problem framing processes), and governance processes (for example, processes of collectively searching and creating solutions). This creates complex co-evolutionary dynamics that under specific conditions can create a transitional pattern: after a long period of optimisation and dynamic equilibrium a relatively short and disruptive period of destabilisation and reconfiguration after which a new dynamic equilibrium might emerge.

As societal transitions in large scale systems are by definition complex, uncertain and contested, they are also unmanageable from a traditional perspective. Not only because there is no one point of origin for interventions as every actor influences the dynamics, but also because most of the more powerful actors are part of the system facing structural changes. This means they are by definition adverse to disruptive and swift transitions. A governance approach for transitions thus requires a new perspective toward governance of planetary problems as follows:

▶ Action needs to tap into and be in confluence with ongoing dynamics in order to steer the system with incremental steps toward a new sustainable (system) state (co-evolution rather than revolution) (Rotmans *et al.*, 2001)

▶ Small-scale actions need to be directed to domains in which a small intervention can result in tipping toward larger changes or, simply, seek for such changes that can cascade toward broader system innovation (tipping innovation's cascade) (Frantzeskaki *et al.*, 2012a; Loorbach *et al.*, 2011)

▶ Actions need to also refer to processes that will couple with or reroute ongoing processes in a co-evolutionary continuum (feed in and onto co-evolutionary processes) (Loorbach 2010; F. Frantzeskaki *et al.*, 2012) taking into account existing power-relations as well as path-dependencies (Avelino *et al.*, 2011)

Given the ambiguities and uncertainties in transitions, transition governance views sustainability as a characteristic of the process of change itself, both in terms of the extent to which it helps to move away from unsustainability and in terms of the extent to which the process is able to accommodate and generate diversity, inclusivity and reflexivity. Given that there are different approaches to dealing with transitions focused on different aspects of sustainability (for example, climate change, recycling, carbon emissions, pollution, biodiversity, and so forth), the aim is to achieve as many interconnected aspects of sustainability as possible within the scope of the intervention space (Loorbach and Frantzeskaki 2012; Frantzeskaki and Loorbach 2010; van Buuren and Loorbach 2009; Loorbach and Wijsman 2013).

Experiences with transition governance show that a plurality of societal systems have different dynamics between different actors on different levels and in different domains. They partially have to put their personal interests and aspirations aside, or forward, when transition pathways to sustainability are drawn up and decided on. Actors have divergent backgrounds and interests, thus they seek different windows of opportunity in systemic societal change toward sustainability (Brown *et al.*, 2013; Smith and Raven, 2012). Transition governance builds on the adaptive and transformative capabilities of actors in the context of societal systems under transition pressures.

Basic tenets for transition governance

The characteristics of societal transitions have led to the formulation and experimental application of **tenets for transition governance** (Loorbach 2007, 2010; Frantzeskaki *et al.*, 2012) much like related change-oriented approaches based on complex systems thinking (see for example Scharmer and Yukelson, this issue). The tenets for transition governance are distinct in that they have a normative orientation towards the particular pattern of transitional change as well as a broad focus on agency and (meta-) governance:

▶ The dynamics of the system create feasible and non-feasible means for steering. This implies that content and process are inseparable. Process management on its own is not sufficient; insight into how the system works is an essential precondition for effective management

▶ Long-term thinking (at least 25 years) is preferably used as a framework for shaping short-term policy in the context of persistent societal problems. This means reflection and forecasting: the setting of short-term goals based on long-term goals and the reflection on future developments through the use of scenarios

▶ Objectives should be flexible and adjustable at the system level. The complexity of the system is at odds with the desire to formulate specific objectives and blueprint plans. While being directed, the structure and order of the system are also changing, and so the objectives set should change too

▶ The timing of the intervention is crucial. Immediate and effective intervention is possible in both desirable and undesirable crisis situations

▶ Managing a complex, adaptive system means using disequilibria as well as equilibria. Relatively short periods of non-equilibrium therefore offer opportunities to direct the system in a desirable direction (toward a new attractor)

▶ Creating space for actors to build up alternative regimes is crucial for innovation. Actors at a certain distance from the regime can effectively create a new regime in a protected environment to permit investment of sufficient time, energy, and resources

▶ Steering from 'outside' a societal system is not effective. Structures, actors, and practices adapt and anticipate in such a manner that these should also be directed from 'inside'

▶ A focus on (social) learning about different actor perspectives and a variety of options (which requires a wide playing field) is a necessary precondition for change

▶ Participation from and interaction between stakeholders is a necessary basis for developing support for policies and to engage actors in reframing problems and solutions through social learning

Transition management: experimental governance in practice

These relatively abstract governance tenets have been translated into a practical management framework that intends to offer the space for experimental application as well as scientific reflection on these experiments. The framework was developed based on theoretical reasoning (following the line of reasoning and conceptual integration described earlier) combined with practical experiment and observation. It is an analytical lens to assess how societal actors deal with complex societal issues at different levels, but consequently also to develop and implement strategies to influence these 'natural' governance processes. In the transition management framework, four different types of governance activities (Van der Brugge and Van Raak 2007) are identified that are relevant to societal transitions: strategic, tactical, operational, and reflexive (Loorbach 2007).

In practice, transition management comes down to a combination of developing around a common understanding of a transition challenge and a shared ambition to drive it toward sustainability. By using the transition perspective as a lens, transition teams develop an analysis of a particular persistent problem in a complex societal system. This could be a geographical area (from neighbourhood to city, country, or region), sector, or societal issue. Based on the preliminary analysis, the transition team can identify regime and niche-actors that are potential contributors to a desired transition, who are brought together in so-called transition arenas or experiments. In and around these arenas and experiments, a shared discourse, ambition, and agenda is developed in such a way that it empowers participants and enables them to translate it to their own daily environments. Through such a social learning process, individuals start to relate to a broader common context and ambitions, creating the conditions for diffusion, self-organisational processes, and emergent innovation (Loorbach, 2007).

Transition management thus proposes to develop **informal networks** in which individuals and, later, organisations are provided the mental, social, and physical space to develop new ideas, common language, and ambitions, as well as new joint projects (Nevens *et al.*, 2013). In doing so over a longer period of time, participants will increasingly translate the transition perspective and ideas into their own operating context, while understanding the complexities, unpredictability and non-linear causalities involved (see also Snowden, this issue). These transition management processes therewith indirectly influence and change regular policies in government, business, research, and civil society. Below, the main ingredients of a transition management process are described, which in practice blend and are enacted often in parallel or at least not in specific sequential order.

Establishing a transition team

Transition management processes can be developed in any complex societal system in which individuals or organisations experience both persistent problems and the possibility of a transition; in other words, a context in which current common approaches and solutions do not suffice, future developments are highly uncertain, and major sustainability challenges are present. It therefore starts with people, individuals who seek more fundamental alternatives or are convinced these are necessary. To actively engage with the emerging transition so as to influence its speed and direction, a transition team needs to be formed that can manage both content and participatory process. The transition team needs to include people with different backgrounds: a representative of an initiating organisation or problem owner (often a governmental organisation, but also increasingly businesses or NGOs); experts in the particular transition arena; and transition management experts. It is crucial that the transition team be allowed the necessary space for experimentation and learning—through funding as well as mandate. The transition team is in charge of bringing together the first rough integrated analysis of the transition at hand, analysing the governance and actor-networks, identifying and selecting frontrunners, and managing the different phases and dimensions of the transition management process. These include problem structuring and establishment of a transition arena; developing sustainability visions, images and transition pathways; initiating and executing transition experiments; and transition monitoring and evaluation.

Problem structuring and establishment of a transition arena

Transition management boils down to creating space for frontrunners (niche-players and regime-players) in transition arenas. Formed in transition arenas for a specified issue are: a vision, an agenda, and a social commitment to sustainability values. A transition arena can be also seen as a constellation of governance innovations toward sustainability. A transition arena aims at creating a sustainability partnership that identifies and reframes a persistent problem, and articulates and commits to a vision of sustainable development and to a shared agenda for moving in this direction. The common perspective and terminology developed in the transition arena group relates to the shared belief in the possibility of transition in the near future and the need to develop strategies to guide this transition toward sustainability. Through the process of exchange of perspectives, framing societal complexity in terms of transitions, and developing a strategy of multiple pathways and experiments, transition arenas simultaneously develop a sensitivity for complexity and uncertainty inherent to societal change processes, as well as an action perspective related to insights about how (small scale) strategic interventions might fundamentally alter system trajectories over time. In this way, a transition arena differs from a network of actors, since actors in a transition arena are tied by a common belief (even when having divergent interests), and it is not tied by common or complementary interests like a network of actors.

Developing sustainability visions, pathways, and a transition agenda

Problem structuring and envisioning are very important processes for transition management. The actors involved in the envisioning process are stimulated and supported to reflect on their everyday routines. What is actually realised is a deeper understanding from the actors of the complexity of the challenge (societal problem). The involved actors understand the challenge and realise that their small-scale, everyday actions do have a cumulative impact on the societal system. Throughout the envisioning process, actors shift from passively observing societal problems to realising that their actions reinforce those societal phenomena. An outcome of the envisioning process is that actors who are involved in transition arenas change their daily routines after reflecting on them. What is thus realised is a change or reflection of short-term actions of actors that contemplate and align with the long-term vision that is a product of the envisioning process.

Typical outcomes of such transition arena processes are the following:

▶ The basic transition narrative that is a mapping of the pathologies/flaws of the current system and answers the question, 'why a transition?'

▶ The sustainability criteria that are the conditions under which the same societal function can be provided in the future in a sustainable way, for example, the energy system needs to include clean energy, the health care system needs to be oriented to the individual level and not to systems

▶ The formulation of areas that require changes, expressed in the form of transition images. If for example, one considers the clean energy vision, biomass or wind energy can be included as transition images that link to such a transition vision

The initiation and execution of transition experiments

Transition experiments are high-risk experiments with a social learning objective that are supposed to contribute to the sustainability goals at the systems level and should fit within the transition pathways (Kemp and Van den Bosch 2006). It is important to formulate sound criteria for the selection of experiments and to make the experiments mutually coherent.

The crucial point is to measure the extent to which the experiments and projects contribute to the overall system sustainability goals and to assess in what way a particular experiment reinforces another experiment. Are there specific niches for experiments that can be identified? What is the attitude of the current regime toward these niche experiments? The aim is to create a portfolio of transition experiments that reinforce each other and contribute to the sustainability objectives in significant and measurable ways. Around and between these experiments all sorts of actors can be involved who do not engage regularly in debates about long-term issues; these can be small business, consumers, citizens, or local groups, for example. Here as well the emphasis is on involving first movers.

Monitoring and evaluating the transition process

Continuous monitoring is a vital part of the search and learning process of transitions. Monitoring the transition process itself and monitoring transition management are distinct processes. Monitoring the transition process involves physical changes in the system in question, slowly changing macro-developments, and fast niche-developments—seeds of change as well as movements of individual and collective actors at the regime level. This provides the enriched context for transition management.

Monitoring of transition management involves different aspects and tasks in the following order:

1. The actors within the transition arena must be monitored with regard to their behaviour, networking activities, alliance forming, and responsibilities, and also with regard to their activities, projects, and instruments

2. The transition agenda must be monitored with regard to the actions, goals, projects, and instruments that have been agreed on. Transition experiments need to be monitored with regard to specific new knowledge and insight and how these are transferred, but also with regard to aspects of social and institutional learning

3. The transition process itself must be monitored with regard to the rate of progress, the barriers, and the points for improvement, and so on. Integration of monitoring and evaluation within each phase and at every level of transition management may stimulate a process of social learning that arises from the interaction and cooperation between different actors involved.

In each of the above activity clusters, coalition and network formation is of vital importance combined with the systemic structuring and synthesising of discussions. The transition arena is meant to stimulate the formation of new coalitions, partnerships, and networks. Most often, coalitions emerge around transition pathways or experiments, or around specific sub-themes, where arenas arise from arenas. The very idea behind transition management is to create new coalitions, partnerships and newly formed networks that allows for building up continuous pressure on the political and market arena to safeguard the long-term orientation and goals of the transition process.

Applying transition management: the case of Rotterdam City Harbours

The Cityharbors[1] is an area in Rotterdam of about 1600 hectares located on both banks of the river Meuse and within the city limits. It is still largely used for harbour activities, but will transform over the next 25 years as harbour activities move outward to the sea. The city and the harbour at first failed to come to a joint approach via formal routes and then decided to establish a small office that was asked to develop a new strategic vision. This office adopted the transition management approach and started a broad transition arena process in 2008 in which innovative stakeholders were involved at the strategic level to develop

---

1 http://stadshavensrotterdam.nl/en/

a more ambitious long-term perspective and multiple groups were formed at the tactical level, discussing specific parts of the area or specific sub-themes. Out of this process, a vision emerged of a sustainable city harbour in which an innovative mix of living, working and recreation should develop. This vision 'Creating on the edge', which was presented in 2009, emphasises the need for experiment and innovation and the unique features of this area in terms of the interconnectedness with the water, the availability of space and the urgency to ensure sustainable development of the area. Some of the guiding principles defined were energy self-sufficiency, closed material loops, living on and with water, new communities and clean mobility.

The vision explicitly positioned the area development as a transition process, requiring not only an inspiring vision and ambition, but also an innovative approach. It tied the economic development to sustainable innovation for the area and therefore makes a strong case to see the area development itself as booster for the regional economy and development. The area itself was presented as an experiment zone and a lobby started to create as much space in terms of finance and regulation as possible. The process of developing the vision and following strategy involved over a hundred representatives from different city departments (economic, housing, mobility, social), from the harbour company, from local business and industry, from research and from NGOs. During this process, the discussion on the vision, the need for structural change and the required governance approach created enthusiasm and a new spirit, including ensuring the necessary political support.

The overall vision is now in the process of being translated to different areas on a lower level (Cityharbors is divided into five sub-areas), which all have their own specific characteristics and time-horizon on which harbour activities will gradually disappear, through a variety of transition experiments and networks. Some of the examples are:

▶ **A floating city.** In fall 2009, building started on a first floating building of what could evolve into a floating city. The basic rationale is that increasing water levels in the river and of groundwater will necessitate more innovative living concepts that are able to adapt to this. In the Cityharbors, thousands of people could possibly live on water. The 'floating pavilion' serves as an education and meeting centre and has paved the way for the current contracting of a floating district.

▶ **Clean Tech Delta**[2]. A consortium of companies and other actors involved in the transition arena (like Van Gansewinkel, Waste Incineration Rijnmond AVR, Arcadis, BP, Shell, IBM, Eneco, the city of Rotterdam and three universities) started a cooperative enterprise to develop the area into a laboratory for smart energy, water and materials solutions

---

2 http://www.cleantechdelta.nl/?lang=en

▶ **RDM Campus**[3]. One of the areas has been developed over the past few years as an education and innovation hub around sustainable technologies and practices. It clusters manufacturing, applied higher education and research as a motor for the area's development

These are just some of the initiatives that came out of the transitioning process of the past years. They are examples of how long-term visions and ambitions can be linked to short-term innovative experiments. But also how the transition arena process serves as a way to develop a social learning context in which a shared understanding of the necessary type of change and its direction can emerge in the form of shared language, expectations and goals. These in themselves help to orient short-term actions by actors that not necessarily cooperate but are part of the same larger societal system. The transition arena created mental, physical and financial space for projects that would otherwise never have been developed this quickly or at this level of ambition. Obviously it remains to be seen where this will all lead, but by now it is safe to say that counterweight has been developed against the usual tendencies to develop the area in an ad-hoc manner. By choosing the best economic benefits on the short-term (meaning sell to the highest bidding project developer which will try to maximise its own profits on realisation of construction works instead of maximising the value over the entire life-span), usually city development leads to sub-optimal development from the perspective of sustainability. One of the examples of this counterweight has been the adoption by the city of sustainability criteria to which all developers that want to do something in the area need to subscribe and need to follow.

Taking stock from 14 years of transition management applications

Based on experimental applications such as those described above, there are a number of observations and insights that emerged and seem worthwhile to highlight. They are based on experiences primarily in developed (Western-) European contexts in projects such as MUSIC[4] and InContext[5] as well as in many projects in the Netherlands and Belgium. The basic principles for governance in transitions as well as the ingredients for transition management seem to provide a basic set of guiding principles to develop context sensitive

---

3 http://www.rdmcampus.nl/
4 http://www.themusicproject.eu/
5 www.incontext-fp7.eu

implementation in very different contexts. Ranging from very local to nations, from energy and mobility to education and welfare and from highly urban to very rural, in each of these dimensions the need for exploring more fundamental change processes and empowering social innovation has proven to be of added value. It does imply however the need to underline the necessary absence of any blueprint or standard recipe. But also that application in developing countries, in spite of recent positive experiences in Ecuador and Vanuatu, is still an open question. In general, there are a number of basic challenges that can be identified as central to any governance intervention in transitions and transition management specifically aiming to accelerate sustainability pathways.

Inclusivity

The premise of transition management is that it is based on selective participation and involves frontrunners, especially in earlier stages of the process. So far, this has been argued as a legitimate strategy based on the need to break out of existing dominant paradigms and routines, but in practice this does not always leads to including marginalised perspectives and opinions. Especially in countries with more authoritarian policy regimes, the danger lies in transition management being hijacked and used as another legitimisation for dominant perspectives. Therefore the question is not only practical (how to involve outsider, marginalised, and less articulated perspectives and interests in the process) but also fundamental (how and where transition management can be positioned so that it creates a really protected space for such interests to freely and openly participate).

Democracy

Also related to inclusivity, questions may arise regarding leadership of the transition management process—it can be challenged as undemocratic and the sources of legitimacy questioned. In the experiences and literature so far, the main argument is that the 'informal' status of the transition management process ensures that outcomes will only be adopted when supported by other actors inside the policy arena or society at large. It is argued that the approach seeks to offer a 'supplementary democracy'; that is, a semi-structured arena in which societal actors can collectively identify problems and solutions and discuss implementation. However, this presupposes an institutionalised, formal democratic system that is relatively open to such 'shadow processes'. In lower and middle income countries, where democratic traditions are often relatively young, transition management could easily provide a mechanism to help build such a tradition and engage larger parts of civil society, but it could also easily lead to a too technocratic and functionalistic implementation with hardly any impact beyond the participants.

Diversity and openness

In predevelopment phases of transition, there is a clear drive for more diversity and for exploring multiple pathways, but toward the acceleration stage there is a tendency toward homogenisation of systems of provisioning, in part a consequence of mainstream proclivity toward uniformity, centralisation, and standards setting. Yet, diversity is arguably an important characteristic that needs to be maintained in order that sustainability initiatives are embedded in—and sensitive and adapted to—local contexts, in a way that promotes their longevity and system reflexivity in the long term. The conditions to ensure diversity in the context of coupling and rescaling transition initiatives are yet to be explored, but seem critical given the importance of space and place in engendering acceleration. Especially when it comes to external initiation of transition management, the process is framed toward specific solutions/outcomes. In practice, the challenge is to provide throughout transition management processes a context to reflect, open up, and explore variety.

Speed of change

Transitions are defined as systemic changes in which economic, technological, social, cultural, and ecological changes co-evolve. While this has been true in historical transitions, in most sustainability transitions—and especially in the context of lower and middle income countries where modernisation and sustainability transitions emerge simultaneously—it can be questioned as to whether gradual co-evolution is possible, given the different paces of change in different dimensions. Sociocultural changes take place on a much longer time horizon than technological ones. In these contexts, transition management is challenged to play into these different speeds, identify the tensions they create, and try to address them.

Social learning and capacity building

Transition management is mostly about social learning: collectively trying to understand systemic challenges and seek strategic actions that play into complex processes of social change in order to influence them in a certain direction. Often transition management is interpreted as instrumental: developing a vision and innovation networks is the end goal. Using transition management tools to support and help guide social learning requires skills and competencies, both among participants as well as within the transition team. In many countries, neither the expertise nor the knowledge and facilities to acquire such competencies may be available. Such competencies may be developed through experience, but a certain level of social entrepreneurship, scientific knowledge, and process/governance capacity are a prerequisite of successful transition management.

The resilience of the regime

The (quasi-)autonomous character of a transition trajectory often makes the regime nervous. This reflects the tensions between regular policy and a transition shadow trajectory with a different time horizon, objective and set of policy instruments. As a response to these emerging tensions, the regime has the almost unstoppable tendency to turn (back) into a command-and-control mode. The manifestation of such a command-and-control mode is the attempt to build up new institutional constituencies, such as task forces, advisory boards, sounding boards, etc. This arises mainly out of fear to give away the steering and control of the transition process: it is a mere reflex to remain a handle on a complicated process the regime wants to be in charge of. These institutional constituencies reduce the free space created for innovative niche players, even if they are established to support the transition process and the frontrunners involved. From a transition management viewpoint the only adequate response is to build up a close relationship with (parts of) the regime and maintain the autonomy of the transition project by tuning the free space, agenda and responsibilities of the transition process compared to the regular policy process.

Context specificity

Every transition project is unique in terms of context and participants and therefore requires a specific contextual and participatory approach. At the sector level, mainly professionals will be involved, but in a regional transition arena participants are often more emotionally connected to the subject for example. This means that there is no such thing as a standard recipe for how to manage transition projects. That also means that one will also be surprised by the developments within a transition trajectory, in particular within a transition arena. Arena processes are quite intense and sometimes emotional, full of tensions within participants and tensions between the environment and the arena (Loorbach, 2010). These informal aspects of such a transition trajectory are at least as important as the formal aspects. Preferably these transition projects should be guided by a team of experienced people with a variety of complementary skills and backgrounds.

Empowering frontrunners is key to a transition process

Key to transition management is the empowerment of frontrunners (pioneers, innovative niche players). With empowerment we here mean providing them with multiple resources in order to be better equipped to play the power games with the regime. In the Dutch energy transition, for instance, through development of new regulation and changes in funding schemes conditions were created that open up space for more innovation. But with resources we do not refer only to financial resources such as subsidies, but also to mental resources.

Such as a deeper insight into the complexity and persistency of the problem in question, by reframing that problem and by transforming it into a sustainability challenge, including the possibilities to relate the rather abstract vision to concrete projects that partly shape that visionary future (Grin *et al.*, 2010). After all, a transition arena is to be considered as an empowerment environment for the frontrunners selected and is meant to provide frontrunners with an action perspective.

Discussion: moving forward?

The transition approach is based on the conviction that policy alone cannot solve persistent sustainability problems. So instead of starting from a policy or market-based approach, the transitions approach starts from the conceptualisation of persistent challenges as embedded in the dominant regimes in complex societal systems. Transition scholars have found that in historical cases the societal process of problem structuring gradually creates a deeper awareness of complex problems and the urgency for change. Simultaneously alternatives start to emerge: new technologies, networks, business models, practices, and so on, always in a decentralised and context-specific manner. Transition governance takes these dynamics as starting point as they create resilience and sustainability at the local scale and start to contribute to solutions on a global scale, increasing the likelihood of disruptive changes in the dominant unsustainable regimes. Transition governance in this sense is a 'glocal approach', as it brings in the more generic and global issues as drivers, and uses external challenge as a context to create space for bottom-up context-specific solutions. This in itself is a major transition challenge for governance institutions addressing global issues: they need to shift from seeking generic solutions to offering more generic frameworks that create space for and help to enable bottom-up social innovation.

Depending on the specific context, transition processes can be organised so that frontrunners, champions, and entrepreneurs with different backgrounds are brought together to develop society-based transition agendas. Over the past decade, a lot of experience has been built up with this approach, leading to substantial input into policy agendas. The approach empowers, stimulates, and facilitates social innovation beyond policy. The tools and instruments of transition management help to collectively set boundaries, develop deeper and shared understanding of challenges, share inspiring visions for the future, and create scenarios and pathways toward strategic innovation. Governments and policy-related institutions can find tools that support the different roles they can play in transitions: from facilitating to empowering, from regulating to enforcing, and from initiating to coordinating.

It is however also clear from the 15 years of experimentation that while transition management is successful in empowering transformative social innovation, it is so far not achieving the aspired large scale systemic changes (Loorbach 2014). Over the past years therefore the research agenda has broadened to explore issues of institutional change, top-down strategies, new forms of power, the role of scale and the psychology of transitions. It seems that through this opening up a whole new range of questions emerges as well as fruitful interconnections to other disciplines and parts of the world.

References

Avelino, F. and Rotmans, J. 2011. A dynamic conceptualization of power for sustainability research. Journal of Cleaner Production, 19 (8), pp. 796-804.

Biermann, F. 2007. '"Earth System Governance" as a Crosscutting Theme of Global Change Research.' *Global Environmental Change* 17 (3–4): 326–37.

Biggs, D., R. Biggs, V. Dakos, R. J. Scholes, and M. Schoon. 2011. 'Are We Entering an Era of Concatenated Global Crises?' *Ecology and Society* 16 (2): 27. http://www.ecologyand society.org/vol16/iss2/art27/

Brown, R. R., M. A. Farrelly, and D. Loorbach. 2013. 'Actors Working the Institutions in Sustainability Transitions: The Case of Melbourne's Stormwater Management.' *Global Environmental Change* 23 (4): 701–18.

Dadush, U., and B. Stancil. 2010. 'The World Order in 2050.' *Policy Outlook*, Carnegie Endowment for International Peace, Washington, DC. http://carnegieendowment.org/ files/World_Order_in_2050.pdf

De Dreu, C. K. W., and M.A. West. 2001. 'Minority Dissent and Team Innovation: The Importance of Participation in Decision Making.' *Journal of Applied Psychology* 86 (6): 1191–1201.

De Graaf, R., and R. van der Brugge. 2010. 'Transforming Water Infrastructure by Linking Water Management and Urban Renewal in Rotterdam.' *Technological Forecasting and Social Change* 77 (8) 1282–91.

Frantzeskaki, F., and H. de Haan. 2009. 'Transitions: Two Steps from Theory to Policy.' *Futures* 41(9): 593–606. http://dx.doi.org/10.1016/j.futures.2009.04.009.

Frantzeskaki, N., and D. Loorbach. 2010. 'Towards Governing Infrasystem Transitions: Reinforcing Lock-In or Facilitating Change?' *Technological Forecasting and Social Change* 77 (8): 1292–1301.

Frantzeskaki, F., Thissen, W., and J. Grin. 2012. 'Drifting between Transitions, The Environmental Protection Transition in Greece.' 3rd International Conference of Sustainability Transitions, Copenhagen, August 26–28.

Frantzeskaki, N., D. Loorbach, and J. Meadowcroft. 2012a. 'Governing Transitions to Sustainability: Transition Management as a Governance Approach towards Pursuing Sustainability.' *International Journal of Sustainable Development* 15: 19–36.

Frantzeskaki, N., J. Koppenjan, D. Loorbach, N. Ryan, and M. Charles. 2012b. 'Theoretical and Empirical Contributions to an Understanding of the Governability of System Transitions to Sustainability—Lessons and Next-Step Challenges.' *International Journal of Sustainable Development* 15: 173–186.

Frantzeskaki, N., Wittmayer, J., and Loorbach, D., (2014) 'The role of partnerships in "realizing" urban sustainability in Rotterdam's City Ports Area, the Netherlands', *Journal of Cleaner Production*, 65, 406-417.

Geels, F. W. 2004. 'From Sectoral Systems of Innovation to Socio-Technical Systems: Insights about Dynamics and Change from Sociology and Institutional Theory.' *Research Policy* 33 (6–7): 897–920.

Geels, F. W. 2005a. 'Processes and Patterns in Transitions and System Innovations: Refining the Co-Evolutionary Multi-Level Perspective.' *Technological Forecasting and Social Change* 72 (6): 681–96.

Geels, F. W. 2005b. *Technological Transitions and System Innovations*. Cheltenham, UK: Edward Elgar Publishing.

Geels, F. W. 2011. 'The Multi-Level Perspective on Sustainability Transitions: Responses to Seven Criticisms.' *Environmental Innovation and Societal Transitions* 1 (1): 24–40.

Geels, F. W., and J. Schot. 2007. 'Typology of Sociotechnical Transition Pathways.' *Research Policy* 36 (3): 399–417.

Gell-Man, M. ed., 1994. *Complex Adaptive Systems*. Addison-Wesley, Reading MA.

Genus, A., and A. M. Coles. 2008. 'Rethinking the Multi-Level Perspective of Technological Transitions.' *Research Policy* 37 (9): 1436–45.

Grin, J., F. Felix, B. Bos, and S. Spoelstra. 2004. 'Practices for Reflexive Design: Lessons from a Dutch Project on Sustainable Agriculture.' *International Journal of Foresight and Innovation Policies* 1 (1–2): 126–48.

Grin, J., Rotmans, J. and J. Schot. 2010. *Transitions to Sustainable Development: New Directions in the Study of Long Term Transformative Change*. New York: Routledge.

Hendriks, C. M. 2009. 'Policy Design Without Democracy? Making Democratic Sense of Transition Management.' *Policy Sciences* 42 (4): 341–68.

Karlsson-Vinkhuyzen, S. I., N. Jollands, and L. Staudt. 2012. 'Global Governance for Sustainable Energy: The Contribution of a Global Public Goods Approach.' *Ecological Economics* 83: 11–18.

Kates, R. W., Clark, W. C., Corell, R., Hall, J. M., Jaeger, C., Lowe, I., McCarthy, J. J., Schellnhuber, H. J., Bolin, B., Dickson, N. M., Faucheux, S., Gallopin, G. C., Grubler, A., Huntley, B., Jager, J. and Jodha, N. S., Kasperson, R. E., Mabogunje, A., Matson, P., Mooney, H., Moore, B., O'Riordan, T. and Svedin, U. 2001. 'Environment and development: Sustainability science'. *Science*, 292 (5517), pp. 641-642. Available at: <http://dx.doi.org/10.1126/science.1059386>.

Kaul, I., I. Grunberg, and M. A. Stern, eds. 1999. *Global Public Goods: International Cooperation in the 21st Century*, Oxford, UK: Oxford University Press.

Kaul, I., P. Conceicao, K. Le Goulven, and R. U. Mendoza, eds. 2003. *Providing Global Public Goods: Managing Globalization*. Oxford, UK: Oxford University Press.

Kemp, R., and S. van den Bosch. 2006. 'Transitie-experimenten. Praktijkexperimenten met de potentie om bij te dragen aan transities.' Kenniscentrum voor duurzame systeeminnovaties en transities. Rotterdam, Netherlands.

Kemp, R., J. Rotmans, and D. Loorbach. 2007. 'Transition Management as a Model for Managing Processes of Co-Evolution towards Sustainable Development.' *International Journal of Sustainable Development & World Ecology* 14 (1): 78–91.

Kooiman, J., 1993. *Modern Governance: New Government-Society Interactions*. London: Sage.

Loorbach, D. 2007. 'Transition Management: New Mode of Governance for Sustainable Development.' PhD thesis, Erasmus University, Rotterdam. http://repub.eur.nl/res/pub/10200/.

Loorbach, D. 2010. 'Transition Management for Sustainable Development: A Prescriptive, Complexity-Based Governance Framework.' *Governance* 23 (1): 161–83.

Loorbach, D., 2014. 'To Transition! Governance Panarchy in the New Transformation', inaugural address. Rotterdam: DRIFT - Erasmus University Rotterdam.

Loorbach, D., and N. Frantzeskaki. 2012. Why Taking Complexity Seriously Implies a Paradigm Shift for Policy Studies. In *COMPACT I: Public Administration in Complexity*, ed. by L. Gerrits and P. Marks, 327–45. Litchfield Park, AZ: Emergent Publications.

Loorbach, D., and R. Lijnis Huffenreuter 2010. 'The Practice of Transition Management: Examples and Lessons from Four Distinct Cases.' *Futures* 42 (30): 237–46.

Loorbach, D., and R. Lijnis Huffenreuter. 2013. 'Exploring the Economic Crisis from a Transition Management Perspective.' *Environmental Innovation and Societal Transition* 6: 35–46.

Loorbach, D., and K. Wijsman. 2013. 'Business Transition Management: Exploring a New Role for Business in Sustainability Transitions.' *Journal of Cleaner Production* 45: 20–28.

Loorbach, D., R. van der Brugge, and M. Taanman. 2008. 'Governance in the Energy Transition: Practice of Transition Management in the Netherlands.' *International Journal of Environmental Technology and Management* 9 (2): 294–315.

Loorbach, D., N. Frantzeskaki, and W. Thissen. 2011. 'A Transition Research Perspective on Governance for Sustainability.' In *European Research on Sustainable Development— 1: Transformative Science Approaches for Sustainability*, C. C. Jaeger, David J. Tàbara, and J. Jaeger, (Eds.), 73–89. Berlin: Springer.

Midgley, G., 2003. System Thinking: An Introduction and Overview. In: G. Midgley ed., *Systems Thinking*. Thousand Oaks: Sage. pp. xvii.

Nevens, F., N. Frantzeskaki, L. Gorissen, and D. Loorbach. 2013. 'Urban Transition Labs: Co-creating Transformative Action for Sustainable Cities.' *Journal of Cleaner Production* 50: 111–22, doi: 10.1016/j.jclepro.2012.12.001.

O'Riordan, T. and Lenton, T., 2013. *Addressing Tipping Points for a Precarious Future*. Oxford University Press.

Perkins, S. 2013. 'Global Temperatures Are Close to 11,000-Year Peak.' *Nature*, March 7.

Pierre, J., 2000. *Debating Governance: Authority, Steering and Democracy*. Oxford: Oxford University Press.

Raven, R. P. J. M., S. van den Bosch, and R. Weterings. 2010. 'Transitions and Strategic Niche Management: Towards a Competence Kit for Practitioners.' *International Journal of Technology Management* 51 (1): 57–74.

Rotmans, J., and D. Loorbach. 2009. 'Complexity and Transition Management.' *Journal of Industrial Ecology* 13 (2): 184–96.

Rotmans, J., R. Kemp, M. B. A. van Asselt, F. W. Geels, G. Verbong, and K. Molendijk. 2000. *Transitions & Transition Management: The Case of an Emission-Poor Energy Supply*. Maastricht: ICIS (International Centre for Integrative Studies).

Rotmans, J., R. Kemp, and M. van Asselt. 2001. 'More Evolution Than Revolution: Transition Management in Public Policy.' *Foresight* 3 (1): 15–31.

Schuitmaker, T. J. 2012. 'Identifying and Unravelling Persistent Problems.' *Technological Forecasting and Social Change* 79 (6): 1021–31. http://dx.doi.org/10.1016/j.techfore.2011.11.008.

Smith, A., and R. Raven. 2012. 'What Is Protective Space? Reconsidering Niches in Transitions to Sustainability.' *Research Policy* 41: 1025–36.

Sondeijker, S., J. Geurts, J. Rotmans, and A. Tukker. 2006. 'Imagining Sustainability: The Added Value of Transition Scenarios in Transition Management.' *Foresight* 8 (5): 15–30.

Unruh, G. C. 2002. 'Escaping Carbon Lock-In.' *Energy Policy* 30 (4): 317–25.

Van Buuren, A., and D. Loorbach. 2009. 'Policy Innovation in Isolation?' *Public Management Review* 11 (3): 375–92.

Van den Bosch, S., Breze, H., and Vergragt, P. 2005. 'Rotterdam case study of the transition to a fuel cell transport system.' *Fuel Cells Bulletin*, 6: 10–16.

Van der Brugge, R., and R. van Raak. 2007. 'Facing the Adaptive Management Challenge: Insights from Transition Management.' *Ecology and Society* 12 (2): 33. http://www.ecologyandsociety.org/vol12/iss2/art33/.

Van Eijndhoven, J., N. Frantzeskaki, and D. Loorbach. 2013. 'Connecting Long and Short-Term via Envisioning in Transition Arenas.' In *Connective Capacity in Water Governance*, ed. by J. Edelenbos, N. Bressers, and P. Scholten, Chapter 9, 172–190. London: Ashgate Publications.

Van Knippenberg, D., C. K. W. De Dreu, and A.C. Homan. 2004. 'Work Group Diversity and Group Performance: An Integrative Model and Research Agenda.' *Journal of Applied Psychology* 89 (6): 1008–22.

Westley, F., Olsson, P., Folke, C., Homer-Dixon, T., Vredenburg, H., Loorbach, D,. Thompson, J., Nilsson, M,. Lambin, E., Sendzimir, J., Banerjee, B., Galaz, V., van der Leeuw, S., 2011. 'Tipping toward sustainability: emerging pathways of transformation'. *Ambio* 40 (7): 762-780.

Wiek, A., C. Binder, and R. W. Scholz. 2006. 'Functions of Scenarios in Transition Processes.' *Futures* 38 (7): 740–66.

DOI: [10.9774/GLEAF.4700.2015.ju.00009]

Scaling Out, Scaling Up, Scaling Deep[*]
Strategies of Non-profits in Advancing Systemic Social Innovation

Michele-Lee Moore
University of Victoria, Canada

Darcy Riddell
Waterloo Institute for Social Innovation and Resilience, Canada

Dana Vocisano
Concordia University, Canada

To effect large system change, "niche" or local-level innovations must span spatial and institutional scales to achieve broader systemic impact. Leaders of social innovation, in particular those who work in non-profit organizations and funders of non-profit and civil society organizations, are increasingly concerned with scaling the positive impact of their investments.

This study examines the case of the J.W. McConnell Family Foundation and the implementation of a deliberate strategy, named the Applied Dissemination initiative, to build grantee capacity and to accelerate their initiatives to achieve systemic change. One part of the strategy involved an "educational intervention", where leaders of more than a dozen national-level initiatives in Canada convened regularly over a period of several years to learn from each other's efforts to achieve scale. The group was successful not only in their efforts to scale for positive impact on their respective issue areas, but also in catalyzing a field of practice in Canada with a growing expertise in scaling innovation for systemic change. The findings show the success of six different strategies that may be adopted to scale innovation on the pathway to large-scale or systemic impact, which cut across three different types of "scaling": scaling out, scaling up, and scaling deep.

- Social innovation
- Scaling
- Impact
- Transitions studies
- Scaling strategies

[*] The authors would like to thank the J.W. McConnell Family Foundation, our project Advisory Board, the participants, and the detailed comments of three anonymous reviewers for sharing their insights and supporting this study.

Michele-Lee Moore is an Assistant Professor in the Department of Geography at the University of Victoria, and she leads the Water, Innovation, and Global Governance Lab at the Centre for Global Studies.

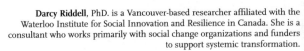

Dept of Geography, University of Victoria, CANADA

mlmoore@uvic.ca

Darcy Riddell, PhD. is a Vancouver-based researcher affiliated with the Waterloo Institute for Social Innovation and Resilience in Canada. She is a consultant who works primarily with social change organizations and funders to support systemic transformation.

Dana Vocisano is an organizational development consultant with 30 years of experience in the non-profit sector. She has a long-time interest in scaling social innovations and most recently has focused on social enterprises. She is a MA candidate in Human Systems Intervention at Concordia University, Canada.

H OW CAN BRILLIANT, BUT ISOLATED experiments aimed at solving the world's most pressing and complex social and ecological problems become more widely adopted and achieve transformative impact? Leaders of large systems change and social innovation initiatives often struggle to increase their impact on systems, and funders of such change in the non-profit sector are increasingly concerned with the scale and positive impact of their investments. As Bradach and Grindle (2014, p. 7) state, the catchphrase 'scaling what works' has become 'a rallying cry to direct more funding to interventions that actually get results'. But questions remain about how funders and social change leaders can work together to have an impact across scales and what 'scale' or 'scaling' actually involves.

In this article, we argue that the process of scaling social innovations to achieve systemic impacts involves three different types of scaling—scaling out, scaling up, and scaling deep—and large systems change (LSC) is likely to require a combination of these types. Although large systems change processes in any complex problem domain will be emergent, we found that certain strategies are associated with each type of scaling process. This argument is based on experiences from social innovation experiments conducted by charitable organisations and funded by the J.W. McConnell Family Foundation, over more than a decade in Canada.

To clarify terminology, we define social innovation as 'any initiative, product, programme, platform or design that challenges, and over time changes, the defining routines, resource and authority flows, or beliefs of the social system in which the innovation occurs' (Westley and Antadze, 2010). We believe social innovation is required to create large systems change.

This paper first examines the literature on management strategies for scaling the process of social change. In particular, we focus on the scholarly fields of strategic niche management (SNM) and social innovation and discuss the challenge of applying existing ideas for scaling from these fields to large systems change. Next, we describe the methods of this study and our case study of the J.W. McConnell Foundation and their grantees, as they collectively set out to learn how to scale the impacts of initiatives to achieve broader systems change. Following that, we present the study results, describing six strategies employed by these systems-change leaders.

Literature review

With the growing interest in scaling, questions arise about how leaders of social change initiatives may achieve scale, and thus, affect large systems change. Two bodies of literature have sought to address such questions: strategic niche management and the broader literature on social innovation.

Strategic niche management (SNM) is a sub-field of transitions studies that emerged in the 1990s (see Rip and Kemp, 1998). The conceptual logic on which SNM hinges, is that organisations interested in supporting the development of innovations must work to create innovation 'niches' (Kemp *et al.*, 1998, Verbong *et al.*, 2010, Hegger *et al.*, 2007). These niches are understood as 'safe' spaces—places that are protected from the daily operational concerns of the organisation, even though the work being undertaken may not yet be profitable, or even feasible (van der Laak *et al.*, 2007; Schot and Geels, 2008; Smith and Raven, 2012). This strand of research primarily focuses on socio-technical transitions—the pathways involved in new technological adoption, and their role in breaking institutional lock-in within a given 'regime', which refers to the reinforcing social, economic, cultural and technological systems in a given organisational field (Geels and Schot, 2007).

SNM scholars have devoted considerable effort to understanding how to create a 'niche' that is safe and have provided detailed understanding about the mechanisms of shielding, nurturing, and empowering (Smith and Raven, 2012). Secondly, consideration has been given to the types of organisations that are able to generate an innovation within that 'niche' (Caniëls and Romijn, 2008), which is understood to involve organisational capacities to articulate expectations and a vision, build social networks to create support for a new technology, and facilitate learning processes within and among niches (Schot and Geels, 2008). However, due to the overt focus on the management of technological niches, questions remain about how or whether these mechanisms and capacities apply beyond the technological, to the scaling of *social* innovations. Despite this, multidimensional systems change has been widely recognised as necessary to address some of our most complex social and ecological challenges (Folke *et al.*, 2011), and thus, cultivation of innovation in technological niches alone will be insufficient.

Later work in transitions studies builds on a framework to address how niche innovations interact with different scales, known as the multi-level perspective (MLP). The MLP depicts three scales or levels to consider when managing an innovation or transition for system-wide change—niche, regime, and an exogenous landscape depicting the broader environment and accrued social trends (Geels, 2002). Van den Bosch and Rotmans (2008) describe the mechanisms by which transition experiments can successfully contribute to transitions, including: deepening (described as learning about culture, norms, values), broadening (repeating an experiment in different niche contexts), and scaling up (embedding a transition experiment into dominant thinking within a niche or regime). However, efforts to explain when or how an innovative initiative moves across scales have been much more limited, as have analyses of the deliberate scaling strategies involved, beyond nurturing smaller-scale niche technologies until they are ready to compete with the dominant technology in a regime. Two studies have illustrated that knowledge translation and the process of 'anchoring' or linking are important mechanisms for connecting the niche to the regime level (Smith and Raven, 2012; Elzen *et al.*, 2012, respectively). But overall, analysis of the processes or agency required to impact the broader system or regime are underdeveloped in SNM and transition studies, despite the fact that large systems change likely involves all three scales. Moreover, further explanation is needed to describe the multiple paths leaders may take to link across scales, and the strategies that may generate large systems change beyond new technology adoption.

Beyond the SNM literature and transitions studies, scholarship in social innovation and social enterprise has focused on the strategic agency required to move ideas from one context to a larger scale (Bradach, 2010; Evans and Clarke, 2011; McPhedran et al., 2011; Mulgan et al., 2008). From a social innovation perspective, large-scale change will necessarily involve changes to rules, resource flows, cultural beliefs and relationships in a social system at multiple spatial or institutional scales. However, in social entrepreneurship and social enterprise studies, the emphasis on 'scaling for impact' reflects a product and consumer orientation, synonymous with diffusion or replication of a programme, product, or organisational model in multiple geographic locations and contexts to maximise the number of people that a social innovation reaches (Dees et al., 2004; Wei-skillern and Anderson, 2003; Mulgan et al., 2008). Even authors who recognise that transformative social innovation will require more than just replicating a programme (e.g. Bradach and Grindle, 2014; Ross, 2014), tend to emphasise diffusion. However, scaling social innovations to effect large-scale change will necessarily involve a more complex and diverse process than simply 'diffusing' a product or model. Therefore, we contend that empirical investigations of deliberate strategies that social innovators use when attempting to create systemic change are also needed—in particular ones that go beyond a focus on geographic and numeric dissemination of a product or service, to impact social systems or institutions.

Westley et al. (2014) characterised the dynamics and pathways of scaling in cases of social innovation by describing five unique pathways to advance systemic change. They differentiate between two kinds of scaling: 'scaling out', where an organisation attempts to affect more people and cover a larger geographic area through replication and diffusion, and 'scaling up', where an organisation aims to affect everybody who is in need of the social innovation they offer, or to aims to address the broader institutional or systemic roots of a problem (Westley et al. 2014). Our research builds on the distinction between scaling out and scaling up, adding new insights by describing associated strategies, and adding the further distinction of 'scaling deep' to create a typology of three approaches to scaling. In so doing, we contribute new research and theoretical perspectives that address gaps in the SNM and social innovation literatures. Moreover, our typology underscores the complexities and complementary nature of the strategies involved in advancing large systems change, opening up new avenues for research on how different scaling strategies relate to one another, and illuminating the role of funders and conveners in amplifying the system-wide impacts of social change initiatives.

Case study and methods

This case study involves a group of grantees in Canada, funded by the Montreal-based J.W. McConnell Family Foundation (herein referred to as McConnell Foundation), who sought greater systemic impact through social innovation. In 1998, the McConnell Foundation began pursuing a deliberate strategy for moving beyond discrete project-based funding, in order to enable broader impact by their grantees. The strategy was called **Applied Dissemination** (AD) and supported social innovators in disseminating new programmes, processes, skills or knowledge in their work with communities and organisations, and to apply or adapt innovations in different settings (Pearson, 2006). As one part of the AD strategy, the McConnell Foundation hosted a community of practice, convening diverse grantees to learn from one another, to integrate concepts of systems change into their practice, and to accelerate the impacts of funded innovations.

Organisations were awarded AD grants after an in-depth review. Selection criteria included showing: a deliberate strategy, demonstrable demand (McConnell Foundation, 1998), and completed evaluations that showed impact and distilled the 'minimum specifications' (Zimmerman, 1998) or variable and fixed elements of an innovation. From 2002 until 2007, the McConnell Foundation formally convened annual meetings with this AD learning group, and many participants continued in peer-support roles beyond this period. Organisations had diverse social change missions, governance and organisational structures and strategies, but shared a focus on scaling their work. Participating organisations included Caledon Institute of Social Policy, Child Development Institute, Tamarack, PLAN, L'Arche Canada, JUMP, L'Abri en Ville, Community Health and Social Services Network, Roots of Empathy, Santropol Roulant, Meal Exchange, and Engineers without Borders. Note that several of the same organisations also participated in the Westley *et al.* (2014) pathways study on social innovation, in which additional case data and organisational descriptions are provided. At the learning group, participants shared experiences and dilemmas, and learned from experts about topics including scaling, developmental evaluation, social marketing, complexity theory, and policy advocacy. Although some efforts did not succeed, almost 17 years later, many participants from the AD learning group have scaled their initiatives through a variety of means: by reorienting their mission to address root systemic issues; by spreading geographically; and by leading the development of new policies and cultural shifts.

Methods

Given the lack of baseline data on scaling strategies for large, complex systems change, we adopted a case study method (Yin, 2014) to begin building a theory of scaling, as per Plummer and Fennel's (2007) theory development approach which consists of concepts, variables and relational propositions. Here, we align with Flyvbjerg (2006) who argues it is possible to begin building theory from a single exploratory case study. As Yin (2014) states, the case study approach investigates a particular phenomenon of interest within its 'real-life context'. Because many study participants are still involved in scaling their social innovations (given that such a process has no endpoint), the phenomenon of scaling could only be studied as it unfolds in its real-life context.

In July 2013, 15 original AD learning group participants were invited to participate in this research. Because most participants were involved over long periods, they brought broad perspectives on changes in their initiatives, organisation, and their own practices over time. We asked them to reflect on the full arc of their own deliberate learning process on scaling. Participants completed a structured survey that used open-ended questions, including: What did 'going to scale' involve for your organisation? How did the AD learning group contribute to your perspective? And, what methodologies or understandings influenced how you grew or scaled your work? Participants were also invited to participate in a small focus group session (max. focus group participants = 4). Some participants chose to only complete the survey (14), but eight participants completed the survey and the focus groups. In total, three focus group sessions of 1.5 to 2 hours in duration occurred in August–September 2013. Focus group questions were: 1) What did you learn about scaling your initiative? 2) How do you now think about 'scale' and 'scaling' in your work? 3) What unintended consequences arose as you attempted to scale innovative initiatives? and 4) What leadership challenges did you face as you undertook this work?

We coded and analysed the survey responses and focus group transcripts, using first an open coding process, and then selective coding, as recommended by Dey (1999). As patterns emerged, we tested themes against the data to further substantiate the theme or refute it. Following the case study approach of Crutchfield and McLeod Grant (2008), we noted where patterns did not hold, helping us to identify differences in the strategies employed, their relationship to different types of scaling, and how these types of scaling differed from one another. We emphasise that our findings focus on the phenomenon of scaling, and the strategies by which actors can move social innovation impacts across scales. It is beyond the scope of this paper to describe the details of each social innovation and organisation involved; rather, we describe the patterns across the different initiatives.

A group of external advisers familiar with the AD learning group reviewed and responded to our preliminary findings.

Results and discussion

Many social change practitioners and funders are focused on scaling their impact, in order to meet the scope of contemporary social and environmental challenges. Executives within the McConnell Foundation believed that while the Foundation had invested resources into several initiatives, which successfully generated new models, these initiatives failed to address the roots or complexity of many social problems. That is, the Foundation was effectively supporting 'niche' development, but there were limited impacts on the broader regime or system. Our findings revealed that through the intensive learning process in the AD learning group, participants began to recognise opportunities to scale the impacts of their initiatives beyond their own 'niche' (whether that was a single school, a community, or a narrow programme area).

Not all participants pursued the same type of 'scale' or strategies to advance systemic impact. The strategy of choice was dependent on many factors: the founding conditions of their organisation; the context surrounding their issue; the resources and support they could access; choices they made about partners and strategies; and the windows of opportunity—political, cultural and social— that emerged. But we contend that several cross-cutting strategies were patterns in the various initiatives and that three different types of scaling emerged from our data: scaling out, up, and deep (Figure 1). The next section provides an overview of the three types of scaling and the strategies that align with each, as well as a short discussion of the leadership challenges involved with scaling.

A typology of routes to systemic impact: scaling out, scaling up and scaling deep

Our research found cross-cutting scaling strategies, and unique strategies that we have categorised into three broad types, refining Westley et al.'s (2014) distinction between scaling out and up, where scaling up refers to institutional changes—in cultural beliefs or rules and policies. Because of the unique strategies involved in these two kinds of institutional change, we suggest the third category of 'scaling deep'.[1] 'Scaling out' was the approach that McConnell Foundation staff and the AD learning group focused on originally, emphasising replication of successful innovations in different communities (or 'niches'), with the hopes of spreading those same results to more people. While at least one organisation has found this to be an enduring means to deal with context-specific issues that affect the system they are trying to change, the majority of participants found that replication might never address the root of the problem if these lay within broader institutions. For many initiatives, the route to greater impact lay in changing institutions and laws, or 'scaling up' to affect policies. Many participants described the shift in their scaling efforts to focus on the policy level because it has 'the largest impact' and was capable of changing the 'rules of the game'. Strategies for 'scaling deep', built on earlier work by Van den Bosch and Rotmans (2008), are related to the notion that durable change has been achieved only when people's hearts and minds, their values and cultural practices, and the quality of relationships they have, are transformed (see Figure 1 and Table 1).

---

1 This term was coined by Tatiana Fraser, the former Executive Director of GirlsAction, during the AD learning group.

Figure 1 Scaling out, scaling up and scaling deep for social innovation

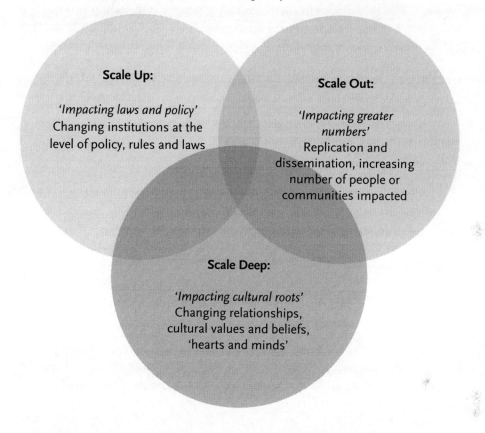

Scale Up:

'Impacting laws and policy'
Changing institutions at the
level of policy, rules and laws

Scale Out:

*'Impacting greater
numbers'*
Replication and
dissemination, increasing
number of people or
communities impacted

Scale Deep:

'Impacting cultural roots'
Changing relationships,
cultural values and beliefs,
'hearts and minds'

Strategies for social innovation and large systems change

Tips for diffusing innovation are abundant. But the findings in this study reveal a new and far more complex picture of what is entailed with 'scaling impact' depending on the type of scaling. Some of the strategies that have been well documented by other scholars consider the skills and agency of actors who are navigating complex systems, trying to stimulate or support large systems change, and leverage the necessary resources to achieve this change (Moore and Westley, 2011; Marshall *et al.*, 2012; Westley *et al.*, 2013; Geobey *et al.*, 2012). For instance, participants routinely cited the need to build and engage networks for all three types of scaling activities. Networking across sectors (rather than within sectors) was noted as especially valuable for focused collaboration, resource-pooling, extending the organisation's sphere of influence, and developing unusual alliances. Our findings specifically confirmed Waddell's (2014, p. 22) previous work, in that networks were not used merely for coordination, but for 'generating coherence through targeted interventions and stewarding development of particularly critical ingredients of a complex change system'.

Moreover, all participants acknowledged that once they re-focused their organisational purpose on scaling, as opposed to simply generating an innovative initiative within a niche, their ideas, process, or programmes required either new funding, or entirely new funding models than what their original initiative required. Funding was not only perceived to support the scaling process, but it was also sometimes perceived as a necessary precursor to scaling in order to build internal capacity for systems approaches. As one participant stated:

> We came to understand that in order to grow, we had to build organisational capacity and we have done so in an effective manner over several years. As a more mature organisation we needed to allocate new resources to growth and development.

But beyond confirming strategies that have been well-documented elsewhere, several other strategies were found to be essential for the scaling process. One cross-cutting strategy served as an important starting point for all participants when they first began to attempt to scale their initiatives. This was the strategy of broadening the framing of the problem to reveal it systemic or root causes.

Cross-cutting strategy 1. Broaden the problem frame

The organisations involved in the AD learning group began with a particular issue-focus such as girl's empowerment, preventing youth incarceration, building networks of support around people with disabilities, and reducing poverty in communities. Their organisational strategies were most often focused on particular populations, in specific regions. However, through participation with the AD learning group, participants realised that they could not achieve their goals of scale and impact unless they broadened their problem-framing.

Several participants described how adopting a systems-change perspective (using systems and complexity frameworks introduced by Westley *et al.*, 2006) was critical to building this consciousness and intention to change. It is beyond the scope of this article to detail the material and exercises the AD learning group undertook to develop a large-systems change perspective. However, in general, the learning process widened previously narrow constructions of problems and solutions, enabling organisational leaders to consider different types of scales (e.g. organisational scales, temporal scales, political scales), and to understand the complex interrelated layers of variables and phases of change that could influence their issue as they tried to scale their impact.

Broadening their problem definition led several organisations to re-conceptualise their goals, as they shifted from being focused on a specific issue, to being more deliberately focused on solving the roots of the problem. For example, the Executive Director of Meal Exchange observed,

> It allowed me to evolve Meal Exchange beyond an emergency food charitable organisation to a food security/food systems organisation. It provided me the mental model and questions to guide the work: 'how do you make access to healthy food systemic? To what end?

Different organisations expressed their new commitment to scaling and systemic impact in different ways. For instance, two organisations formally re-drafted their organisational vision/mission statements to incorporate clear intentions to effect systemic change rather than focusing on a single issue. Other participants used internal communication processes (both formal and informal) to establish agreement among staff to reorienting for greater impact.

Strategies for scaling out, up, and deep

After broadening their problem frame to pursue large systems change, participants described different strategies depending on whether they attempted to
scale out, up, or deep. Table 1 summarises the strategies described below.

Table 1 Three types of 'scaling' and their main strategies

	Description	Main strategies
Scaling out:	**Impacting greater numbers.** Based on the recognition that many good ideas or initiatives never spread or achieve widespread impact	**Deliberate replication.** Replicating or spreading programmes geographically and to greater numbers while protecting the fidelity and integrity of the innovation
		Spreading principles. Disseminate principles, but with an adaptation to new contexts via co-generation of knowledge, leveraging social media and learning platforms: 'open scaling'
Scaling up:	**Impacting law and policy.** Based on the recognition that the roots of social problems transcend particular places, and innovative approaches must be codified in law, policy and institutions	**Policy or legal change efforts.** New policy development, partnering, advocacy
Scaling deep:	**Impacting cultural roots.** Based on the recognition that culture plays a powerful role in shifting problem-domains, and change must be deeply rooted in people, relationships, communities and cultures	**Spreading big cultural ideas** and reframing stories to change beliefs and norms. Intensively share knowledge and new practices via learning communities, distributed learning platforms and participatory approaches
		Invest in transformative learning, networks and communities of practice
Cross-cutting		Seek alternative resources Build networks and partnerships Broaden the problem frame

Scaling out strategy 1. Deliberate replication

Initially, organisations participating in the AD learning group were focused
on the types of diffusion activities documented in previous scaling literature
(Dees *et al.*, 2004; Bradach, 2010). That is, efforts focused on expanding the
geographic scale of programmes or initiatives, and increasing the number of
people impacted by a social innovation. Leaders made decisions about whether
to grow in a centralised manner, to franchise, to pursue other 'social enterprise'

models, or to 'seed' like-minded organisations through affiliation, branching, or accreditation systems. Although this is similar to the approach of many social enterprises, our findings indicated that given the systems-change perspective and years of testing different dissemination approaches, participants began recognising the limitations of a replication or dissemination approach. Participants began to critique the isolated use of scaling out strategies and emphasise the impact and durability of a change. For example, one participant reflected:

> You can't just transport it in a box. And I think there's a lot of confusion in some places with the concept of scale and impact that, in some cases, impact is simply defined as the number of widgets you've spread.

Prioritising system-wide change also led to emphasis on fidelity and integrity for some innovations. One participant stated:

> As we learned that we were replicable and we could scale (1 site to over 100), we realised that the number was not as important as the impact and the sustainability factor. If you cannot replicate your programme and ensure it is done with high integrity and fidelity (achieve positive outcomes you know the programme can achieve) and ensure the programme can be sustainable, then your efforts of scaling are fruitless.

Protecting the integrity and fidelity became referred to in the AD learning group as Zimmerman et al.'s (1998) 'min specs' or minimum specifications. That is, leaders needed to determine what the non-negotiable aspects were, and what could vary when replicating, to ensure they were achieving a sustainable impact along with scale. This led some organisational leaders to jettison programme scaling and focus on spreading principles.

Scaling out strategy 2. Spreading principles

In recognising the limitations of a geographic replication approach, some organisations pursued more of an 'open scaling' model, where the core principles and approach of the innovation were spread, leaving it to the local community to adapt it to local conditions: 'You can scale an idea that lives out differently in every context'.

Shifting to focus on scaling impact demanded that organisational leaders distil the essence of their innovation and hone their capacity to disseminate the knowledge and principles associated with it:

> We had to be very careful about articulating clearly the principles guiding our actions and that we always made sure to stick to those principles to the extent that we could. Those were our real guide-posts. And so groups could feel free to undertake whatever activity they wanted to, but they couldn't deviate from the overarching principles that we had set that bound us together as a collective, as a group.

A potential drawback of this approach is the intensive work involved in translating an approach in numerous different contexts, when there is no specific 'product' to simply adopt. Tamarack addressed this in part by creating a national-scale learning community for anti-poverty initiatives in hundreds of communities in Canada and the United States—blending a scaling out strategy with a scaling deep strategy.

Scaling up strategy 1. Scale up through policy or legal change

Our findings showed that scaling out mostly concentrates impacts on the niche scale, through developing more niches. For many social innovators, an equally powerful opportunity lies in impacting higher levels of institutions through policy change—referred to as the regime by SNM and transitions studies scholars. We refer to this cross-scale dynamic as scaling up. As one participant claimed: 'We don't have to have more chapters or more people involved, or expand to new regions—we can take the issue and get it into the policy domain, have public policy discussions and scale those up.'

Participants described at least two approaches for scaling up. In the first approach, pointed to in the quotation above, social innovators working at the level of families or communities shifted their work to higher levels in government in order to address root causes in larger-scale institutions that affected an entire population. One example of this is the work of Planned Lifetime Advocacy Network (PLAN) in their creation of the world's first Registered Disabilities Savings Plan, which changed the financial regulations guiding savings and benefits for people with disabilities and enabled them to escape financial dependency on the state. Creating new policy or regulatory frameworks was seen as part of disrupting existing systems and transforming them into something better. This differed from replication strategies, since it often meant leaving behind the initial innovative initiative, and starting an entirely new initiative focused on policy change.

The second approach focused on linking together community-level policy interventions into a more coherent movement. Interestingly, just as application within the local context is important when disseminating new ideas and programmes, it was also seen as critical when scaling policy change from one jurisdiction to another. One participant described how 'one of the things that we learned in trying to scale up in terms of policy-related work was that context really mattered'. Those leaders who were seeking to scale policies faced challenges because municipal contexts and systems vary greatly across Canada, and approaches had to be adapted to new jurisdictions each time.

Scaling deep strategy 1. Generating big cultural ideas

> Our language changed—from feed the hungry to 'good food for all'

Closely linked to the cross-cutting strategy that involved broadening the problem frame, many participants and organisations found that scaling the impacts beyond the niche to the regime required scaling deep into the beliefs, ideas, and narratives of dominant social structures. Working with norms and values as vehicles for scaling innovations was described as critical because ideas live differently in every context but can spread rapidly. One strategy that was employed involved deliberately reframing predominant narratives that existed about the social issue participants sought to address. By changing the narrative, participants described how they could successfully begin to change cultural norms and beliefs about the issue. As one example, a leader with L'Arche, an organisation focused on people with intellectual disabilities, described the following:

> We have, with others, been successful in reframing the goal of disability support from charity to contribution, from group to individual, from need to asset, and to significantly reduce the stigma attached to intellectual disability. Much more work to do, but today, as opposed to 10 years ago, the goals of belonging and citizenship for people with intellectual disabilities are widely accepted.

Culture change strategies varied tremendously, but one example included using stories as a method for sharing and co-creating ideas. One practitioner explained that amalgamating stories from the individuals affected by the relevant social issues, and translating them into a resonant framing enabled individual anecdotes to tell a more systemic story about the need for change. Therefore, our findings indicate that creating new stories and amplifying those that exist becomes an important vehicle for generating cultural ideas and thus, scaling deep to affect the 'regime' level of institutions, and even to the broader cultural landscape.

Scaling deep strategy 2. Invest in transformative learning

> What we learned was how to develop a community of learning that in turn develops the growth and development of the networks we created. It is the connectedness that is the strength of our networks and this connectedness can only be created through sharing experiences and best practices.
>
> What it was we wanted to scale was an experience rather than a particular programme or process

A common strategy to increase the scale and impact of socially innovative initiatives is to invest in learning processes (e.g. Dweck, 2007; Crutchfield and McLeod Grant, 2008). But cultivating learning became a specific strategy used to build shared mind-sets across a range of sectors and organisations, to ensure the impact of their initiative is scaled deep into the defining routines and practices and beliefs of partners and collaborators. Participants described how learning processes for scaling can be supported by a range of methods, including: mentorship, deliberate transfer of practices, capturing and sharing organisational or community culture, and shared reflection and evaluation practices. Interestingly, many AD learning group participants who used learning communities as a central means of scaling credited their experience in the AD learning group itself as the inspiration or model.

Our findings suggest that less mature forms of scaling focus on replication, and as social innovators begin to take seriously the need for large systems change, their approach transforms to include scaling up and/or scaling deep. This occurs as leaders of change gain confidence, grow partnerships and networks, and aim more consistently to change the system dynamics that gave rise to the problem in the first place. Consequently though, our findings revealed that large systems change impacts could occur when participants moved from scaling out to scaling up, or from scaling out to scaling deep. No single participant immediately jumped to scaling up or scaling deep, and thus, we believe that large systems change involves at least a combination of the three types of scaling. Relating to the transitions studies literature and SNM, scaling across multiple niches remains a critical step before being able to scale impacts to the regime, landscape, or both.

Challenges in scaling

While the strategies described above were utilised to achieve different types of scaling, they were not without significant challenge. Inevitably, ambitious large systems-change goals can present leadership, organisational and social challenges.

Often, a socially innovative initiative is managed and implemented by a small portion of a larger organisation. As cited earlier, research in SNM emphasises the importance of safe spaces for innovation (e.g. Schot and Geels, 2008; Caniëls and Romijn, 2008). But in practice, this creates tension, both with other staff in the other sections of the organisation, or with board members who see the initiative as an anomaly from the organisation's central mission. As one participant stated: 'We ended up with a "business" operating inside of a non-profit. We had conflicts between the "old" and the "innovative". Our operational needs were different than other departments in the organisation'. These internal tensions were sometimes the most time consuming part of scaling processes. As one person described: 'I underestimated the time, skills, and talents required to get other colleagues within the organisation to understand and support what we were trying to do'.

Participants noted that the time and energy required for scaling was one of their greatest scaling challenges, as it placed demands on the growth and sustainability of their own capacity to act as leaders. Here, the support of like-minded peers was essential to sustain the innovators as they pursued a path of systemic change and scaling. As two participants described:

> ...to me this question of stress and the capacity to manage the ambiguity and to inspire others to stay with you in the ambiguity, is a key capacity. And when we talk about key leadership challenges, it's certainly maintaining in oneself that capacity over time. Because none of this work, if we're really talking about impact, durability and scale, is in any way a short fix.
>
> Note to self: Do not underestimate the resistance that will come from within and without. It takes great commitment and time and energy to grow into the new. In our larger and decentralised organisation, we are not always unified as we struggle to hold together the old and the new, the 'system' and the individual, growth in numbers and growth in character and leadership, the simplicity with running alone and the complexity of partnering with others for greater impact, and the longing for stability and completion with the reality that change is our constant companion.

Conclusion

While previous research on strategic niche management and social innovation has shown the benefits of replication and diffusion strategies, or of creating 'safe' spaces for experimentation within an organisation, we conclude that these only contribute to systemic change when used in conjunction with a variety of other strategies that ensure impacts are scaled up or deep. While both sets of literature widely acknowledge the importance of recognising scale and the general mechanisms needed within a niche to ensure an innovation's 'readiness' to be taken to scale, little insight has been provided about the strategies of actors to cross those scales.

This study of the AD learning group participants found that scaling for impact involved a combination of strategies. One of the key, but often overlooked, changes required when an organisation chooses to scale an innovative initiative involves re-framing the problem, and therefore the purpose of the organisation and their initiative.

Different strategies may then be used to scale out, up, or deep, but a formula does not exist for their precise combination. Rather, an important finding is that the three types of scaling and their strategies can interact in powerful ways to advance systemic change goals. The different types of scaling reveal at least three dimensions of systems that need to be engaged in large-scale change efforts: the quantifiable breadth of people and systems included; the institutional shifts in law, policy and resource flows that are necessary; and the subjective and inter-subjective transformations in values, relationships and cultural practices that support durable system-wide change. Furthermore, by tracing the patterns of scaling, this study highlighted that it is a combination of scaling out, up, and deep that is most likely to lead to large systems change, rather than any single strategy. That is, an organisation cannot simply expect to scale up to effect systems change without having gone through the lessons and capacity building experiences that occur when scaling out, or scaling deep.

Additionally, as scaling occurs, it is essential to ensure that the endurance and stamina of leadership can persist for the duration of time that is required for scaling an initiative. Applied learning processes, such as the AD learning group, can serve as an important forum to address this type of challenge.

However, theoretical and practical questions remain. First, additional research would be helpful to discern how the different types of scaling interact in other contexts, and whether these patterns are similar in cultural and policy contexts outside of North America. Second, these conclusions are based on more than a decade of experience; much of which involved learning by doing. The question that remains for the future is, how much of this can be 'taught', so that non-profits and funders today can leapfrog on the scaling successes of the past.

References

Bradach, J. (2010). Scaling impact: How to get 100x the results with 2x the organization. *Stanford Social Innovation Review*, 6, (3): 27-28.

Bradach, J. and Grindle, A. (2014). Emerging pathways to transformative scale. *Stanford Social Innovation Review*, Spring, (Supplement): 7-11.

Caniëls, M. C. J.and Romijn, H. A. (2008). Strategic niche management: Towards a policy tool for sustainable development. *Technology Analysis & Strategic Management*, 20, (2): 245-266.

Crutchfield, L. R.and Mcleod Grant, H. (2008). *Forces for good: The six practices of high-impact nonprofits*, San Francisco, CA, John Wiley & Sons.

Dees, G., Anderson, B. B.and Wei-Skillern, J. (2004). Scaling social impact: Strategies for spreading social innovations. *Stanford Social Innovation Review*, 1, (4): 24-33.

Dey, I. (1999). *Grounding grounded theory*, Millbrae, CA, California Academic Press.

Dweck, C. (2007). *Mindset: The new psychology of success*, New York, NY, Ballantine Books.

Elzen, B., Van Mierlo, B.and Leeuwis, C. (2012). Anchoring of innovations: Assessing Dutch efforts to harvest energy from glasshouses. *Environmental Innovation and Societal Transitions*, 5, (1): 1-18.

Evans, S. H.and Clarke, P. (2011). Disseminating orphan innovations. *Stanford Social Innovation Review*, 9, (1): 42-47.

Flyvbjerg, B. (2006). Five misunderstandings about case study research. *Qualitative Inquiry*, 12, (2): 219-245.

Folke, C., Jansson, A., Rockstrom, J., Olsson, P., Carpenter, S. R., Stuart Chapin Iii, F., Crepin, A.-S., Daily, G., Danell, K., Ebbesson, J., Elmqvist, T., Galaz, V., Moberg, F., Nilsson, M., Osterblom, H., Ostrom, E., Persson, A., Peterson, G., Polasky, S., Steffen, W., Walker, B.and Westley, F. (2011). Reconnecting to the biosphere. *Ambio*, 40, (7): 719-738.

Geels, F. W. (2002). Technological transitions as evolutionary reconfiguration processes: A multi-level perspective and a case study. *Research Policy*, 31, (8-9): 1257-1274.

Geobey, S., Westley, F. R.and Weber, O. (2012). Enabling social innovation through developmental social finance. *Journal of Social Entrepreneurship*, 3, (2): 151-165.

Hegger, D. L. T., Van Vliet, J. and Van Vliet, B. J. M. (2007). Niche management and its contribution to regime change: The case of innovation in sanitation. *Technology Analysis and Strategic Management*, 19, (6): 729-746.

Kemp, R., Schot, J.and Hoogma, R. (1998). Regime shifts to sustainability through processes of niche formation: The approach of strategic niche management. *Technology Analysis & Strategic Management*, 10, (2): 175-198.

Marshall, N. A., Park, S. E., Adger, W. N., Brown, K.and Howden, S. M. (2012). Transformational capacity and the influence of place and identity. *Environmental Research Letters*, 7, (3): 034022.

Mcconnell Foundation, J. W. (1998). *Should you sow what you know?* Montreal, QC. JW McConnell Family Foundation.

Mcphedran, J., Waitzer, J. M.and Paul, R. (2011). Scaling social impact: When everybody contributes, everybody wins. *Innovations*, 6, (2): 143-155.

Moore, M.-L.and Westley, F. R. (2011). Surmountable chasms: Networks and social innovation for resilient systems. *Ecology and Society*, 16, (1): art 5.

Mulgan, G., Tucker, S., Ali, R.and Sanders, B. (2008). *Social innovation: What it is, why it matters, and how it can be accelerated*. London, UK. The Basingstoke Press.

Pearson, K. (2006). *Accelerating our impact: Philanthropy, innovation and social change*. The J.W. McConnell Family Foundation.

Plummer, R.and Fennell, D. (2007). Exploring co-management theory: Prospects for sociobiology and reciprocal altruism. *Journal of Environmental Management*, 85, (4): 944-955.

Rip, A.and Kemp, R. (1998). Technological change.) *In:* Rayner, S. & Malone, E. L. (eds.) *Human choice and climate change*. Columbus, OH: Battelle Press.327-399

Ross, R. K. (2014). We need more scale, not more innovation. *Stanford Social Innovation Review*, Spring, (Supplement): 18-19.

Schot, J.and Geels, F. W. (2008). Strategic niche management and sustainable innovation journeys: Theory, findings, research agenda, and policy. *Technology Analysis & Strategic Management*, 20, (5): 537-554.

Smith, A.and Raven, R. (2012). What is protective space? Reconsidering niches in transitions to sustainability. *Research Policy*, 41, (6): 1025-1036.

Van Den Bosch, S.and Rotmans, J. (2008). *Deepening, broadening and scaling up: A framework for steering transition experiments*. Delft, Netherlands. Knowledge Centre for Sustainable System Innovations and Transitions (KCT).

Van Der Laak, W. W. M., Raven, R. P. J. M.and Verbong, G. P. J. (2007). Strategic niche management for biofuels: Analysing past experiments for developing new biofuel policies. *Energy Policy*, 35, 3213–3225.

Verbong, G. P. J., Christiaens, W., Raven, R. P. J. M.and Balkema, A. (2010). Strategic niche management in an unstable regime. Biomass gasification in India. *Environmental Science and Policy*, 13, (1): 272-291.

Waddell, S. (2014). *Addressing the world's critical issues as complex change challenges: The state of the-field*. NetworkingAction and Ecosystems Labs.

Wei-Skillern, J.and Anderson, B. B. (2003). *Nonprofit geographic expansion: Branches, affiliates, or both?* Center for the Advancement of Social Entrepreneurship. The Fuqua School of Business, Duke University.

Westley, F. R.and Antadze, N. (2010). Making a difference: Strategies for scaling social innovation for greater impact. *The Public Sector Innovation Journal*, 15, (2): art 2.

Westley, F. R., Antadze, N., Riddell, D., Robinson, K.and Geobey, S. (2014). Five configurations for scaling up social innovation: Case examples of nonprofit organizations from Canada. *The Journal of Applied Behavioral Science*, 1-27.

Westley, F. R., Tjornbo, O., Schultz, L., Olsson, P., Folke, C., Crona , B.and Bodin, Ö. (2013). A theory of transformative agency in linked social-ecological systems. *Ecology and Society*, 18, (3): 27.

Yin, R. (2014). *Case study research design and methods, 5th edition*, Thousand Oaks, CA, SAGE Publications Inc.

Zimmerman, B., Lindberg, C.and Pilsek, P. (1998). *Edgeware: Lessons from complexity science for health care leaders*. Dallas, TX. VHA Inc.

DOI: [10.9774/GLEAF.4700.2015.ju.00010]

Transformative Capacities of Global Private Sustainability Standards

A Reflection on Scenarios in the Field of Agricultural Commodities

Pieter Glasbergen
ICIS-Maastricht University, the Netherlands

Greetje Schouten
Wageningen University, the Netherlands

Since the mid-1990s, private sustainability standards and certification schemes have aimed to introduce a new paradigm in the trade of agricultural commodities. However, there is still a lot of uncertainty about the transformative capacity of these arrangements. This paper discusses three plausible scenarios for the future of governance in the field of sustainable agriculture: leaving it to the market; bringing the state back in; and new forms of meta-governance. These scenarios are evolving concurrently but also build upon each other. Contingencies that are important are consumer power, the proliferation of corporate social responsibility, and the enclosure of new markets for sustainable products. It is concluded that, because of their limitations, none of the scenarios will be able to realise a system change on its own.

- Sustainability standards
- Certification
- Sustainable agriculture
- Scenarios
- Transformative capacity

Pieter Glasbergen is Honorary Professor of Governance for Sustainable Development at ICIS-Maastricht University (2011–present) and Emeritus Professor at Utrecht University and the Open University, the Netherlands. He chairs the Maastricht-Utrecht-Nijmegen Research Programme on Partnerships (www.munpop.nl).

Maastricht University, ICIS, PO Box 616, 6200 MD Maastricht, The Netherlands

pieter.glasbergen@ maastrichtuniversity.nl

Greetje Schouten is a postdoctoral research fellow at both the Public Administration and Policy Group at Wageningen University and at the Partnerships Resource Centre, which is part of the Rotterdam School of Management of Erasmus University Rotterdam. In 2013, she defended her PhD thesis on processes of legitimisation of private multi-stakeholder governance arrangements at Utrecht University. This research was part of the Maastricht-Utrecht-Nijmegen Programme on Partnerships (MUNPOP).

Public Administration and Policy Group, Wageningen University, PO Box 8130, 6700 EW, Wageningen, the Netherlands

Greetje.Schouten@wur.nl

O VER THE PAST FEW DECADES, private actors, particularly industry consortia and partnerships between businesses and NGOs, have become vital elements in the search for a more sustainable future. These private governance arrangements are now active in a great, and still expanding, variety of economic sectors, such as forestry, fisheries, agriculture, mining, tourism, and apparel production. Using mainly certification as a regulatory tool, many of these private governance arrangements have become focal points in terms of sustainability standard-setting, enforcement of these standards, and in monitoring compliance.

In the literature a range of factors explaining the proliferation of private actors' roles in governance arrangements can be found. Many scholars point to the decreasing capacities of states to solve the various problems posed by processes of globalisation (cf. Bitzer 2012, p. 16). Others refer to their inability to provide a regulatory framework for intervening in the global market sphere (Tallontire 2007; Reed 2012). At the same time, firms aspire to promote themselves as socially and environmentally responsible actors (Tallontire 2007). Combined with the international growth and changing role of civil society organisations, this has led to a fundamental change in the relations between state, market, and civil society, and to the proliferation of private actors in global governance (see also Pedersen and Pedersen, 2013).

Different from government regulation, the intervention strategy of private governance arrangements is based on the idea that market principles can be used to promote more sustainable practices and their authority is largely derived from the supply chain (Cashore 2002). In essence, the initiators recognise an economically (i.e. sales-related or image-wise) profitable *and* environmentally and socially friendly opportunity in a market sector, which they regard in combination important enough to promote a collaborative change in management practices.

In this paper we particularly address the changes in the governance of agricultural commodities through the introduction of private certification schemes. Characteristic of the certifications in this field is that the standards they define originate mainly from Northern-based companies and NGOs, while they address production in the South (Schouten, 2013). In that sense they connect Northern consumption to Southern production. Although participation in the schemes is voluntary, they de facto aim to change the conditions of agricultural production and opportunities for market access.

Sustainability standards can be defined as 'external points of reference by which a product or a service's performance, its technical and physical characteristics, and/or process and conditions under which it has been produced or delivered, can be assessed' (Nadvi and Waltring, 2004, p. 56). Bartley (2010) conceptualises private certification schemes as consisting of different types of regulation. Private arrangements can be characterised as market-based instruments, as regulation by information and as voluntary programmes. First, certification is market-based since it derives its authority for a large part from the supply chain (Cashore 2002). Furthermore, the costs of non-compliance arise from market forces, instead of hierarchical government authority (Bartley

2010). Second, certification as regulation by information means governing by disclosure of information. In the certification schemes discussed in this paper this disclosure of information pertains to the sustainability of production processes. If standards or the auditing process are not effective or credible, certification may run the risk of generating disinformation and being regarded as 'greenwashing' (Bartley 2010, p. 6). Third, certification is voluntary and therefore stakeholders must see individual benefits in order to participate. This creates a tension between the stringency of the standard and participation (Bartley 2010, p. 6).

The literature is ambiguous in its assessment of private certification schemes: some believe monitoring and certification will provide consumers with a false sense that problems have been solved and will de-mobilise international labor and environmental campaigns, while others see the information generated by non-governmental regulation as key to transforming how we produce, consume and regulate global products and processes (O'Rourke 2006, p. 899).

Otieno and Knorringa (2012) also distinguish between two opposing views on the developmental relevance of standards. The first emphasises the exclusionary effects of standards resulting from a lack of resources and capacities of actors from developing countries to comply with these new requirements. The second view focuses on the potential opportunities of standards and the competitive advantage they can bring to developing countries. However, many researchers point primarily to the limitations and weaknesses of private certification. According to Ponte et al. (2011, p. 300) 'it is becoming clearer that standards are unable to substantially address some of the more complex social and environmental problems'. They argue that this is partly due to their voluntary nature and their limited capacity to promote systemic change. Djama et al. (2011, p. 205) state that 'sustainability standards are dominated by a neoliberal political rationality'. They argue that standards are essentially not designed to solve environmental and social problems, but are rather created for managerial reasons. Moreover, there is an increasing concern that these global standards are geared towards Northern priorities and fail to substantially include Southern perspectives (Otieno and Knorringa 2012). Furthermore, only a limited number of business actors will have sufficient incentives to join a certification initiative, which limits the scope of these initiatives (Marx 2008, p. 268). Marx et al. (2012) conclude that although private standards are an important governance instrument, their global impact might be further limited as they are mainly active in a selected number of (developed) countries.

Similar to other large system changes, the intention to transform agricultural production processes to become more sustainable induces much uncertainty, since the governance of agricultural production and trade can be conceptualised as a complex system in which many components (producers, consumers, organisations, institutions, norms, etc.) interact at multiple levels (local, national, regional and global) (Waddell et al. 2014). For different actors this large system change has different meanings and many tensions among these meanings can be found, even within the same actor category. Participating NGOs generally place them in a broader pro-poor sustainable development strategy or focus on environmental conservation. However, there are also many NGOs campaigning against (often the same) sustainability standards. Companies regard them as a tool to manage reputational risks and secure future supply, but in general commercial benefits need to be higher than expected costs. Farmers in developing countries sometimes see in them an opportunity to access markets and improve living conditions by receiving a higher price for their products, but also fear the new bureaucratic prerequisites, which are often difficult to implement. Governments in developing countries hope for new markets, but fear that private certifications threaten their sovereignty. Governments in some developed countries view them as means to express their worries about current unsustainable practices, but feel that they are restricted to really participate by international trade regulations.

Global sustainability standards aim to introduce a new paradigm in trade that considers environmental and social impacts of production. This change process is not a technical process, but a very complex and highly controversial one. In the current transition phase, different scenarios to a more sustainable agriculture are possible. Each of them has its specific transformative capacity, understood as the ability to bring about substantial sustainable system changes at the production level in a development context. Therefore, we need not only focus on present problems, but also on long-term development impacts. These impacts encompass the promotion of more environmentally friendly and socially responsible production practices, the increase of market access and revenues for Southern farmers, and the empowerment of smallholders in agriculture.

This paper reflects on these capacities, answering the question: what are possible developments and how should they be valued in terms of transformative capacity? It is not our intention to predict the future but to imagine what plausible futures are. Foresights with this intention generate insights regarding the dynamics of change, future challenges, and options for further change. The analysis produces mirrors to the current situation that can be used as tools to suggest potential intervention points and to design policy agendas (Kuosa, 2011; Van Lente, 2012).

Based on dynamics in our focal field we argue that three alternative scenarios are plausible. The first one relates to the current trend and refers to private actors from businesses and NGOs that take the lead. The second one relates to the role of public actors and refers to bringing the state back in. The third one takes the institutionalisation of some form of meta-governance into account. Each of these 'futures' has some opportunities and creates some dilemmas when reviewed in terms of transforming agricultural production in a sustainable way. A further analysis of the factors that drive the transformative capacity in this field reveals some contingencies that need to be taken into account when deliberating opportunities for system change.

The scenarios in this paper were first indicated in the context of an analysis of sustainability standards on palm oil and soy (Schouten, 2013). They were further elaborated using a series of complementary analyses in the fields of coffee, cocoa, cotton, tea, palm oil, and soy of the Maastricht-Utrecht-Nijmegen research programme on partnerships.[1] Each scenario starts with an analysis of current events and emerging trends by looking for existing themes and patterns already evident in the field of sustainable agriculture. The scenarios are further developed and elaborated by exploring what these emerging trends would look like when they are imagined to take place on a larger scale. We then assess the scenarios in terms of strengths and weaknesses regarding the possibilities to create an effective governance system for sustainable agricultural commodities.

Leaving it to the market

The first scenario anticipates an increased institutionalisation of private governance arrangements as important regulators of sustainable agriculture. Around the mid-1990s private actors, particularly NGOs and businesses, became involved in the global arena as promoters of more sustainable production processes in Southern, often developing countries. Apart from older standards such as organic and Fair Trade, the Forest Stewardship Council (FSC) (1994) and the Marine Stewardship Council (MSC) (1999) confirmed a new trend of business–NGO collaborative arrangements, such as the later Roundtable on Sustainable Palm Oil (RSPO) (2007), the Roundtable on Responsible Soy (RTRS) (2010) and the Aquaculture Stewardship Council (2012). In the same time period many more standard-setting and certifying partnerships developed for coffee, cocoa, tea, cotton, etc.

We observe at least five trends over the last two decades. First, a double process of expansion that may be characterised as a process of succession and a process of enlargement. Succession takes place when new certifications in a specific value chain are introduced as a reaction to earlier ones. An example gives the sustainability certification of tea by Unilever. Because this certification was successfully introduced, and Unilever is the market leader in the chain, other companies followed suit to introduce their own sustainable tea certifications (Glasbergen, 2013). Enlargement takes place when the tool of certification spreads from one value chain to another. For example, sustainable standards for tea followed the pattern of coffee certification, while regarding spices and aquaculture initiatives were more recently taken. Emerging gradually as a result of many uncoordinated actions of various independently operating actors, all agricultural commodity chains now face multiple standards with different and often competing sustainability claims.

Second, we observe a process of consolidation that takes place in commodity chains that are already rich with certifying schemes. The coffee chain might be exemplary for the pattern that develops over time. Regarding coffee, there are tens of different sustainability standard setting arrangements with different

---

1 www.munpop.nl

levels of ambition. However, some have become the dominant actors in the value chain. Fair Trade is one of the oldest, and sustains fairer trade relations and empowerment of poor farmers who work in small-scale cooperatives. One of the other older schemes, organic standards and certifications, focus more on ecological issues. This emphasis also plays a role in the Rainforest Alliance certifications (RA). UTZ-certification puts more emphasis on an increased quality and productivity as the basis for improving farmers' livelihood. The scheme of 4C introduces a low level set of standards that can be used as a general stepping stone towards more stringent sustainability prerequisites.

Third, while keeping their specific focus the dominant ones tend to become more 'all-inclusive', in the sense that they expand their original narrow focus (i.e. either organic, social, or ecological) towards a more inclusive set of criteria that connect social, environmental and economic issues (Vermeulen and Kok, 2012, p. 190). These are also the schemes that spread their activities gradually to other agricultural commodities such as tea and cocoa. In that way they further confirmed their leading role.

Fourth, the first contours of a saturation point become visible. Again coffee serves as an example since coffee standards and certifications set the trend for more sustainable agricultural commodities produced in the South and this sector is the most developed one. Next to the dominant ones referred to above, two other categories of standards and certifications seem to develop. The first are the specialities such as bird-friendly, shade grown and eco-friendly coffee. The second may be called the responsible coffees, which are labelled by consumer related companies, such as Starbucks' C.A.F.E. Practices and Nespresso's AAA. This structuration of the field of standards becomes also visible in cocoa certifications.

Fifth, we observe a trend of increasing relationships among the private sustainability arrangements regarding a specific commodity. This is particularly visible in the world of arrangements for a more sustainable cocoa production. An analysis of tens of arrangements in this issue field shows a growing network, with a lot of overlapping membership (several actors partner in various arrangements), and growing collaboration regarding agricultural field schools and issues of child labour. However, the relationships are far more competitive when it comes to sustainability standards, which is closely related to competition for market share (Bitzer et al. 2012).

This scenario has several strengths and weaknesses in terms of the possibilities to create an effective governance system for sustainable agricultural commodities. It is promising in the sense that it presents a continuing institutionalisation of sustainable development in the private sector. Next to business actors, also (international) NGOs play a prominent role in defining the terms of sustainable agriculture. Companies may further be able to assume responsibilities for sustainable production and consumption and further internalise environmental and social costs of agricultural production. The market for certified products is large enough to accommodate a number of different systems. Competition between these schemes may spur innovation, such as in the Unilever tea case referred to above, and consumers will be able to make a choice from a lot of different options. However, the reverse process is also possible. The market strives for creating niches. Though expanding much faster than conventional agricultural commodity markets, the overall market share of certified products is still small. These shares are estimated 10% for tea, 22% for bananas, 9% for coffee, 13% for cocoa, and 15% for palm oil (Steering Committee, 2012). Moreover, the demand for certified products is currently lower than the supply, which implies that certified commodities are not sold as such. Estimates of overproduction run from 30 to 50% of certified coffee, cocoa and certified palm oil ((KPMG, 2013). As a consequence, producers are not sure of a premium fee which may easily disrupt their positive attitude towards sustainability standards. The many different and competing certification schemes that result from free market development also induce a differentiation that may easily result in an unnecessary and inefficient duplication of efforts. Consumers have already become confused about the differences and the reliability of labelled products and there are signs of a 'certification fatigue' (Bartley, 2010).

Bringing the state back in

The promotion of sustainable agriculture can be seen as a general interest or public good regarding which governments necessarily need to play a role. Over the years, this role has been more or less crystallised for developed countries, while some developing countries are currently in the process of defining their role. Particularly governments in Western Europe approach a more sustainable agricultural sector as a public good. However, their main stance is that this good can and needs to be realised by markets actors themselves. The role of governments should be restricted to sustaining those initiatives that fit into their national sustainable development strategy. Underlying this restricted stance is the free market ideology, which found its expression in the international trade regulations. According to Ulrich Hoffmann, it is feared that sustainability standards directly or indirectly undermine the hard-won disciplines in the WTO agreements (UNFSS, 2013). Despite this restricted stance, however, a set of sustaining activities developed over time, which reflects some agreement about possible roles on how to engage with private standards and certifications (regarding general overviews see Steering Committee, 2012; Gulbrandsen, 2012; Vermeulen and Kok, 2012).

First, governments may have a role to play in information dissemination and training as well as facilitating services to bring standards down to the farmers. The exchange of information could also be aimed at facilitating 'public contestation' about private standards and certifications as a tool to induce a more sustainable agriculture.

Second, generally applicable principles and procedures may be developed derived from public law in areas such as transparency and accountability. Such an institutional benchmark enables the assessment of the credibility of certification initiatives. Additional requirements may stipulate the disclosure of information. Governments may formally approve the schemes that meet such requirements. Moreover, governments could develop an overall monitoring and evaluation strategy and in that way also improve the public visibility and accountability of private regulations.

Third, governments may also stimulate the use of the potentials of the private spheres for public objectives by creating complementarities between private regulations and state regulations. Most certifications cannot ever be successful if governments do not sustain them with policies related to sound land use planning, clear property rights, a well-functioning physical infrastructure, etc. For example, to sustain forestry certifications the EU and the USA recently developed a set of rules that forbid the import of timber if not legally (according to the rules of the country) logged.

Fourth, governments are also clients of the certified products and can be central to the uptake of certification on the demand side. They may require state-owned companies to adopt the standards and with public procurement policies they can stimulate the purchase of certified products. In some sectors, public institutions are big purchasers that can set a trend for a more sustainable market.

Last, governments can sustain private sustainability standards and certifications as a donor or by creating an institutional context to work on them. For instance, the Dutch Government initiated and to a large part funds the Sustainable Trade Initiative (IDH, Dutch for Initiatief Duurzame Handel), which focuses on market solutions to issues of sustainable production and consumption. IDH supports, among others, several roundtables, including the RSPO and RTRS. Other European governments also are donors of several roundtables and private governance arrangements as part of their sustainability strategy.

Although these roles *as a set* suggest the possibility of the development of a coherent governmental approach to sustainable agriculture, the reality is different. In practice, aspects of these activities are taken up ad hoc and incrementally. Even governments sustaining the idea of private regulation are lacking a strategic approach with a deliberate course of action and a consistent combination of governmental interventions.

The roles defined above, although mainly related to governments in developed countries, can also be fulfilled by governments in producer countries. Some even need to be fulfilled by them, to realise a sustainable system change. In general, the developing countries' evaluation of private regulation of agricultural commodities is not that different from governments of the developed world, albeit there are some important nuances in the argumentation. As the new sustainability standards, which are far ahead of public regulation, directly penetrate into their most important economic sectors, many governments fear that they may be used as anti-competitive instruments, with a risk of excluding parts of their products from export markets.

More fundamental is the question of sovereignty in developing sustainability standards, which may be seen as a fundamental public responsibility that is threatened by the imposition of external private standards (TSPN, 2011).

However, this does not mean that developing countries fully oppose sustainability standards. Some of their governments already work in projects with NGOs and companies, such as the recently (2013) consolidated long-term collaboration agreement of UTZ and the government of Minas Gerais, Brazil. The alliance, which relies on the alignment of the UTZ Code of Conduct and the Certifica Minas Café certification standard, is supposed to benefit over 1,800 Minas Gerais coffee-farming producers by facilitating them access to international markets through the network of UTZ. The UTZ/Certifica Minas Café alliance is the first one in its type and marks a milestone in the way voluntary standards align with national and regional certification schemes. It is supposed to work as a model for effective collaboration elsewhere.[2]

An even more fundamental change is taking place where national governments of developing countries (re-)take their role as central actors in regulating sustainable agriculture, presumably at the detriment of private governance arrangements. This development can be observed in Indonesia and Malaysia. The national governments of these countries are far in the process of introducing their own standards for sustainable palm oil and reduced their relations with the RSPO. Indonesia is also planning to develop its own sustainability certification regarding sustainable coffee and cocoa. Although it is expected that the first standards will not be very stringent in sustainability requirements, they will be mandatory and include smallholder production.

The scenario of 'bringing the state back in' also has several strengths and weaknesses in terms of possibilities to create an effective governance system for the trade in sustainable agricultural commodities. On the one hand, this scenario is promising, since sustainable agriculture will not be dependent anymore on the rather unpredictable market dynamics. Because this regulation is mandatory, it can potentially transform a whole sector within a specific territory. Moreover, it is promising that sustainable production in this scenario is not only on the agenda of consuming countries, but also on the agenda of Southern production countries. On the other hand, there are no signs that governments of developed countries will take responsibility for large-scale system change. The ones that take a positive stance towards sustainability certification follow the market trend with ad hoc sustaining activities. Moreover, there are many governments of export markets (i.e. India, China, Pakistan, and Russia) that are not interested yet in sustainability standards and certification. It is in fact the existence of these non-Western markets that is one of the drivers of the Indonesian and Malaysian governments to keep all their options open with their own standards. Thus far it is also not fully clear what their regulations will actually look like and if they really have the potential to transform the production of agricultural commodities in a more sustainable way. Implementation and enforcement of public certification can be problematic in states that have weak administrative structures and are afflicted by corruption. It is therefore

---

2 https://www.utzcertified.org/

difficult to assess whether these public certification schemes will be really more effective than the private ones.

Institutionalising meta-governance

The third scenario assumes that actors from both the public and the private sphere may play a more prominent role in regulating sustainable agriculture by taking on a meta-governance role. Meta-governance refers to the management of plurality with the aim to induce more coherence in the governance of an issue area. In our case this concerns collaborative efforts aimed at enhancing coherence in the voluntary standards landscape to explore opportunities for mutual learning and closer cooperation, agree on benchmarks for convergence, and develop mechanisms for furthering such convergence (Derkx and Glasbergen, 2014).

Meta-governance can take different forms. Some private standards schemes aim to fulfil a platform function for a commodity. For example, the Common Code for the Coffee Community (4C), a German-based public–private initiative which later became an independent association, fully operational since 2006, aims to make the coffee sector as a whole more sustainable. It serves as a platform for discussion and collaboration of actors along the coffee chain and developed a baseline standard. 4C positions itself in the market as the first step for further improvements. While other already existing standards are only able to reach a niche market, 4C reaches out to producers and industry actors in the 'mainstream market'. Over the last years, it enhanced efforts to align audits and benchmarking with other standards, such as RA and UTZ. The goal is to avoid multiple audits and to give already certified producers also access to 4C markets. This means that a producer who holds another certification can apply for a 4C licence without additional costs or efforts, which increases marketing possibilities for producers and greater supply diversity for buyers. 4C has always emphasised that it is a verification, not a certification and that 4C is only the baseline and further improvement is recommended. Although 4C brought a lot of actors in coffee around the table it has not yet realised the status of worldwide accepted baseline standard.[3]

Another example relates to the multiplicity and duplication of organic standards and certifications. This inefficiency induced a collaborative partnership of IFOAM, FAO and UNCTAD to search for opportunities to create more coherence in the field. In 2003 they founded the International Task Force on Harmonisation and Equivalence in Organic Agriculture (ITF) to address and seek solutions to trade barriers arising from the many different standards, technical regulations and certification requirements that function in the organic sector, and to enable developing countries to have more access to organic trade. Within

3 www.4c-coffeeassociation.org/

its mandate the ITF has been very successful as it brought together a large group of stakeholders in the field, including (inter)governmental, civil society, and private sector experts. It developed baseline requirements an organic certification body conducting third party conformity assessments should meet if it is to be recognised as competent. It also developed equivalence rules to enable recognition and acceptance of standards among each other. Only near the end of its existence did the ITF really start to raise awareness of and mobilise political support for its outputs; a process that was continued by its successor (convened by the same partners), the three-year Global Organic Market Access project (GOMA). GOMA (2009–2012) kept the topic of harmonisation and equivalence visible, strengthened the motivation to reduce trade barriers and has seen some uptake worldwide, though the process is still going slowly (Derkz and Glasbergen, 2014). In 2013 the aims of harmonising and creating equivalence among organic standards has been incorporated into the United Nations Forum on Sustainability Standards (UNFSS; see below).

Some frontrunner private sustainability standards joined forces around 2000 to learn from each other's programmes and cooperate on the identification of best practices. They established the International Social and Environmental Accreditation and Labelling (ISEAL) Alliance. This third private answer to the fragmentation in standards and certifications revolves around the development, implementation, and stewardship of internationally applicable good practice guidance on standards systems. Its main aim is to improve the authority of the standards in the market place and to become a trustworthy partner of governments. ISEAL developed so-called Codes of Good Practice, which serve to improve the credibility of standard-setting arrangements. There currently are Codes of Good Practice for standards setting, impact assessment, and compliance assurance (certification and accreditation). As ISEAL primarily pursues procedural rather than content-based harmonisation, its work does not directly touch upon the substantive standards of its members. However, the choice for a 'neutral convener' role, with a focus on the technicalities of standards-setting and implementation, is also a risk. Two of the founding fathers of ISEAL left the arrangement. One of the reasons is supposed to be ISEAL's reluctance to define sustainability clearly and concretely. Content-neutrality thus may induce many standards-setting arrangements to join, but at the risk of losing some others (Bernstein, 2011; Loconto and Fouilleux, 2013; Derkx and Glasbergen, 2014).

Currently, we see that several intergovernmental agencies are also looking into the option to bring more coherence in the field of sustainability standards. The United Nations Forum on Sustainability Standards (UNFSS, 2013) has the potential to become a prominent actor in this endeavour. The overall goal of the UNFSS is to make private sustainability standards a driver to sustainable development in developing countries instead of an obstacle. It aims to achieve this by actively engaging developing countries in international dialogues on private standards harmonisation and equivalence. The steering committee consists of five UN agencies: the Food and Agriculture Organisation (FAO), the UN

Conference on Trade and Development (UNCTAD), the UN Environment Programme (UNEP), the UN Industrial Development Organisation (UNIDO), and the International Trade Centre (ITC). However, UNFSS actively engages with all kinds of stakeholders. Up to now it has mainly served as an informed policy dialogue that is still young and of which the results still need to materialise.[4]

This scenario also has its strengths and weaknesses in terms of the possibilities to create an effective governance system for sustainable agriculture. Meta-governance approaches by intergovernmental organisations or by private arrangements might present a favourable future pathway to overcome some of the limitations of individual private governance approaches. Moreover, producing countries in the tropics seem to increasingly reclaim regulatory power, while consuming countries seem to mitigate their sustainability impacts by supporting private governance arrangements. This might lead to increasing tensions between Northern and Southern approaches to sustainable development. Hence, a more coherent approach, particularly addressing the credibility of private standards at the global level seems promising. However, all of the initiatives only focus on harmonisation and equivalence, being the technical aspects of standard setting arrangements, which is more a response to democratic pressures than an attempt to create coherence regarding the great confusion about the substantial aspects of the many sustainability standards. As far as the content of the standards is discussed this only regards the minimum requirements. The contexts of the meta-governance attempts are free trade and the assumption that voluntary standards and certifications are effective instruments to realise a more sustainable agriculture. Both are not questioned; therefore, it remains to be seen if meta-governance arrangements will get the power and mandate to adequately play a dominant role in bringing about large-scale system change.

Discussion and conclusions

We started this paper with a question about possible future developments in the domain of the governance of sustainable agriculture and how they should be valued in terms of transformative capacity. To this end, we have sketched three alternative plausible scenarios: 'leaving it to the market'; 'bringing the state back in'; and 'institutionalising meta-governance'. Table 1 gives a summary of the main characteristics of the different scenarios.

4 http://unfss.org

Table 1 Main characteristics of the three different scenarios

	'Leaving it to the market'	**'Bringing the state back in'**	**'Institutionalising meta-governance'**
Main promoter(s)	Businesses and NGOs	Southern states	Public or private governance actors
Object of regulation	Supply chain	Territorial area	Private governance arrangements
Source of legitimacy	Market demand	Sovereignty	International/ inter-organisational negotiations
Organising principle	Horizontal	Hierarchy	Orchestration
Strengths in terms of transformative capacity	Continuing institutionalisation of sustainable development Companies take responsibility Competition may lead to innovation	Mandatory regulation Sustainability is on the agenda of developing countries	Overcoming limitations of individual governance approaches Resolving North–South tensions
Weaknesses in terms of transformative capacity	Creation of niche markets Low market uptake of certified products Duplication of efforts Confusion among consumers	Doubt whether these states will take responsibility for large system change Implementation and enforcement might be problematic	Procedural focus (instead of substantive focus) Debatable power and mandate to bring about large system change
Examples	FSC, MSC, RSPO, RTRS, UTZ, ASC, etc.	Indonesian Sustainable Palm Oil, Malaysian Sustainable Palm Oil	ISEAL, UNFSS

Our analysis shows that there is evidence for all three scenarios evolving concurrently, albeit advocated by different protagonists and originating from different regions and policy levels. This indicates that private actors have become legitimate governance actors in global governance although they are not undisputed. Our analysis also shows that the scenarios are not independent, but build upon each other: elements of scenario two have started materialising as a reaction to emergent elements of scenario one. Governments of producing countries established national sustainability standards in reaction to global private standards. Scenario three, institutionalising meta-governance, seems to develop as an attempt to regulate the governance arrangements emerging in scenarios one and two. All three scenarios indicate that a process of change towards a more sustainable production and trade in agricultural commodities has been set in motion. However, none of the scenarios has the transformative capacity to become a leverage point for a large system change on its own.

The 'leaving it to the market' scenario has already created vested economic interests in the development and protection of niche markets for sustainable products. Therefore, the further institutionalisation of this scenario is expected to result in even more fragmentation in standard-setting and certification procedures. The institutionalisation of the second scenario 'bringing the state back in' and particularly the development of less stringent standards of producing countries may create a further differentiation and fragmentation of the governance of sustainable agricultural commodities. Stringent standards might be created for consumers in one part of the world and other, weaker sustainability standards might be created for other consumer markets. The 'institutionalising meta-governance' scenario, if further elaborated, leaves the content of standards and therefore the fragmentation of the market intact. However, this scenario, with its focus on harmonisation, lays an important foundation under a potential large system change. With its prerequisites about procedures for standard-setting, transparency, auditing, etc. it has the potential to rule out unreliable standards and strengthen the legitimacy of the strong ones.

Although none of the scenarios is a leverage point for large system change in itself, each of the scenarios provides a potential building block for such a large-scale change. What seems to be essential is building bridges across public and private initiatives for large system change. Such an approach might, similar to the development of mandatory food safety standards, require an intergovernmental attempt to define basic sustainability standards for the trade in agricultural commodities. It might thereby 'raise the floor' and provide a basic level of sustainability in the agricultural sector. Such a basic standard leaves the market intact to offer more stringent or further differentiated certificates for niche markets. However, such an approach will not develop spontaneously. As sustainability is a less urgent issue from the perspective of many stakeholders compared to food safety, there are some very important contextual conditions to be fulfilled, including consumer power, the proliferation of corporate social responsibility, and the enclosure of new markets for sustainable products.

Consumer power is generally regarded an important driver of change, although many sustainability standards address business-to-business products, with no direct relationship to consumers, since these products are largely invisible to them (Schouten and Glasbergen, 2012). Moreover, only a small part of the category of consumers, particularly middle- and upper-class consumers, is concerned about the reliability of information about the conditions under which goods have been produced and want to know what credible standards are. Therefore, consumer demand seems more to follow the creation of the standard-setting arrangements than initiating them or being a strong constituting factor (Glasbergen, 2013). This does not, however, imply that consumer power can be neglected, particularly in combination with corporate social responsibility (CSR). The past few decades saw the proliferation of CSR strategies of companies to contribute to social and environmental sustainability goals while avoiding negative sustainability impacts (Giovannucci *et al.* 2014; Williams, 2014). The CSR concept thereby stretches the societal responsibility of companies beyond economic and legal responsibilities only. However, CSR strategies, which are inherently connected to private certification schemes, tend to address sustainability issues for as long as they do not jeopardise the economic gains of a company or industry. Nevertheless, these processes can be self-reinforcing, especially when first movers are lead firms in the value chain that are able to establish a trickle-down effect.

Third, sustainability standards and certifications particularly represent Northern values and appeal to Northern markets. In other large markets, including China, Russia, India and Pakistan the demand for more sustainable agricultural products is fairly non-existent so far. These markets understandably have different priorities. However, for large scale transformations to take place in the field of sustainable agriculture, these markets should necessarily become engaged in the acceptance of sustainability standards. Here again lies an important role of intergovernmental initiatives. Important to note is that recent research among a sample of participants of the UN Global Compact (1,000 executives, across 27 industries, and over 100 countries) showed that almost all CEOs believe that sustainability will be important to the future success of their businesses. Many of these CEOs are already in the forerunning category, but hesitant on further progress. Almost all observe that governments and intergovernmental organisations did not make good progress in the last years on promoting sustainable production (UN Global Compact, 2013).

Up to now, we have seen ad hoc responses to the unsustainable trade in agricultural commodities rather than a coherent process of planned institution building for large scale system change. The different scenarios represent different vested interests. One might even point to a risk of stalemate between the different protagonists of each scenario. According to our view, the question therefore is not so much 'which scenario is the best one', but rather 'how to utilise their respective strengths'. This implies establishing connections across the public–private divide, while at the same time some structural conditions need to be addressed. This strategy could give private certifications a place in the governance of sustainable agriculture, albeit with much more coherence in the content of standards and the way they are developed and implemented than is currently available and with a frame-setting role of (inter)governmental organisations regarding basic standards to prevent unsustainable practices.

References

Bartley, T (2010), 'Certification as a mode of social regulation', Jerusalem Papers in Regulation and Governance. Working paper no. 8.

Bernstein, S (2011), 'Legitimacy in intergovernmental and non-state global governance', Review of International Political Economy, 18, 1, 17-51.

Bitzer V (2012), 'Partnering for Change in Chains: the Capacity of Partnerships to Promote Sustainable Change in Global Agrifood Chains', International Food and Agribusiness Management Review, 15, 13-38.

Bitzer V, Glasbergen P, Leroy P (2012), 'Partnerships of a feather flock together? An analysis of the emergence of networks of partnerships in the global cocoa sector, Global Networks, 12, 355-374.

Cashore B (2002), 'Legitimacy and the Privatization of Environmental Governance: How Non-State Market-Driven (NSMD) Governance Systems Gain Rule-making Authority', Governance: An International Journal of Policy, Administration, and Institutions, 15, 503-529.

Derkx B, Glasbergen P (2014), 'Elaborating global private meta-governance: An inventory in the realm of voluntary sustainability standards', Global Environmental Change, 27, 41–50.

Djama M, Fouilleux E, Vagneron I (2011), 'Standard-setting, certifying and benchmarking: a governmentality approach to sustainability standards in the agro-food sector'. In: Ponte S, Gibbon P, Vestergaard J (eds) Governing through standards: origins, drivers and limitations, Palgrave MacMillan, Basingstoke, 184-209.

Giovannucci D, Von Hagen O, Wozniak J (2014), 'Corporate Social Responsibility and the Role of Voluntary Sustainability', Schmitz-Hoffmann C, Schmidt M, Hansmann D, Palekhov B, Voluntary Standard Systems: A Contribution to Sustainable Development, Springer-Verlag, 359-383.

Glasbergen, P (2013), 'Legitimation of certifying partnerships in the global market place', Environmental Policy and Governance, 23, 354-367.

Gulbrandsen, L. H. (2012), 'Dynamic governance interactions: Evolutionary effects of state responses to non-state certification programs', Regulation & Governance, 1-20.

KPMG, (2013), Improving smallholder livelihoods: Effectiveness of certification in coffee, cocoa and cotton, Study commissioned by SUSTAINEO.

Kuosa, T (2011), 'Evolution of futures studies', Futures, 43, 327-336.

Loconto A, Fouilleux E, (2013), 'Politics of private regulation: ISEAL and the shaping of transnational sustainability governance', Regulation & Governance, 1-21.

Marx A (2008), 'Limits to non-state market regulation: A qualitative comparative analysis of the international sport footwear industry and the Fair Labor Association', Regulation & Governance, 2, 253-273.

Marx A, Maertens M, Swinnen J, Wouters J (2012), 'Conclusion: private standards - a global governance tool?' In: Marx A, Maertens M, Swinnen J, Wouters J (eds) Private Standards and Global Governance: Economic, legal and political perspectives, Edward Elgar, Cheltenham, 293-309.

Nadvi, K., & Waltring, F. (2004), 'Making sense of global standards', In H. Schmitz (Ed.), Local enterprises in the global economy: Issues of governance and upgrading, Cheltenham: Edward Elgar.

O'Rourke D (2006), 'Multi-stakeholder Regulation: Privatizing or Socializing Global Labour Standards?' World Development, 34, 899-918.

Otieno G, Knorringa P (2012), 'Localizing Global Standards: Illustrative examples from Kenya's horticulture sector', In: Dijk MPv, Trienekens J (eds) Global Value Chains: Linking local producers from developing countries to international markets, Amsterdam University Press, 119-135.

Pedersen ERG, Pedersen JT, (2013), 'Introduction: The rise of business-NGO partnerships', Journal of Corporate Citizenship, 50, 6-19.

Ponte S, Gibbon P, Vestergaard J (2011), 'Conclusion: The current status, limits and future of "governing through standards"'. In: Ponte S, Gibbon P, Vestergaard J (eds) Governing through standards: origins, drivers and limitations, Palgrave MacMillan, Basingstoke, 289-304.

Reed D (2012), 'Development and the problematic of non-state regulation', In: Reed D, Utting P, Mukherjee-Reed A (eds) Business regulation and non-state actors. Whose standards? Whose development? Routledge, Abingdon, 19-37.

Schouten G (2013), 'Tabling Sustainable Commodities through Private Governance: Processes of Legitimization in the Roundtables on Sustainable Palm Oil and Responsible Soy', Gildeprint, Utrecht.

The Journal of Corporate Citizenship Issue 58 *June 2015* © Greenleaf Publishing 2015

Schouten G, Glasbergen P, (2011), 'Creating legitimacy in global private governance: The case of the Roundtable on Sustainable Palm Oil', Ecological Economics, 70, 1891-1899.

Schouten G, Glasbergen P. (2012), 'Private multi-stakeholder governance in the agricultural market place: an analysis of legitimization processes of the roundtables on sustainable palm oil and responsible soy', International Food and Agribusiness Management Review, 15B, 53-78.

Steering Committee of the State-of-Knowledge Assessment of Standards and Certification, (2012), Toward sustainability: The roles and limitations of certification, Washington, DC: RESOLVE, Inc.

Tallontire A (2007), 'CSR and regulation: towards a framework for understanding private standards initiatives in the agri-food chain', Third World Quarterly, 28, 775.

TSPN, (2011), Food-related voluntary sustainability standards: A strategy guide for policy makers, Draft for discussion.

UN Global Compact, (2013), Accenture CEO Study on Sustainability. Architects of a better world.

UNFSS, (2013), Launching Conference of the United Nations Forum on Sustainability Standards (UNFSS). Summary report. Geneva.

Van Lente, H (2012), 'Navigating foresight in a sea of expectations: lessons from the sociology of expectations', Technology analysis and strategic management, 24:8, 769-782.

Vermeulen W.J.V., Kok, M.T.J. (2012), 'Government interventions in sustainable supply chain governance: Experience in Dutch front-running cases', Ecological Economics, 83, 183–196.

Waddell S (2014), 'Turning point – large systems change producing the change we want', Journal of Corporate Citizenship, 53, 5-8.

Williams OF (2014), 'CSR: Will it change the World? Hope for the future: An emerging logic in business practice', Journal of Corporate Citizenship, 53, 9-26.

DOI: [10.9774/GLEAF.4700.2015.ju.000011]

Exploring Social Movements Thinking for Leading Large-Scale Change in Health and Social Services Systems

Judith A. Holton
Mount Allison University, Canada

The purpose of this paper is to explore social movements thinking as an approach to leading large-scale change in health and social services. Based on key informant interviews, publicly available documents and pertinent literature, this paper uses a case study approach to explore two examples of health and social system change that have leveraged social movements thinking in mobilising energy for large-scale system change. The two cases offer insights into the efficacy of a social movements perspective in mobilising energy and commitment for large-scale system change. While the intention of large-scale change is to impact a system at the macro-level, it is inevitably enacted through multiple actions at the micro-levels of a system; individual acts of commitment that resonate with deeply held personal values, inspiring the articulation of shared values and connecting those values with the need for change. The power in social movement thinking is in the ability to elicit those values as inspiration for mobilising a system's energy toward a desired future. The paper proposes 'lessons' that may serve as guide posts for those initiating large-scale change efforts in other jurisdictions.

- Social movements
- Health and social systems
- Change management
- Large-scale change
- Shared values
- Public narratives

Judith A. Holton, PhD is Associate Professor of Management at Mount Allison University, Canada where she teaches organisation theory, strategy, leadership and the management of organisational change. Her research interests include leadership in complex environments, informal networks, learning and innovation in knowledge work as well as research methodology. She has published in *The Learning Organization, Leadership and Organization Development Journal, Advances in Developing Human Resources, Team Performance Management* and *The Grounded Theory Review*.

Ron Joyce Centre for Business Studies, Mount Allison University, 144 Main Street, Sackville, NB, E4L 1A7, Canada

jholton@mta.ca

> For the simplicity on this side of complexity, I wouldn't give you a fig. But for the simplicity on the other side of complexity, for that I would give you anything I have.

THIS QUOTATION, ATTRIBUTED TO OLIVER Wendell Holmes, nicely captures the elusive quest of those charged with leading large-scale change, whether in the public or private sphere. Indeed, large-scale change in complex systems remains one of our greatest challenges as a global society. Despite continuing technological advances that have extended the reach of activity in public, private and not-for-profit sectors, leveraging the opportunities of such extended reach means that any effort to solve the kinds of social, environmental and business issues that reside at the heart of complex systems calls forth a need for multiple perspectives from an ever-widening range of stakeholders. As the focus and reach of change efforts extends beyond traditional, 'containable' boundaries, their complexity grows exponentially—and with it, the challenges to leadership.

Healthcare is perhaps one of the most challenging arenas for the initiation and management of large-scale change efforts. While escalating pressures for change compete for scarce resources, system leaders acknowledge that traditional planned approaches to change fail to recognise the complex nature of such systems. Large-scale change in health and social services calls for leaders to be *connoisseurs of chaos* who are comfortable with systems non-linearity and who are sensitive to the importance of attending to systems perturbations in time- and error-sensitive contexts (Petrosky, 1985 in Issel and Narasimha, 2007, p.168). New thinking, new models and approaches are needed that transcend traditional theories of change management to offer a more intelligent response particularly to stakeholder engagement for leveraging both cost reduction and quality improvement.

Waddell *et al.* (2014) suggest that we simply do not know how to create change initiatives at the scale required of the challenges we currently face. They advocate a focus on change systems rather than individual change initiatives all the while recognising that the scale of change required is intimidating in its need to bring together personal change methodologies, programme and services change processes as well as significant shifts in values, policies and programmes. The burning questions: If traditional approaches are no longer appropriate as strategy maps for leading large-scale change, where does this leave us in our efforts to successfully lead such change efforts? Does social movements thinking offer possibilities for more effectively leading and managing the complexities of large scale change?

To begin to address these questions, we explore efforts in the UK in applying social movements thinking for mobilising large-scale change in health and social services. We begin by offering a brief review of the literature on social movements thinking and aligning it with literature on complex systems management. Following this, we draw on empirical data from key informant interviews and publicly available documents to briefly introduce two change initiatives, exploring these in their rich contexts in an effort to shed light on specific contingent conditions (Tsoukas, 1989). Doing so allows us to offer an assessment of achievements at both the micro- and macro-system levels from which we propose 'lessons' that may serve as guide posts for others initiating large-scale change efforts. Our focus on managing change in health and social services systems reminds us of the complicated and contested nature of such endeavours.

A social movement lens for exploring change

The current state of the world reflects a problem-solving methodology never seen in nature: remedies from above imposed upon the excluded (Hawken, 2007, p. 179).

Throughout history, social movements have played a key role in societal change (Crossley, 2002; Hawken, 2007). Their features of community organising and voluntary, coordinated and cause-oriented mobilisation have attracted commitment and engagement across a diverse range of participants and causes (e.g. political independence, women's rights, climate change) that have frequently resulted in sustained social change. This capacity for engaging a diverse range of stakeholders holds particular attraction in its potential for facilitating deeper enquiry into multiple, localised contexts and cultures. Orchestrated social movements are especially amenable to mobilising the energy for learning within organisational systems (Strang and Jung, 2002). Their particular blend of shared understanding and persuasion built on the beliefs and values that people hold can create a greater sense of engagement and commitment to turning shared goals into coordinated action. Barley and Tolbert (1997) draw on the notion of scripts as 'observable, recurrent activities and patterns of interaction characteristic of a particular setting' (p. 98) and script enactment as, over time, producing institutional logics that shape identities and material practices. A social movements' perspective may offer insight into ways of flexibly enacting such logics embedded in complex institutional systems, thereby leveraging large-scale transformational change.

Waddell (2007) suggests that traditional approaches to large-scale change 'arise from an array of change theories that are often not explicit' (p.71). Snowden and Boone (2007) suggest that those tasked with leading such change efforts tend to '...fall back into habitual, command-and-control mode; [with the] temptation to look for facts rather than allowing patterns to emerge; [and a] desire for accelerated resolution of problems or exploitation of opportunities' (p.73). Kurtz and Snowden (2003) posit that traditional approaches to decision making and policy formulation rest on three assumptions—the assumption of order, the assumption of rational choice and the assumption of intentional capability—and that these assumptions are only true in highly constrained systems. Snowden (this issue) reminds us that change in complex systems is emergent with possibilities captured through narrative techniques, essential to gaining multiple perspectives from which patterns can be sensed and explored (Kurtz and Snowden, 2003). 'The nature of the complex domain is the management of patterns' (Snowden, 2002, p.107).

Organisations tend to focus on the past in creating 'predictive and prescriptive models for future decisions based on the assumption that they are dealing with a complicated system in which the components and associated relationships are capable of discovery and management' (Snowden, 2002). Such approaches focus on specification, often relying on strong central system ties through the creation of inter-agency organisations to lead complex system change. Such strategies, however, do not deliver the radical reorientation necessary to produce the 'second order' sustainable responses characteristic of the complexity domain (Sun and Scott, 2005). The complexity domain favours the strength of weak (distributed) ties (Granovetter, 1973, 1983; Kurtz and Snowden, 2003) with social movements thinking focused on system energy through words like 'contagion', 'epidemic', 'explosion' to describe the power and spread of that energy (Bate et al. 2004, p.63).

Ganz (2000, 2007, 2010) has studied the impact of social movements in addressing socially complex issues including migrant workers' rights in California, the American civil rights movement and the environmental movement. He is also widely recognised as the architect of the social media campaign that has been widely attributed as instrumental in the election success of Barack Obama in 2008 (MacGillis, 2008; Vaccari, 2010). Ganz describes the power of social movements thinking as framed not in a traditional rational-analytic problem-solving mode but rather as an exercise in emergent creative thinking and flexible adaptation. What Ganz suggests aligns with the complex domain of Kurtz and Snowden's (2003) Cynefin sense-making framework where patterns emerge through the interaction of many agents and cannot be predicted in advance. At the heart of this process is the need to surface and articulate stories of personal experience and values—a 'story of self' (Ganz, 2010). Multiple personal narratives are then aligned to create a shared narrative grounded in shared values—the 'story of us'—to create momentum and energy to take action for change—the 'story of now' (Ganz, 2010). As such, the mimetic effect of small, local actions evoked through shared narratives can be amplified and replicated across a system and beyond, providing powerful imagery for carrying system change forward to the next stage. The use of personal narratives in mobilising latent energy is similar to generative approaches such as appreciative inquiry and world cafe that rely on layered conversations to surface possibilities for systems change (Cooperrider et al. 2008; Grandy and Holton, 2010; Hurley and Brown, 2009). The idea resonates as well with the concept of open innovation in technology development which strategically leverages internal and external sources of ideas to foster innovative solutions by diffusing internal silos of expertise through personal networks that reach beyond narrow specialisations (Chesbrough, 2010).

Narrative as captured in conversations is at the heart of McAdam et al.'s (1996) framing processes where different parties with different views attempt to shape the conversation in a contested field. As the conversation is increasingly framed, it must contend with existing political, institutional and social structures and leverage opportunities presented through established networks where such opportunities can mobilise energy through positive role models, peer pressure, forums for learning and dialogue that keep the momentum for change moving forward (Waddock, 2009). The process is similar to Ganz's

(2010) three-stage process of alignment in facilitating a deep-level system inquiry through values-based framing of an issue, building solidarity through mobilising narratives and sustaining engagement through a collective identity, commitment and shared purpose.

Traditional approaches to managing change in health and social service systems have relied on planned, incremental programmes to streamline and control activities while rationalising costs (Bevan, 2012). At the same time, these organisations are facing unprecedented challenges in terms of economic constraints, demographic shifts and rising public expectations that render traditional approaches insufficient to address such complexity (Bevan *et al.* 2013). Despite clear goals and considerable financial investments, change efforts realise only limited improvements when patterns of work are deeply ingrained in protocols and best practices (Baker, 2012). Tucker and Edmondson (2003) suggest that health systems are slow to learn and offer three reasons for this failure: the reliance on individuals to solve problems; the lack of slack resources due to efficiency concerns; and the emphasis on worker empowerment but without providing necessary organisational information to actually manage change. They further suggest that the pressures to demonstrate benefits from change initiatives overshadow willingness to acknowledge errors and failures and to learn from efforts at system change. One can imagine that such pressure is especially strong when change agents are reminded that politicians, funders and the public in general prefer good news stories to tales of system dysfunction. The fallibility of the largely human dimension in health and social services, however, requires adaptive as well as technical change (Heifitz, 1994) for 'identifying and triaging multiple health and social problems of individual programme clients and community needs' (Issel and Narasimha, 2007, p.167).

Social movements efficacy depends on a broad development of strategic leadership practices that align and motivate individual and collective energies, encouraging risk taking and imagination aligned through shared values. It is important to consider from the outset how stakeholder communities are identified, how they are engaged, what meaningful engagement entails and how often challenging and conflicting perspectives are not only to be heard and respected but embraced. Heifetz (1994) suggests that leaders should in fact encourage conflict as a means of 'ripening' issues. Such diversity can foster reflexivity, soften resistance to change and open us to the possibility of learning (Cortese, 2005). There is an inherent liminality in doing so, however, that can be both uncomfortable and liberating as 'normal order is suspended and…experienced as both unsettling and creative' (Sturdy et al. 2006). Those charged with formal leadership may find themselves 'temporarily undefined, beyond the normative social structure. This weakens them since they have no rights over others. But it also liberates them from structural obligations' (Turner, 1982, p. 27). The challenge then for those charged with leading large-scale change in such systems may be in balancing the need to be seen as demonstrating leadership from the perspective of the formal organisation while at the same time seeking to discover where the system as a whole desires to focus energy for change and mobilising that energy to move the system toward its desired, not predestined, future.

Two Case Studies in Managing Change

We highlight here two empirical examples of efforts to manage system change in the provision of health and social services. Both cases are situated within England but differ in the system level of change (micro vs. macro) and the origin of the initiative (emergent vs. planned). C2 Connecting Communities is a grassroots initiative that emerged over 20 years ago from frustration with the inadequacy of disconnected system-level efforts to address local community needs and has since been replicated in several communities across the UK as a model for regenerating local communities by improving social conditions and enhancing health outcomes. The initiative was an emergent change process that resembles closely principles of social movements thinking. The second case, NHS Change Day, is a planned, system-wide initiative launched in 2013 and intentionally aligned with a social movements approach.

C2 Connecting Communities: An emergent micro-level initiative

While acute care settings have been the subject of much attention in terms of healthcare reforms, community-based health and social services programmes have frequently been overlooked but offer space for a range of 'safe-to-fail' experiments (Kurtz and Snowden, 2003). A powerful example of safe-to-fail experimenting is C2 Connecting Communities (C2), an exciting and profoundly transformational example of community regeneration initiated through the efforts of two community nurses, Hazel Stuteley and Philip Trenoweth, working in the Cornwall area of the UK during the 1990s (Durie and Wyatt, 2007). Stuteley and Trenoweth were deeply troubled by the health and social conditions on a local council estate in Falmouth; an estate that had been cited as the most deprived in the area (Gordon et al. 1996):

> In the mid-1990s, the Beacon and Old Hill Estate in Falmouth in Cornwall was in the depths of despair. Although located in the affluent South West of England, it was nicknamed 'Beirut' by residents and was among the most deprived areas of Britain. On a spiral of decline, its problems were akin to those of inner cities. In a climate of mistrust between the police and community, violent crime, drug dealing and intimidation were rife. With little central heating, the cold, damp homes had resulted in a sharp rise in childhood asthma and respiratory problems. Largely abandoned by the statutory agencies, it was an estate that had become isolated. Above all, the community had lost its spirit and its people were no longer holding their heads high (Connecting Communities, 2008).

In their case study of the Beacon and Old Hill Estate, Durie and Wyatt (2007) apply a complexity framework to elicit the conditions and responses to those conditions that allowed for the emergence of 'adjacent possibilities' (Kauffman, 1995, 2000). Their analysis pointed to weak community/system connections and to community feelings of isolation and abandonment by various system agencies resulting in locked-in behaviours that were preventing any meaningful change (Durie and Wyatt, 2007, p.1934). That sense of isolation and abandonment, however, also served as the 'point of criticality' in producing 'an overwhelming sense that *something had to be done*' (p.1934). Their analysis suggests that Stuteley and Trenoweth's intervention had focused the system's attention to this point of criticality, producing a 'shift from the poverty of relations [on the estate] to the formation of a series of richly diverse *new* relations' (p.1935) through which 'adjacent possibilities' for change would emerge as novel and creative yet practical solutions that reversed the community's cycle of decline.

> With the active creation of new relations between residents, resulting from the ongoing door-to-door conversations, and the various public meetings and consultations, as well as the new relations between residents and agencies, a rich reservoir for innovating with new behaviours was created. Just as significantly, however, these new relations ensured that the influence of these new behaviours could spread throughout the system (Durie and Wyatt, 2007, p.1937).

From a Cynefin perspective (Kurtz and Snowden, 2003), the Beacon and Old Hill case illustrates complexity in the range of clients and their needs, the service providers, the jurisdictional authorities, the scarcity of resources, the mutual dysfunction and cumulative human despair from a multitude of failed initiatives. Solutions, if they were to work, had to emerge from active and open experimentation based on salient information, heuristic facility and genuine motivation (Ganz, 2000) as rooted in what the community valued, not what the system ordained. Stuteley and Trenoweth had no particular model for change in mind but simply used their knowledge of local conditions, their professional expertise and their earned and trusted connections within the community to mobilise efforts toward addressing a maze of issues and problems that appeared to be beyond the remit or resources of any specific public authority. As Durie and Wyatt (2007) suggest, the case is a clear example of emergent structure within the system (p.1937). By 'managing in the present, amplifying and dampening as appropriate to allow a more sustainable, but unpredictable future to emerge' (Snowden, 2011, p.145), Stuteley and Trenoweth intuitively embraced principles of social movements thinking. They invited the community to attend a series of listening forums. Tea and biscuits and a raffle were offered as incentives. The process was slow to begin but once the community came to realise that someone was actually listening, the energy accelerated:

> There was one meeting of nearly one hundred and fifty people. That was the fiercest, the angriest. Once they got going there was no stopping them. They laid into the police, housing and local government but it was healthy. Nobody had listened to them before. That night, sitting at the back of the hall, I really felt for the first time that things would change (Hazel Stuteley, July 2013).

People needed to be heard, they needed better housing and neighbourhood security and they needed to work together to prioritise how those needs were addressed through the local allocation of finite resources. Listening forums allowed Stuteley and Trenoweth to capture the community's micro-narratives (Snowden, this issue), using these as the basis for building grassroots support and mobilising resources. The system—via the local regional council—responded by leveraging resources through an energy conservation initiative to address deplorable housing conditions on the estate and delegating some of its powers to manage the resources to a tenant-led-partnership. 'This was the first step in the community really believing in itself. Knowing it could achieve something. We were overjoyed!' (Hazel Stuteley, July 2013). Over time, efforts grew through a 'cycle of virtuous change' (Gillespie and Hughes, 2011), generating local pride and the energy to tackle even more complex issues facing the community. Today, the Beacon and Old Hill Estate not only boasts a vibrant grassroots-led and -governed community services centre but its model of success—now known as C2—has been shared and replicated in over 20 communities throughout the United Kingdom and has been recognised with a number of national awards (Durie and Wyatt, 2007, p.1931).

Zald *et al.* (2005) acknowledge that social movement agendas can become part of managerial strategy, but often initially present themselves outside the parameters of anticipated organisational policy. 'As a result, managers are often in the position of reacting to unanticipated agendas and collective action' (p.278). This relational complexity of large-scale change initiatives renders strategy a particularly dynamic process, full of possibilities and rife with uncertainty as emergent issues bring into play diverse values at both the individual and system levels. To avoid both premature and defensive responses, managers need to facilitate processes for gathering in as much intelligence as possible from within the system and its environment rather than simply 'broadcasting out'.

Durie and Wyatt (2007) cite three factors as key to shifting the energy from decline to regeneration: trust in those who initiated the intervention (i.e. Stuteley and Trenoweth); their commitment to the future of the community instilling a desire within itself to make a difference; and the recent arrival of new residents who were not already locked in to dominant system behaviours and thus more open to 'adjacent possibilities'. Stuteley and Trenoweth, as local leaders, recognised that the change required didn't fit neatly into any existing policy or programme budget; what was needed was basic and straightforward at the local level but challenging at the macro-level with its siloed responsibilities and pre-defined resource allocations. Listening broadly and openly to individual concerns, focusing collective attention to the articulation of shared values and opening up to creative solutions from those in the community who were not already 'locked in' to the dominant dysfunctions would facilitate the emergence of adjacent possibilities for prioritising needs and allocating finite resources, therein providing a rationale for decision-making: those whose needs were greatest would be accommodated first with a shared commitment to continue working together to secure sufficient funds to address additional needs. Early successes fostered community confidence and the energy to stay the course. Over time, leadership from within the community would emerge to replace Stuteley and Trenoweth and in so doing would foster the community's self-sustainability. Twenty years on, the Beacon Community Resource Centre continues to be a self-organising focus for generating creative and innovative solutions to emergent community needs. Stuteley and community leaders from Beacon and Old Hill estates have continued, as well, to share their experiences with other interested communities and community-based organisations through the creation of C2,[1] a social enterprise focused on tackling health and social inequalities in disadvantaged communities across the UK, based on a seven-step model developed from the Beacon and Old Hill experiences: 1) locating energy for change; 2) creating vision; 3) listening to communities; 4) formalising a partnership; 5) sustaining momentum; 6) taking action; and 7) continuing a trajectory of improvement (Gillespie and Hughes, 2011). Within this model, we see elements of both the Ganz (2010) three stage process (i.e. eliciting personal values, discovering shared values and mobilising action for change) and McAdam *et al.*'s (1996) social movements approach of framing processes, political opportunity structures and mobilising structures.

NHS Change Day: A planned macro-level initiative

The NHS is the largest health system in the world, serving a population of 54 million, with 1.7 million employees (Bevan *et al.*, 2013). Founded over 65 years ago, the NHS has continued to provide free healthcare to Britons through direct taxation, without regard for individual ability to pay and, in so doing, has achieved the status of a 'sacred cow' (Wheeler, 2013). Like many health and social services organisations, the NHS has traditionally framed leadership in terms of structures and positional authority (Bevan *et al.*, 2013). Brookes (2011) suggests there is an increasing need for formal leaders in organisations to work in partnership, 'often in settings where there is no formal or appointed leader' (p.177). This can be a tough lesson for many leaders in large-scale health and social services systems who have honed their skills and reputation on exercising authority and devising emphatic, rapid response solutions in organisational systems where efficiency and accountability remain the primary values.

For over a decade, however, the NHS has been studying the application of organising principles from social movements theory for enhancing its innovation and improvement change initiatives; many of which can only be described as increasingly complex in their scope, intention and constraints (Bibby *et al.* 2009; NHS Institute for Innovation and Improvement, 2010) and requiring a conceptualisation of 'leadership everywhere' (Bevan *et al.*, 2013). The work, under the leadership of Helen Bevan and the Institute for Innovation and Improvement[2] is grounded in social movements thinking, particularly the work of Marshall Ganz (2010). The approach is highly inclusive, endeavouring to tap

---

1 www.c2connectingcommunities.co.uk/
2 Due to a major restructuring of the NHS as of 31 March 2013, the Institute for Innovation and Improvement no longer exists. Its work is now being administered by NHS Improving Quality (www.nhsiq.nhs.uk/)

into individual passions and values. Commitment is individual; the aim is to engage, persuade and embrace collective goals and values to build strong, 'like us' internal network ties by engaging employees at all levels while at the same time fostering and mobilising community network ties through broad stakeholder engagement. The intention is to build system resilience by connecting and mobilising a range of latent change agents and collaborators—'leaders everywhere' (Hilton and Lawrence-Pietroni, 2013). The intention is to shift focus from compliance with accepted practice and accountabilities—the 'Known' domain (Kurtz and Snowden, 2003)—to a commitment to innovation and service improvement—the 'Complexity' domain (Kurtz and Snowden, 2003). Strategic capacity comes through greater access to salient information, heuristic facility and motivation that can effectively compensate for what is often lacking in the way of traditional project resources (Ganz, 2000). To date, NHS change efforts using social movements thinking have ranged from re-energising nursing and midwifery services to enhancing end-of-life care and the use of patient care decision aids to assist individuals in making their own decisions about their care. One early success often cited in NHS publications is a 'call to action' aimed at reducing the prescription of anti-psychotic drugs for people with dementia. Launched in 2011, the initiative is reported to have reduced such prescriptions by 51% (Boyd et al. 2013).

As part of its efforts to build this culture of commitment to change, in 2012, the NHS, under the direction of Helen Bevan, launched a new model for organisational large-scale change (see Fig. 1). The model is intended to address failures in earlier efforts to enact systems change by achieving change through multiple mechanisms that leverage shared purpose; a deeply rooted and widely held desire to improve patient care (NHS Improving Quality, 2013).

> If we look at the whole history and the evidence base around large-scale change what we can see very clearly is that if we want to build the energy, the creativity and the innovation for creating change at scale we need to be able to hook in with people's intrinsic motivators for change...connecting with a shared purpose, a higher purpose that no matter where we are in the system we can appreciate the shared purpose that we are trying to achieve. It's about engaging, mobilizing and calling people to action. It's about creating the kind of motivational leadership that is needed for transformational change. We know that all those things are very important but we also recognize that we are part of a system and what we also know is that if we are going to create the focus and momentum for delivery at scale we need to work with the drivers of extrinsic motivation—the things in the system that move us all together in the right way...regulation, systems that incentivize financial and otherwise, performance management, accountability measures...if all we had were intrinsic motivators, we could have a lot of people energized about change but we would not all be heading in the same direction. Often, however, what happens is that a system's extrinsic motivators 'eat up' or kill off the intrinsic motivation. What I think is the genius of our new change model is that for the first time, it gives us a framework that aligns and connects our intrinsic and extrinsic motivators for change as part of a whole system for change (Helen Bevan, September 2012).

Figure 1 NHS Change Model

Source: www.nhsiq.nhs.uk/capacity-capability/nhs-change-model.aspx

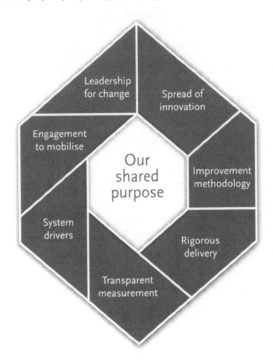

Building on the new change model, Bevan and associates launched a system-wide call to action inviting all NHS employees to commit to individual acts of positive change within the NHS and to declare their commitment publicly through a socially mediated website. Described as a grassroots initiative that started with a conversation on Twitter between trainee doctors (Bevan *et al.*, 2013), the intention was to create—in one day—a mass movement of NHS staff proving that large-scale change can be enacted through multiple single acts by individuals (Hilton and Lawrence-Pietroni, 2013, p.4). It was a bold experiment in applying social movements thinking to mobilise system energy for change. The hope was that the effort would reach beyond the formal system's 'strong ties' (i.e. employees) to also leverage latent energy within the overall system (i.e. patients, community) by tapping into the capacity within patient and community-based loosely connected 'weak ties' (Granovetter, 1973, 1983).

In contrast to C2's emergent community-based approach, the NHS Change Day employed a more traditional centrally initiated approach relying extensively on social media to accelerate culture change across the organisation. As a centrally planned initiative, Change Day required a balancing act 'between frontline action AND using the leverage of the hierarchy to make positive change happen without destroying the grassroots power' (Bevan *et al.*, 2013). The key was shifting from the traditional reliance on compliance to a commitment-based approach anchored in a shared purpose of improving patient care that had been articulated widely, both formally and informally, throughout the system.

The goal for NHS Change Day 2013 was to secure 65,000 individual action pledges; this number was intended to be symbolic of the organisation's 65 years of service to the British people. The effort was officially launched in January 2013. Considered an ambitious goal at the outset, it would prove slow to gain traction. The energy was latent and required persistent messaging to overcome the prevailing NHS culture of compliance. An unexpected learning for the organising team was to discover how deeply engrained in the organisation's culture was the need to seek consent—to comply before acting. The Change Day call to action had to instil a new belief in the value and power of voluntary action for positive changes for patient care (Bevan *et al.*, 2013). Success came through consistent commitment and encouraging individual action through an aggressive social media campaign that helped to make individual pledges visible and tangible. As the momentum built, the organisation's formal leadership served as 'signal generators' (Bevan *et al.*, 2013) to further amplify the positive energy being created. By pledge day, 13 March 2013, the original goal had been surpassed with over 189,000 pledges to act having been logged on a virtual pledge wall. The success of such macro-level approaches is, of course, more difficult to assess particularly over the short term. NHS Change Day 2013 received considerable praise and recognition (Bevan *et al.*, 2013) with its follow-up Change Day 2014 logging over 800,000 pledges (Roland, 2014); a success repeated with a third Change Day on March 11, 2015.

Conclusion

In this paper, we have explored the potential for social movements thinking as a lens in designing and delivering large-scale change efforts. We have used this lens to discuss two specific change efforts in the area of health and social services. We are not suggesting that embracing a social movements approach is a simple way to solve the challenges of large-scale, complex change initiatives and it would seem that we still have much to learn about managing and achieving change on such a scale but perhaps there are some lessons to be gleaned from the examples offered in this paper.

First, as Kurtz and Snowden (2003) suggest, change in complex systems such as health and social services cannot be predicted in advance but rather emerges as a pattern of coalescing energy from which activity can be mobilised. Those leading change under such circumstances have to be sufficiently humble to acknowledge and respect what emerges as felt needs within the system, grounded in the reality of everyday experience and underpinned by deeply held personal values; values that hold the potential capacity for mobilising a system's energy toward change. The outcome may not be what was initially envisaged as planned strategic system change but once surfaced and fuelled with deeply held and shared values, the system will not move until those needs are addressed. Stuteley and Trenoweth intuitively understood that they did not have the answers to the problems faced by the community, that they could not plan a solution without the community; that they had to listen for adjacent possibilities to emerge as the community self-organised around an emergent shared purpose.

> **The lesson.** Leading complex projects is much less about using positional authority to broker solutions and much more about fostering an enabling culture by listening for passion, posing thoughtful, even provocative questions and then having the commitment and the courage to fully explore the adjacent possibilities around those questions.

Second, a critical perspective on social movements thinking might suggest that change efforts can be hijacked by centrally led, strong-willed and persuasive tactics cloaked in social movements rhetoric but that still end up looking a lot more like traditional approaches to change management. NHS Change Day was designed to inspire a climate where the focus and momentum for change could be achieved by aligning intrinsic motivation through shared purpose with the system's drivers of extrinsic motivation (regulations, incentives, measures) and then stimulating the system's latent energy for change through individual acts of creativity and commitment. Macro-level alignment opened up micro-level initiative.

> **The lesson.** The formal organisation and its leadership cannot intervene directly to create a movement; instead, it must focus on creating the receptive context (organisational, structural, political, and cultural) and triggering conditions that will bring a movement to life (Bate *et al.* 2004).

Third, the question then is what happens when things are genuinely disputed and contested, often from very different perspectives? How do decisions to move forward get made? How are less powerful voices heard? How is consensus reached? As Durie and Wyatt (2007) suggest, a system reaches a point of criticality where despite individual frustrations and perspectives, everyone comes to acknowledge that something must change. Both C2 and the NHS found themselves facing unsustainable futures. Having surfaced multiple perspectives and listened for shared values, each system was poised to move into the realm of uncertainty by listening for what was possible and then being sufficiently bold to believe that what was possible was achievable. As Scharmer and Yukelson (this issue) suggest, the awareness or intention that people bring to a situation has a profound impact on the quality of the results they achieve.

> **The lesson.** Leading from a social movements perspective requires courage to leave behind familiar power-vested responses and directives to trust in the promise that respecting difference, embracing diversity, inviting challenges to the status quo and sitting with uncertainty in service to unorthodox thinking will move complex, large-scale change efforts forward—eventually.

Fourth, undertaking large-scale change can be a daunting effort when stakeholders are geographically dispersed and where opportunities are rare to bring the whole system together. While the availability of a range of social media offers immense potential for galvanising disparate energies into a collective commitment, Piskorski (2011) suggests that this mobilising potential is undermined when approached from a top-down instrumentalism. Merely employing social media to broadcast and to seek feedback generally fails to translate into success for digital strategies. Social strategies that help people create or enhance relationships—arenas where people connect with each other under the auspices of the organisation—generate engagement that can translate into commitment and action. C2's emergence predated current social media capabilities but its local nature allowed it to use the most effective social medium—face-to-face conversations. The power of the C2 story and its model of change have since spread via social media where its replication in a growing number of communities across the UK has taken it from micro- to macro-level impact. NHS Change Day, on the other hand, was planned as a macro-level initiative; the intended scope of which would have been virtually impossible without a social media platform where the medium could also be the message—that change was possible across the organisation through single acts from leaders everywhere (Hilton and Lawrence-Pietroni, 2013).

> **The lesson.** While the intention of large-scale change is to impact a system at the macro-level, it is inevitably enacted through multiple actions at the micro-levels of a system; individual acts of commitment that resonate with deeply held personal values, inspiring the articulation of shared values and connecting those values with the need for change. The power in social movement thinking is in the ability to elicit those values as inspiration for mobilising a system's energy toward a desired future where '…the emergence of problems amounts to the creation of adjacent possibilities' (Durie and Wyatt, 2007, p.1939).

Fifth, sustainability of large-scale change efforts rests within 'the space between' the diversity of interests and concerns that emerge when authentic efforts are invested in engaging relevant stakeholder communities. In both cases presented in this paper, system stakeholders were experiencing conditions with increasing levels of dissatisfaction but were locked into dysfunctional patterns of behaviour. No solution had been devised through the remit of centrally planned agencies. In both C2 and NHS Change Day, strategies emerged to embrace as many stakeholders as possible, with grounded relevance in their everyday realities. Without privileging any particular community, ideas that resided at the edge of the system's assumptions and conventions came into view. What might be possible could then be explored.

> **The lesson.** 'Sustainability and resilience are more likely to be achieved if we enable change rather than trying to determine what that change would be in advance' (Snowden, this issue).

While it may be easy to be sceptical in thinking that social movements thinking is simply another fashionable management trend, the examples we have explored above do suggest that social movement thinking may offer possibilities for generating the energy and early optimism that is a prerequisite to successful achievement of any large-scale change effort; particularly when the change effort entails a diverse range of stakeholders with needs that inevitably exceed resources. As the examples discussed in our paper suggest, however, the real value in social movements thinking may be in its capacity to leverage an often overlooked resource; that of hope and a belief in the possibility that resources needed for change are, in fact, abundant but must be activated through shared purpose and relationships (Bevan *et al.* 2013).

References

Baker, G.R. (2012). The challenges of making care safer: Leadership and system transformation. *Healthcare Quarterly*, 15, 8-11.

Barley, S.R and Tolbert, T.S. (1997). Institutionalization and structuration: Studying the links between action and institution. *Organization Studies*, 18(1):93-117.

Bate, P., Robert, G. and Bevan, H. (2004). The next phase of Healthcare improvement: What can we learn from social movements? *Quality & Safety in Healthcare*, 13: 62-66.

Bevan, H. (2012). *Some Ideas for Complex Projects: Mobilization and strong/weak ties.* WebEx presentation to the Ashridge Leading Complex Projects Action Research Consortium, January 16, 2012.

Bevan, H., Roland, D., Lynton, J., Jones, P. McCrea, J. (2013) Biggest ever day of collective action to improve healthcare that started with a tweet. *M-Prize: Management Innovation Exchange*. Retrieved from http://www.managementexchange.com/story/biggest-ever-day-collective-action-improve-healthcare-started-tweet-0

Bibby, J., Bevan, H., Carter, E., Bate, P. and Robert, G. (2009). *The Power of One, the Power of Many*. Coventry, UK: NHS Institute for Innovation and Improvement.

Boyd, A., Burnes, B., Clark, E. and Nelson, A. (2013). *Mobilising and organizing for large scale change in healthcare: 'The right prescription: A call to action on the use of antipsychotic drugs for people with dementia'*. Manchester: University of Manchester.

Brookes, S. (2011). Crisis, confidence and collectivity: Responding to the new public leadership challenge. *Leadership*, 7(2), 175-194.

Chesbrough, H. (2003). *Open Innovation: The new imperative for creating and profiting from technology*. Boston: Harvard Business School Press.

Connecting Communities: Engaging with challenged communities in the south west of England through sport and physical activity. Final Report. (2008). Exeter: Health Complexity Group. Peninsula Medical School.

Cooperrider, D.L., Whitney, D. and Stavros, J.M. (2008). *Appreciative inquiry handbook: For leaders of change*, 2nd ed. (Chapter 9). Brunswick, OH: Crown Custom Publishing.

Cortese, C.G. (2005). Learning through teaching. *Management Learning*, 36(1), 87-115.

Crossley, N. (2002). *Making sense of social movements*. Buckingham, UK: Open University Press.

Durie, R., and Wyatt, K. (2007). New communities, new relations: The impact of community organization on health outcomes. *Social Science & Medicine*, 65(9), 1928-1941.

Ganz, M. (2000). Resources and resourcefulness: Strategic capacity in the unionization of California Agriculture, 1959-1966. *American Journal of Sociology*, 105(4), 1003-1062.

Ganz, M. (2007). *Telling Your Public Story: Self, us, now*. Kennedy School of Government. Retrieved from: http://www.wholecommunities.org/pdf/Public%20Story%20Worksheet07Ganz.pdf

Ganz, M. (2010). Leading Change: Leadership, organization, and social movements, in Nohria, N. & Khurana, K. Eds., *Handbook of Leadership Theory and Practice: An HBS Centennial Colloquium on advancing leadership*, Boston: Harvard Business Press.

Gillespie, J. and Hughes, S. (2011). *Positively Local: C2 a model for community change*. The Centre for Welfare Reform Policy Paper 09.08.2011. Birmingham: University of Birmingham, Health Services Management Centre.

Gordon, D., Payne, S. and Henson, B. (1996). *Poverty and deprivation in West Cornwall in the 1990s*. Bristol, UK: Bristol University.

Grandy, G. and Holton, J. (2010). Mobilizing Change in a Business School Using Appreciative Inquiry. *The Learning Organization*, 17(2), 178-194.

Granovetter, M. S. (1973). The strength of weak ties. *The American Journal of Sociology*, 78(6), 1360-1380.

Granovetter, M. S. (1983). The strength of weak ties: A network theory revisited. *Sociological Theory*, 1, 201-233.

Hawken, P. (2007). *Blessed Unrest: How the largest movement in the world came into being and why no one saw it coming*. New York: Viking.

Heifitz, R. (1994). *Leadership without Easy Answers*, Cambridge, MA: Harvard University Press.

Hilton, K.B. and Lawrence-Pietroni, C. (2013). *Leaders Everywhere: The story of NHS Change Day—a learning report*. Leeds, UK: NHS Improving Quality.

Hurley, T.J. and Brown, J. (2009). Conversational leadership: Thinking together for a change. *The Systems Thinker*, 20(9), 2-7.

Issel, L.M. and Narasimha, K.M. (2007). Creating complex health improvement programs as mindful organizations: From theory to action. *Journal of Health Organization and Management*, 21(2): 166-183.

Kauffman, S. (1995). *At Home in the universe: The search for laws of self-organization*. Oxford: Oxford University Press.

Kauffman, S. (2000). *Investigations*. Oxford: Oxford University Press.

Kurtz, C. F., and Snowden, D. J. (2003). The new dynamics of strategy: Sense-making in a complex and complicated world. *IBM Systems Journal*, 42(3), 462-483.

McAdam, D., McCarthy, J. D., and Zald, M. N. (Eds.). (1996). *Comparative perspectives on social movements: Political opportunities, mobilizing structures, and cultural framings*. Cambridge, UK: Cambridge University Press.

MacGillis, A. (2008). Obama camp relying heavily on ground effort. *Washington Post*, 12, 2008.

NHS Improving Quality. (2013). *From Shared Purpose to Joint Action: Telling the story and capturing the learning from the NHS Change Model*. Final report prepared by the SAPPHIRE Group, University of Leicester, UK. Leeds, UK: NHS Improving Quality.

NHS Institute for Innovation and Improvement. (2010). *Large Scale Change—NHS Mobilization*. Coventry, UK.

Petrosky, P. (1985). *To engineer is human: The role of failure in successful design*. New York: St. Martin Press.

Piskorski, M.J. (2011). Social strategies that work. *Harvard Business Review*, November, 117-122.

Roland, D. (2014). *NHS Change Day—An unmitigated success* (July 4). Retrieved from: http://www.england.nhs.uk/2014/07/04/damien-roland/

Snowden, D. (2002) 'Complex acts of knowing: paradox and descriptive self-awareness', *Journal of Knowledge Management*, Vol. 6(2), 100-111.

Snowden, D. (2011). Good fences make good neighbors, *Information, Knowledge, Systems Management*, 10(1), 135-150.

Snowden, D.F. and Boone, M.E. (2007). A Leader's Framework for Decision Making: Wise executives tailor their approach to fit the complexity of the circumstances they face. *Harvard Business Review*, November, 69-76.

Strang, D. and Jung, D-I., (2005). Organizational change as an orchestrated social movement in, Davis, G.F., McAdam, D., Scott, W.R. and Zald, M.N. *Social movements and organizational theory*. Cambridge, UK: Cambridge University Press.

Sturdy, A., Schwarz, M and Spicer, A. (2006). Guess Who's Coming to Dinner? Structures and uses of liminality in strategic management consultancy. *Human Relations*, 59(7), 929-960.

Sun, Peter Y.T. and Scott, J. (2005). Sustaining Second-order Change Initiation: Structured complexity and interface management. *The Journal of Management Development*, 24(10), 879-895.

Tsoukas, H. (1989). The validity of idiographic research explanations. *The Academy of Management Review*, 14(4), 551-561.

Tucker, A.L. and Edmondson, A.C. (2003). Why hospitals don't learn from failures: Organizational psychological dynamics that inhibit systems change. *California Management Review*, 45: 55-72.

Turner, V. (1982). *From Ritual to Theatre: The human seriousness of play*, New York: PAJ Press.

Vaccari, C. (2010). 'Technology is a commodity': the internet in the 2008 United States Presidential election. *Journal of Information Technology & Politics*, 7(4), 318-339.

Waddell, S. (2007). Realising global change: Developing the tools: building the infrastructure. *The Journal of Corporate Citizenship*, 26 (Summer): 69-84.

Waddell, S., Hsueh, J., Birney, A., Khorsani, A. and Feng, W. (2014). Large systems change: Producing the change we want. *The Journal of Corporate Citizenship*, 53 (March): 5-8.

Waddock, S. (2009). Making a difference? Corporate responsibility as a social movement. *The Journal of Corporate Citizenship*, 33(Spring): 35-46.

Wheeler, B. (2013, July 17). Why not ... privatize the NHS, BBC News UK Politics. Retrieved from: http://www.bbc.com/news/uk-politics-22528719

Zald, M.N., Morrill, C. and Rao, H. (2005). The impact of social movements on organizations: Environment and responses. In, Davis, G.F., McAdam, D., Scott, W.R. and Zald, M.N. *Social movements and organizational theory*. Cambridge, UK: Cambridge University Press.

DOI: [10.9774/GLEAF.4700.2015.ju.000012]

Navigating Change in Complex Multi-Actor Settings

A Practice Approach to Better Collaboration

Petra Kuenkel

Collective Leadership Institute, Germany

The article examines successful patterns for collaboration in large-scale, multi-actor sustainability initiatives across the boundaries of private sector, public sector, and civil society. Sustainability challenges have moved on the agenda of every nation, every organisation and many citizens. These challenges require new forms of collaborative inventiveness as well as change-makers able to implement change jointly across all levels of the global society. The author presents a methodology, based on extensive literature reviews of conceptual thought as well as research with cross-cultural leaders and intervention strategies of sustainability practitioners, for invigorating human competences that foster result-oriented and value-based collaboration. The methodology presented—the *Collective Leadership Compass*—is a navigating tool enabling leaders to, through constructive and reliable collaboration, effect change in complex multi-actor settings by paying attention to patterns of human competences in the dimensions of *future possibilities, engagement, innovation, humanity, collective intelligence,* and *wholeness.* A case example, showing a practical application by a sustainability platform project leader, explores how the methodology is applied in practice. It suggests further research into the understanding of how to build the capacity of groups of actors to become catalysts for large systems change.

- Collaboration
- Multi-actor
- Complexity
- Leadership
- Competences
- System change

Petra Kuenkel is a full member of the Club of Rome and a leading strategic adviser to pioneering international multi-stakeholder initiatives that address complex sustainability issues. As the co-founder and Executive Director of the Collective Leadership Institute she promotes the scaling-up of collaboration skills for change agents from the private sector, public sector and civil society that have the sustainability of this world and the future of humankind as their focus. She is a pioneering thinker on re-inventing leadership as a collective competence of a group of leaders that catalyse positive change for the common good. Petra Kuenkel is part of an international think tank on large systems change and co-founder of the Partnering Alliance, an initiative aiming at improving the quality of partnering for sustainability between the public sector, the private sector and civil society. Prior to the founding of the Collective Leadership Institute she facilitated value-based leadership development programmes for executives from multinational companies and held a management position at an international development organisation.

✉ Collective Leadership Institute, Eisenhartstrasse 2, D 14467, Germany

🖥 petra.kuenkel@collectiveleadership.com

N JULY 2006, 45 PEOPLE met in Salvador Bahia in a small meeting room of one of the local hotels. Despite the unbearable heat, the group of stakeholders, from across the global coffee chain, passionately concentrated on a written document projected onto the wall. Different versions had been under discussion for months—causing conflicts, threats, and waves of mistrust between the global coffee industry and international NGOs. After a long day they finally agreed on a document that would enable an operational mainstream standard for sustainable green coffee production. The meeting was a breakthrough in a challenging initiative that led to the founding of the Common Code for the Coffee Community Association (4C) in 2007.[1] This association is an international strategic alliance for responsible supply chain management in the coffee sector. More than 100 representatives from over 25 coffee producing countries participated in the development process.[2] Today more than 350 members of the association come from 40 countries and represent producer organisations in all coffee producing countries as well as trade and industry, civil society, research, and support organisations.

The stakeholders involved were frontrunners with regard to acting in a complex multi-actor setting. Since then, engaging with expected impacts of complex sustainability mega-forces has moved on the agenda of every nation, every organisation as well as an increasing number of citizens. Sustainability concerns might lead to a change in how corporations approach business as climate change, ecosystem decline, energy security, water scarcity, resource management, food security, demographic change, and population growth will continue to impact businesses over the next 20 years (de Boer and van Bergen 2012). As these challenges cannot be dealt with in isolation, it is important to develop multi-stakeholder collaboration as a response to the complexity of the challenges ahead (Lozano, 2007; Kuenkel and Schaefer, 2013). This is an emerging field of practice that is characterised by:

▶ Multiple actors, often with conflicting interests, who need to align around a joint improvement approach (e.g. expanding the production and marketing of sustainably produced coffee)

▶ The effectiveness of the collaboration being dependent on engaging actors, who would not normally work together, into a joint approach

▶ Multi-dimensional problems which require solutions that are, first, *complicated*—e.g. ensuring good practices in the production of the commodity; second, *complex*—requiring a testing and learning approach, emerging solutions and innovation for scalability; and, third, *chaotic*—subject to unforeseen market or political influences (see also Snowden, 2007)

Despite a strong belief in the ability of collaboration to solve challenges, the complex multi-dimensionality of problems faced in the sustainability arena is often not considered (Fadeeva, 2005). The question therefore arises how to

---

1 www.4c-coffeeassociation.org
2 4C official press conference, 23 April 2007

best approach multi-stakeholder collaboration in multifaceted environments. A starting point could be a better understanding of different types of complexity. While Otto Scharmer (2007) distinguishes between three types of complexity, generative complexity, dynamic complexity and social or institutional complexity, Barrett (2014) also emphasises value complexity.

▶ **Dynamic complexity** refers to circumstances where cause and effect relationships are not traceable or easily planned. Systemic, whole systems approaches to complex change, such as the above example in green coffee production, require multi-stakeholder collaboration to ensure all aspects of a system are represented

▶ **Generative complexity** implies that past solutions are often not appropriate for the future. Instead, radically new innovations are frequently required in order to shift behavioural habits, solidified mind-sets, and systemic structures and, as a result, collaboration across think-tanks and institutions, research and practitioners is called for

▶ **Social and institutional complexity** refers to the diversity of actors involved in sustainability challenges and extends into different cultures, interests, and territorial boundaries. However, most complex challenges require aligned, yet differentiated action that can most likely be achieved through multi-stakeholder collaboration

▶ **Value complexity** refers to the intricacies introduced by conflicting personal values, institutional values and societal values found both globally and locally. Despite the differences in interest, multi-stakeholder collaboration has the potential to—if not align values—at least negotiate between the differences

Many of the sustainability challenges mentioned above display more than one, if not all types of complexity. Kaufmann (1995) suggests that, where complexity is high, the capacity to adapt, to evolve, to coordinate, to innovate, and to change is equally high. In the case of the Common Code of the Coffee Community initiative this turned out to be true—the actors learned how to successfully navigate all four types of complexity throughout the five-year process. Although the development of the code was not an easy process, but subject to internal and external conflicts, lingering mistrust, and severe differences in opinions, the leaders learned to operate and to deliver in a multi-actor setting, across institutional boundaries, mind-sets, and world-views, and made a decisive step towards managing complex change. But what made success in this multi-actor setting possible?

The call for collaboration in multi-actor settings can be a substantial requirement to realise. The process of partnering between different stakeholders is generally slow, with many different levels of understanding around partnering, high transaction costs and a tendency to duplicate already existing solutions in an inefficient effort. As a result, many existing multi-stakeholder collaborations are not yet delivering at full efficiency or effectiveness (Biermann et al. 2007). Stakeholders can get lost in a jungle of impeding structures, get trapped in the measuring of questionable results, or become severely disappointed by a lack of understanding across sectors, organisations, cultures, race, or gender. This in turn, may well result in their enthusiasm and commitment declining and they might become cynical towards weaker or mistrustful towards stronger stakeholder groups.

This article explores navigating stakeholder collaboration in complex change by looking at underlying effective patterns of collaboration that enable actors to manage all four types of complexity and turn them into opportunities. It does so through presenting a methodological approach to navigating change in a multi-actor setting—the *Collective Leadership Compass*—a framework reflecting mutually supportive factors for effectiveness in collaboration. Used as a guiding tool for mental attention the compass can become critical to the transformation of a group of fragmented, mistrustful or competitive actors into a functioning collaboration pattern. It can also help leaders take the invisible into account, ask new questions, design more successful process intervention strategies and guide collective action. Collective Leadership is here seen as the capacity of a group of leaders to catalyse systems change in a multi-actor setting (Pór, 2008; Kellermann, 2012; Kuenkel and Schaefer, 2013).

The methodological approach presented—the *Collective Leadership Compass*—suggests six dimensions that, consciously attended to, have factually led to more constructive and reliable collaboration efforts in complex multi-actor settings. The methodology is based on 20 years' experience in assisting collaboration efforts to succeed, backed by a large body of literature and research into success factors for collective action. Although the six dimensions are not new, what is new is paying attention to their *joint* presence and the positive effect this has on the quality of collaboration. Such attention invigorates a pattern of interactive human competences that subsequently ease navigating complexity in an integrative and inclusive way. Table 1 shows the dimensions and related competences.

Table 1 The Dimensions of the Collective Leadership Compass

Dimension	Related competence
Future possibilities	Our competence to take responsibility and consciously shape reality towards a sustainable future
Engagement	Our competence to create step-by-step engagement towards building effective collaboration systems
Innovation	Our competence to create novelty and find intelligent solutions
Humanity	Our competence to reach into each other's humanness, both the collective experience and individual experience of being human
Collective intelligence	Our competence to harvest differences for progress
Wholeness	Our competence to see a larger picture and stay connected to the common good

Every change endeavour starts with people considering **future possibilities**. At times individuals sense a potential future and at times a vision for a future is developed by a group of people. Over time the potential then grows into a more structured change initiative or even a movement. The dimension of future possibilities refers to the human competence to take responsibility and consciously shape reality towards a sustainable future. However, even the greatest visions for change are futile if not enough stakeholders are prepared to commit to action.

Effective multi-actor settings therefore require sufficient **engagement** of stakeholders—the powerful and the less powerful, the influential and the affected. Meaningful stakeholder engagement processes can create trust and cohesion, invigorate network connections, and foster collective action that leads to tangible outcomes. The dimension of engagement refers to the human competence to create step-by-step engagement towards building effective collaboration ecosystems.

However, if novelty does not also enter a collaboration system, the process might not move forward, if actions and behaviours that led to the current situation are re-created. Although learning from the past is valuable it should not limit leaders to simply create new variations of existing solutions. The dimension of **innovation** refers to the human competence to create novelty and find intelligent solutions. However, innovation that does not take our shared humanity into account can create unsafe environments.

Awareness of the human story has both an individual and a collective perspective. Collaboration systems are able to shift towards constructive solutions when there is mutual respect and acknowledgment of the intrinsic value of all people, regardless of different opinions and viewpoints. The dimension of **humanity** refers to the ability of each person to connect to their unique human competence in order to reach out to each other's shared humanity. Increasing awareness, however, requires exchange with others about the actions to be taken.

Life thrives on diversity, and so do human collectives. Meaning-making frameworks—offline or online—rooted in dialogue between human beings are essential to multi-stakeholder collaboration—if balanced with all other dimensions. The dimension of **collective intelligence** refers to the human competence to harvest differences for progress.

However, all collective moves towards sustainability need to also be embedded in people's ability to sense **wholeness**. When leaders are able to distance themselves from any given situation, they are often able to shift to new insights, better understand the coherence of a situation or attend to the needs of a larger whole. Gaining perspective and seeing a collaborative change effort from within a larger context is a relative, yet important step, in mastering complexity. Leaders are trained to focus on fragments of reality, on a small fraction of a larger story, or on their own field of expertise. The dimension of wholeness refers to the competence to see a larger picture and stay connected to the common good.

It is important to understand that these six dimensions are interlinked and related. Rather than simply adding to one another they lead to results through their interconnectedness as a recurring pattern of human competences. Once this pattern emerged in the complex sustainability initiative mentioned above, people were more forthcoming, conflicts could be laid to rest with an acknowledgement of difference, and generally collaboration was leading to better results in less time. This gave rise to developing the compass as a navigating framework to enhance collaboration effectiveness based on both observation and research. A model valid for complex multi-actor-settings, however, needs to include these aspects:

▶ Multi-actor settings in complex change endeavours are geared towards an outer change with regards to sustainability—often with sole focus on the issue, the solving of a problem or finding new solutions. Little attention is placed on the process of how individuals and collectives bring about **a more sustainable** future. Hence developing a guiding model needed to **support awareness of co-creative processes**.

▶ Multi-stakeholder collaboration takes place in a rational issue-based environment, yet when it fails, the failure can most often be traced back to non-rational aspects like trust, misunderstanding, pressure, disrespect, etc. Hence, developing a guiding model would need to **integrate rational and non-rational aspects**.

▶ The urgency of addressing sustainability issues often resulted in too little time for extensive and joint reflection. Although it is obvious that, like all other leadership challenges, navigating change in multi-actor settings requires reflection, such could only be partly realised in the collaboration systems I experienced. Hence, a guiding model would need to function both at a **superficial level** by enhancing minimum actions that just about make a collaboration system operational, and at a **deeper, more reflective level** of fostering the cohesiveness and effectiveness of a collaboration system.

▶ Complex challenges around sustainability, as argued, require responses in multi-actor settings which in themselves are complex. A guiding model for multi-stakeholder collaboration needed to **adequately reflect the complexity**, but still be useful and action oriented.

In order to take these aspects into account and with the assumption that multi-stakeholder collaboration is exemplary for co-creative human evolution, respective knowledge streams were explored. To depict all of the literature reviewed would go beyond the scope of this article. The following selected conceptual thought had the most significant influence on developing the Collective Leadership Compass.

Shaping the future

Multi-stakeholder collaboration is a way of forming temporary, goal-oriented systems of human interaction. Because of their temporary nature and—in contrast with institutions—their loose structure, they could become catalysts for changing the behaviour of participating institutions and individuals. Peter Senge argued that the essence of leadership is '...learning how to shape the future. Leadership exists when people are no longer victims of circumstances, but participate in creating new circumstances' (Senge quoted in Jaworski, 1996, p. 3). For a long time, leadership has been regarded as an individual capacity. However, this paradigm is shifting as a result of increasing research into leadership as a competence of a collective—be it a team, the core group of a multi-stakeholder collaboration initiative, or the senior leadership group of a corporation (Kellermann, 2012). Peter Senge further addressed this when he said that leadership '...is the capacity of a human community to shape its future and specifically to sustain the significant processes of change required to do so (Senge, 1999, p. 16). Extending the insights gained through Senge's work through reading widely into a vast number of additional literature on leadership, as well as my personal experience that people are drawn to the potential of making a difference, enabled me to define the dimension of *future possibilities*—with aspects such as **future orientation**, **empowerment** and **decisiveness** as important lenses through which a collaboration system could be enhanced or improved.

Shared value creation

A whole body of literature, particularly in development cooperation, but also in leadership, hints to the importance of participation as a way of ensuring that people are better at implementing that which they have helped to create (Cernea, 1985). This understanding is crucial to the global sustainability challenges, irrespective of whether we are creating responsible supply chains, developing innovative technology for climate adaptation, or coordinating better water resource management. A brilliant example of this is the concept of creating shared value as outlined by Michael E. Porter and Mark R. Kramer (Porter and Kramer, 2011). Multi-stakeholder collaborations not only create learning advantages, for the public sector as much as for the private sector, they can also save time and costs. These savings occur because implementation is eased when people are part of shaping their own future. Combining these insights with my personal experience of the importance of high quality, step-by-step engagement in change management, gave rise to defining the dimension of *engagement* with aspects such as **process quality**, **connectivity** and **collective action** as important lenses through which a collaboration system could be enhanced or improved.

The creation of novelty

Joe Jaworski suggested that '...the deeper territory of leadership [is] collectively "listening" to what is wanting to emerge in the world, and then having the courage to do what is required' (Jaworski, 1996, p. 182). Otto Scharmer further developed this underlying idea into his approach of the Theory U, which is essentially built on the capacity of a group of people to change their structure of attention and subsequently their collective pattern of thought and action (Scharmer, 2007). As individuals and teams carry more and more responsibility in complex multi-actor change initiatives, this capacity to jointly become inventive grows in importance. A whole body of research and practice has emerged around the approach of design thinking (IDEO 2008)—a methodology that systematically involves a collective in creating novelty. The methodology focuses on diverse perspectives by integrating human, business and technological factors as well as multiple levels of expertise into an interactive process of idea creation, prototyping and iterative improvement. Together with my personal experience that navigating result-oriented stakeholder collaboration needs both content expertise and entirely new perspectives, this gave rise to defining the dimension of *innovation* with aspects such as **creativity**, **excellence** and **agility** as important lenses through which a collaboration system could be enhanced or improved.

Ethical know-how

In their dialogue on *The Future of Humanity* (Krishnamurti and Bohm, 1986) the Western physicist David Bohm and the Eastern metaphysician J. Krishnamurti explored the assumption that human thought creates divisions—between 'me' and 'you' and between 'me' and 'the world'. They suggest that people act on these mental divisions as if they were realities, resulting in polarisation in the world: difference, disparity, and conflict. In his lectures on *Ethical Know-How*, Francesco Varela noted that human perception is not the representation of a pre-given external world, but in itself a co-creator of reality (Varela, 1999). We create reality, as we perceive it. Hence, ethical expertise, for Varela, is not a skill, which we acquire, but a natural state that we unearth when we remove layers of obscured consciousness and begin to see into the very nature of reality. We become empathetic with humankind and the world if we enact or free this inner disposition. Together with my personal experience that mutual respect despite difference in opinion is a cornerstone of successful collaboration, this gave rise to defining the dimension of *humanity* with aspects such as **mindfulness**, **balance** and **empathy** as important lenses through which a collaboration system could be enhanced or improved.

Meaning-making interaction

All systems, including multi-stakeholder collaboration systems, need to balance their autonomy with the rules and relational patterns of the larger system they are part of (Sahtouris and Lovelock, 2000). This balance applies to both actors within a multi-stakeholder collaboration, and to a collaboration system in relation to other initiatives. A key to negotiated balance is diversity, in nature a crucial requirement for the resilience of a system. The greater the diversity, the more sustainable a system becomes over time. Similarly, multi-stakeholder collaboration initiatives are built on internal relationship patterns as well as a shared context of meaning (Luhmann, 1990) sustained by continuous conversations. Many authors (Berry, 1999; Elgin, 2001; Capra, 2003) have argued that in order for the collectively meaningful to emerge, diversity must be seen as an asset and endeavours must belong to the collective. The importance of dialogue, as a contributor to quality communication, has long since also been adopted in the corporate world (Isaacs, 1999; Wheatley, 1999; Jaworsky *et al.*, 1996). Together with my personal experience that navigating complex change, in multi-actor settings, requires space for structured dialogue, this gave rise to defining *collective intelligence* with aspects such as **dialogic quality**, **diversity** and **iterative learning** as important lenses through which a collaboration system could be enhanced or improved.

Networked patterns

An important feature of natural (including human) systems is the ability to relate through relational patterns, ordered in the form of networks, with constant internal communication. Multi-stakeholder collaboration can be best understood as networked action (Waddell, 2011) that recognises power differences between actors rather than falling into hierarchical relationships. Consequently the structure supporting co-creation should consist of a networked composition of actors, with differences in power, expertise and influence, rather than the layered organogram typically found in organisations. In my experience, collaboration systems seem to emerge when a sufficient degree of a common identity, even though temporary, develops linked to a pattern of mutual support. As a result, I realised that navigating tools needs to mirror patterns of referential relationships. The most relevant conceptual approach, depicting structured patterns, which create aliveness, can be found in the work of Christopher Alexander (2002). He suggests that vitality (or life) of a given space is the result of the composition of what he calls 'centers', elements of structure in a given space that interact and influence each other. My personal observation was that areas of attention in a collaborative space similarly functioned as a pattern—and subsequently fostered or prevented collaborative effectiveness. This assumption has given rise to developing the six dimensions as centres of attention as a whole as well as defining *wholeness* with aspects such as awareness of the larger **context**, **mutual support** and **contribution** as lenses through which a collaboration system could be enhanced or improved.

From the individual to the collective

The literature reviewed suggests a deeply human capacity to consciously act and reflect as a collective. Multi-stakeholder collaboration within the global sustainability agenda requires us to become more knowledgeable about how to best utilise these capacities. The Collective Leadership Compass (see Fig. 1) suggests one way of unearthing them by paying attention to the joint presence of all dimensions over time. In order to cross-check this proposition and the initial design of the six dimensions arrived at from both literature and the field of collaboration practice, a qualitative study with 30 practitioners, from local and international multi-stakeholder collaboration initiatives (Kuenkel *et al.*, 2013), was carried out. The interviewees reflected that success in their initiative hinged on the application of the following strategies:

- ▶ **Fostering trust building** through respect for difference, invigorating passion for the future and putting effort in finding common ground. This resembled the importance of enhancing *humanity* and *future possibilities*.

- ▶ **Modelling evolutionary change processes** through a step-by-step engagement of stakeholders with focus on creating results collectively and ensuring a good flow of communication. This resembled the importance of enhancing *engagement* and *collective intelligence*.

- ▶ **Invigorating connectivity** through developing personal networks that grow into interconnected movements for change, as a contribution to the common good. This resembled the importance of enhancing *engagement* and *wholeness*.

- ▶ **Creating patterns of vitality** through enabling actions of mutual support, able to create balanced flexible containment by balancing agreed rules and structures with creativity and the capacity to learn and adapt quickly. This resembled the importance of enhancing *innovation* and *wholeness*.

The Common Code for the Coffee Community[3] initiative, mentioned at the beginning of this article, is only one example where the compass yielded results. So far it has also been tested in a variety of other multi-actor settings such as: creating a momentum for public–private partnerships in infrastructure in Southern Africa; enhancing water resource management in Tunisia; building a sustainable textile alliance in Germany; supporting the Government of Laos to build its sustainable forestry strategy; developing a draft land policy in Cambodia; and creating a functioning collaboration system for economic development in Rwanda. The compass has also been applied in situational diagnosis, continuous process planning, team reviews and event planning.

Rather than prescribe action, the application of the compass enables actors to acknowledge reality *as it is* (the current collaboration pattern observed). This opens a pathway into the evolutionary potential (see Snowden, this issue) of a current reality. Once people are able to recognise a present pattern, through the lens of the six dimensions, they are also able to more effortlessly sense what is needed to allow a more collaborative pattern to emerge.

---

3 www.4C-coffeeassociation.org

Figure 1 Collective Leadership Compass

COLLECTIVE LEADERSHIP *COMPASS*

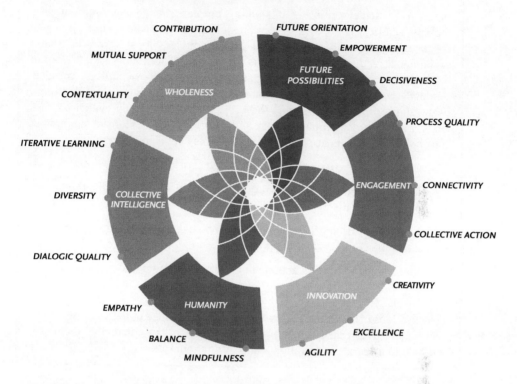

The compass is a navigating tool that gives leaders a frame for evaluating whether they enhance a field for effective collaboration. One way to describe how the compass creates effectiveness is to compare it with a balanced scorecard (Kaplan and Norton, 1996). A balanced scorecard leads to results if all its elements get sufficient attention in an appropriately balanced way. It can be used as diagnostic tool, planning tool and evaluation tool. The same applies to the compass. The decisive difference, however, is that the compass addresses collaboration competence and quality—as important contributors to complex change and the resilience of a system. It does not measure in any way the overall performance of a company, institution or even a multi-stakeholder partnership. Rather than placing key performance indicators behind the six dimensions, it should be used as a lens that guides planning, action and reflection. Rather than serve as a substitute for important management aspects of multi-stakeholder collaboration, such as getting governance structures in place, ensuring sufficient resources, creating agreed upon action plans or keeping communication transparent, the compass places all these issues into the larger context of enhancing a collaborative field. Applying the methodology can help leaders navigate through human difficulties and enhance the vitality of individuals and collectives, especially when applied to collaboration systems. As a collective, collaboration systems become more *resilient*—a capacity needed for driving complex change.

Box 1 Using the Collective Leadership Compass as a navigating tool in complex change

In order to achieve joint results in a complex change environment with multiple actors, it is important to create sufficient cohesiveness in a system of collaborating actors. Trust and mutual respect, coupled with an acknowledgment of difference, reduce the transactions costs of a collaboration system. Rather than preventing conflicts, the compass helps actors move through conflicts productively, while staying in a collaborative field. In the case example, found below, the compass was used by the project secretariat as an overall process guiding tool, a process quality check and a preparatory tool for the planning of stakeholder events. Its application followed this overall sequence:

▶ Observing the current situation with the compass as a lens

▶ Defining the momentary goal or challenge (the more specific the better) in relation to the overall goal of the initiative

▶ Identifying the entry point dimensions—the current starting points to enact the compass and defining correspondent focus actions

▶ Identifying supporting actions in all or at least most dimensions

▶ Evaluating results and starting afresh

Conversations in process planning and evaluation, guided by the six dimensions, gain perspectives that strengthen the awareness of the co-creative processes and help to integrate both rational and non-rational issues.

The following brief exemplary case example shows the practical application of the compass in development of the Common Code of the Coffee Community (referred to throughout the article). Conscious collaboration—setting up a temporary or lasting system of multi-stakeholder actors—is a form of creating life. The ability of leaders to bring a sufficient degree of life to a system determines its success. A people-centred and planet-sensitive future requires us to build many nested **collaboration systems**—issue-based systems of (institutional) actors, aiming to change the status quo (usually a common good) for the better. The example that follows is far from perfect, but it shows that, even under difficult circumstances, navigating change in complex multi-actor settings can make a difference. The compass was used as a navigating tool for process planning by the project secretariat of the initiative.

The Common Code for the Coffee Community Association (4C) developed out of a cross-sector partnership between three stakeholder groups: coffee trade and industry; coffee producer organisations; and international civil society organisations. The 4C association is a remarkable example of the creation of a global community, who joined forces to improve the social, environmental, and economic conditions for those earning their living from coffee. The most important improvements were the application of a code of conduct, support mechanisms for farmers, and a verification system. The 4C initiative, like many other multi-stakeholder initiatives, moved through four different phases (Kuenkel, 2009). Even though it is important to keep the six dimensions of the Collective Leadership Compass in a healthy balance throughout the overall process, the phases require a difference in focus.

Phase 1

Phase 1 (preparing the system for collaboration) was about shaping the idea in dialogue, understanding the context, and initiating the multi-stakeholder initiative. In the 4C initiative the emphasis was placed on building trusting relationships, testing existing and possible future cooperation, and learning from past positive and negative experiences. A small cross-sector team met, exchanged ideas, and received inputs from interested and knowledgeable people. Informal conversations became a melting pot for the screening of possibilities. The idea to develop a mainstream standard for sustainable green coffee production matured, was criticised, was further refined, and developed a healthy level of resilience. As a result, a network of interested people emerged, even prior to the official launching of the initiative. Phase 1 focused on the dimensions and aspects of the Collective Leadership Compass as shown in Table 2.

Table 2 Focus of Collective Leadership Dimensions in Phase 1

Dimension	Aspects	
Humanity	Empathy	Building relationships between diverse and controversial stakeholders
Engagement	Process quality	Building a core group of visionary actors and designing step-by-step engagement of more stakeholders
Future possibilities	Future orientation	Exploring possibilities and variations of what a standard could resemble and the requirements to jointly develop it
Collective intelligence	Dialogic quality	Building resonance for the purpose of the initiative through informal conversations during a number of coffee-related conferences
Innovation	Agility	Being flexible in the process design and utilising emerging opportunities
Wholeness	Contextuality	Researching existing niche market standards and their features in relation to the proposed mainstream standard
	Contribution	Always reminding stakeholders of the potential impact of shifting the dysfunctional structure of an entire value chain towards sustainability

Using the compass for planning and process management helped actors from all sectors stay in dialogue around the initial idea to influence the mainstream market towards greater sustainability. Because people met repeatedly to collaborate on similar issues and specific topics with regards to coffee and sustainability, the idea of developing a mainstream standard slowly began to take root. The challenges were tremendous: The attempt to create an international mainstream coffee standard had to take into consideration that, with several big roasting companies involved, the European and American antitrust authorities would begin to scrutinise the initiative. Any suspicion that the initiative would intervene into the free market laws or distort open competition would have caused an intervention by antitrust authorities. However, despite the challenges and the absence of easy answers, the initiative found support in many different countries in Asia, Africa, and Latin America. People realised that there was a real chance to have a structural effect on the imbalances in coffee production.

Phase 2

Phase 2 (building a collaboration system) was about reshaping the goal, clarifying resources, creating a structure for the initiative, and agreeing on a plan of action. Once the official launching of the initiative took place, most of the stakeholders already felt that they were an integral part of the initiative. Selecting this group of stakeholders was based on finding the right balance between 'engaging the interested' and 'engaging the official representatives'. The former were important to drive the process, the latter crucial for the legitimacy of the process. Because of the quality of the preparatory phase, these two groups of stakeholders had almost merged. The service attitude and expertise of a project secretariat not only ensured consensus-building meetings, integration of multiple perspectives, and reliability of process but were also drivers of the vision and helped to include the expertise needed to explore all possible solutions to coffee mainstream market challenges. Phase 2 focused on the dimensions and aspects of the Collective Leadership Compass as shown in Table 3.

Table 3 Focus of Collective Leadership Dimensions in Phase 2

Dimension	Aspects	
Engagement	Process quality	Developing and jointly agreeing on a roadmap for implementation
	Connectivity	Creating structures (agreement, organisational set-up, working groups) sufficient to ensure the cohesiveness of the collaborating stakeholders
	Collective action	Ensuring that all meetings are focused on jointly agreed results
Collective intelligence	Diversity	Ensuring all perspectives could be heard, appreciating diverse contributions

Dimension	Aspects	
Humanity	Balance	Creating opportunities for informal interaction and people to get to know each other as people during all meetings
Future possibilities	Empowerment	Creating a steering committee composed of all stakeholder groups that functioned as decision-making organ for the implementation process
Innovation	Excellence	Bringing in expertise on the issue of sustainability standards, certification, and capacity building for farmers
Wholeness	Contextuality	Regularly reassessing the stakeholder analysis and the wider field of actors

The result was an agreed implementation plan, a budget plan for future financial contributions by the industry involved, and an allocation of roles between the stakeholders. Expert working groups started to focus on the technical aspects of the standard.

Phase 3

Phase 3 (implementing collaboration) emphasised the development of the standard and the agreement on the rules of participation or for new industry members to join. It required a regular reinforcement of the power of the potential impact during stakeholder meetings, which were not free of conflicts. Mistrust never completely disappeared, yet all stakeholders learned to stay in a collaborative field and move towards tangible results. After two years, the standard had been developed and the initiative moved into phase 4.

Phase 4

In phase 4 (taking collaboration to the next level), the stakeholders unanimously agreed in 2006 to establish a non-profit organisation that would become the future formal structure for the initiative, a global membership organisation—the 4C Association—dedicated to implementing sustainability in the coffee sector and open to coffee chain participants ranging from small coffee farmers to large roasting companies as well as to all others on a supportive basis.

Conclusions and way forward

In order to address global challenges, the joint capacity of leaders to become catalysts for change is called for. Navigating complex change in multi-actor settings, as mentioned at the beginning of this article, is becoming the day-to-day business of most cross-sector initiatives addressing sustainability challenges. If we look at poor collaboration we can easily calculate the opportunity costs of well-intended collaboration initiatives that go astray or do not deliver (see also Tandon, this issue). Some of them may fail because they are poorly designed, but most struggle with impact because of the human factor and not because of a wrong goal. Better building and sustaining humanly driven collaboration systems is an art we need to master, if we want to lead towards a more sustainable future. In the case example the compass was used as a lens to assess and plan a stakeholder process that aimed at addressing complex challenges. It was not a substitute for existing change management tools, but a way of integrating tools and approaches into an overall guiding structure. Almost like a 'balanced collaboration scorecard' the compass functioned as a continuous quality-check for a collaboration pattern to work best. When challenges arose and collaboration efforts became difficult, the compass was an impactful guide that created a field of attention.

Leadership development often refers to the individual; however the article suggests that we need to invest in research on how to build the capacity of groups of actors to become catalysts for large systems change. It proposes to use the Collective Leadership Compass for both research and action in the area of large systems change. Further research could include:

▶ The application of the compass as a diagnosis, planning and evaluation tool as much as for personal leadership development with emphasis on collaboration skills

▶ An updated review of the literature to see what new thoughts and developments have been made in the fields which informed the Collective Leadership Compass

▶ A review of other methodologies and practices focusing on collaboration and how these are different or complement the methodology outlined in the Collective Leadership Compass

▶ An independent study by a researcher/researchers—other than the author— on the application of the methodology in a real environment, in order to gain a better understanding and unbiased opinion of third party application of the compass

Navigating complex change in multi-actor settings requires attention to how leaders from different stakeholder groups become joint drivers for change while navigating their differences, overcoming internal and external conflicts, and keeping the purpose of the joint initiative high on the agenda. Such initiatives are of high value for strategically oriented companies as they provide in-depth experience of stakeholders' perspectives. But the collaboration experience gained is also of value for the strategic moves companies need to make towards sustainability internally, because most of them require cross-departmental—often complex—change. The need for more and better collaboration for sustainability requires us to scale-up both research and practice into better functioning collectives.

References

Alexander, C. (2002): *The Nature of Order: Book One, The Phenomenon of life*, Berkeley: Centre for Environmental Studies.

Barrett, R. (2014): *The Values-Driven Organization: Unleashing Human Potential for Performance and Profit*, Abingdon, Oxon: Routledge.

Biermann, et al (2007): Multistakeholder-partnerships for sustainable development: does the promise hold? in: *Partnerships, Governance and Sustainable Development*, Glasbergen, P. et al, Cheltenham: Edward Elgar Publishing.

de Boer, Y. and van Bergen, B. (2012): Expect the Unexpected: Building business value in a changing world. White Paper, KPMG International. Downloaded 20 September 2013 http://www.kpmg.com/Global/en/IssuesAndInsights/ArticlesPublications/Documents/building-business-value.pdf

Buber, M. (1962): Werke 1. Bd., Schriften zur Philosophie: *Die Krisis des Menschen als eine Krisis des Zwischens*, p. 280, Munich.

Capra, F. (1996): *The web of life: A new understanding of living systems*, New York: Anchor Books.

Cernea, M. M. (Ed.) (1991): *Putting people first: sociological variables in rural development*. Oxford: Oxford University Press

Fadeeva, F. (2005). Promise of sustainability collaboration: potential fulfilled?, *Journal of Cleaner Production* 13.2: 165-174.

IDEO (2008): 'Design Thinking' In *Harvard Business Review* [online] Available from: http://www.ideo.com/by-ideo/design-thinking-in-harvard-business-review [accessed 4 May 2014].

Jaworski, J. (1996): *Synchronicity: The Inner Path of Leadership*, San Francisco: Berrett-Koehler.

Kaplan, R. S. and Norton, D.P. (1996), *The Balanced Scorecard: Translating Strategy into Action*, Harvard Business Review Press, Kindle Edition

Kauffman, S. (1995): *At Home in the Universe: The Search for Laws of Self-Organization and Complexity*. New York: Oxford University Press.

Kellermann, B. (2012): *The End of Leadership*, New York: Harper Business.

Krishnamurti, J. and Bohm, D. (1986): *The Future of Humanity: A Conversation*. San Francisco: Harper & Row.

Kuenkel, P. (2008): *Mind and Heart: Mapping Your Personal Leadership Journey Towards Sustainability*, Potsdam: Collective Leadership Institute.

Kuenkel, P. et al (2009): The Common Code for the Coffee Community, in: Volmer, D., *Enhancing the Effectiveness of Sustainability Partnerships*, Washington: National Academies Press.

Kuenkel, P., et al. (2013): *Shifting the way we co-create: How we can turn the challenges of sustainability into opportunities* Collective Leadership Series, Vol. 1, Potsdam: Collective Leadership Institute.

Lozano, R. (2007): Collaboration as a pathway for sustainability. *Sustainable Development*, 15: 370–381

Luhmann, N. (1990): *Essays on Self-Reference*, New York: Columbia University Press.

Pór, G. (2008): *Collective Intelligence and Collective Leadership: Twin Paths to Beyond Chaos*, University of Amsterdam, Netherlands. Sprouts: Working Papers on Information Systems, 8(2). http://sprouts.aisnet.org/8-2

Porter, M. and Kramer, M. (2011) Creating Shared Value. *Harvard Business Review* [online] Available from: http://hbr.org/2011/01/the-big-idea-creating-shared-value (accessed 4 May 2014).

Sahtouris, E. and Lovelock, J.E. (2000): *Earthdance, Living Systems in Evolution*, San Jose, New York, Lincoln, Shanghai.

Scharmer, C. O. (2007): *Theory U: Leading from the Futures as it emerges*, San Francisco: Berrett- Koehler Publisher.

Senge, P., et al. (1999): *The Dance of Change*. London: Nicholas Brealey.

Snowden, D., and M. Boone, (2007). 'A Leader's Framework for Decision Making of the circumstances they face'. *Harvard Business Review Journal*, (November 2007).

Varela, F.J. (1999): *Ethical Know-how: Action, Wisdom, and Cognition*, Stanford University Press.

Waddell, S. (2011) *Global Action Networks: Creating Our Future Together*, Hampshire: Palgrave Macmillan.

DOI: [10.9774/GLEAF.4700.2015.ju.000013]

Assessing the Performance of Transition Towards Renewable Energy

Case Study of Iran's Fuel Cell Technology[*]

Enayat A. Moallemi
Amirkabir University of Technology, Iran; The University of Melbourne, Australia

Abbas Ahmadi and Abbas Afrazeh
Amirkabir University of Technology, Iran

Naser Bagheri Moghaddam
Iran Fuel Cell Steering Committee, Iran

Transitions towards renewable energies are not mere technological changes; they are tightly intertwined with broader societal and economic changes as well. The interdependency between the socio-technical factors causes inertia inhibiting deviation from the dominant fossil energy system and hindering transition towards renewables. In order to realise the transition, this large-scale system's change should be governed, first of all by diagnosing the current state of the system, and second by designing policy mechanisms to foster the system in transition. This paper concentrates on the first step and aims to present a framework for assessing the performance of energy socio-technical systems in transitions. The framework is applied to fuel cells, as a strategic and emerging energy technology, in the context of a developing country, Iran. It seeks to answer the questions: How successful has the transition been to date, and what have been the main drivers and barriers behind that degree of success? To achieve this, the study provides an expert-based quantitative assessment of the transition, called 'performance mapping', and the qualitative explanation of drivers and barriers in transition, called 'performance analysis'.

- Performance assessment
- Technological innovation systems
- Sustainability transitions
- Fuel cell technology
- Iran

* The authors thank the Renewable Energy Organisation of Iran for providing access to the required data and documents. The authors especially value the extensive review by Steve Waddell and also the constructive comments of three anonymous reviewers.

Enayat A. Moallemi is a recent postgraduate student from Amirkabir University of Technology, Iran. He has been fellow researcher in policy and strategy studies at the National Research Institute for Science Policy (NRISP). His main interests of research are 'modelling of energy transitions' and 'long-term energy policy analysis'. Enayat is currently a PhD Candidate in Energy Policy at the University of Melbourne, Australia.

 Renewable Energy and Energy Efficiency Group, Department of Infrastructure Engineering, The University of Melbourne, Australia, Victoria 3010

Department of Industrial Engineering and Management Systems, Amirkabir University of Technology, 424 Hafez Ave, Tehran, Iran

emoallemi@aut.ac.ir; emoallemi@student.unimelb.edu.au

Abbas Ahmadi received his BSc degree in Industrial Engineering in 2000 at Amirkabir University of Technology, MSc degree in Industrial Engineering in 2002 at Iran University of Science and Technology, and PhD degree in Systems Design Engineering in 2008 at University of Waterloo. He joined the Amirkabir University of Technology, Iran in 2009 where he is at present Professor at the Department of Industrial Engineering and Management Systems. Dr Ahmadi's research interests are in supply chain management, business intelligence, swarm intelligence, computational intelligence, data and information management, system analysis and design, and cooperative intelligent systems. He has authored and co-authored several papers in journals and conference proceedings, chapters in books, and numerous technical and industrial project reports. Under his supervision, several students have completed their degrees.

 Department of Industrial Engineering and Management Systems, Amirkabir University of Technology, 424 Hafez Ave, Tehran, Iran

abbas.ahmadi@aut.ac.ir

Dr **Abbas Afrazeh** is Associate Professor in Amirkabir University of Technology, Department of Industrial Engineering & Management Systems, Tehran, Iran.

His major area of research and teaching are as follows: knowledge management, intellectual capital, human resource management, and productivity at work. He has published about 120 scientific papers in different journals and conferences. He is a member of six scientific societies.

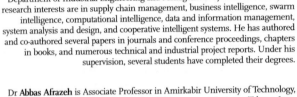

Department of Industrial Engineering and Management Systems, Amirkabir University of Technology, 424 Hafez Ave, Tehran, Iran

afrazeh@aut.ac.ir

Naser Bagheri Moghaddam is a recent PhD graduate from the Department of Management and Accounting, Allameh Tabataba'I University. He is now a senior adviser to the Iran Fuel Cell Committee.

Iran Fuel Cell Steering Committee, Tehran, Iran

nbagheri1382@yahoo.com

THE DEVELOPMENT OF RENEWABLE ENERGIES involves a large number of radical changes to the energy sector as a socio-technical system. It incorporates complex processes of large-scale changes in an inter-correlated set of actors, institutions and technologies, which are called 'transitions'. Transitions are processes which transform large established systems (Scharmer and Yukelson, this issue), break down their structures and result in technological and economic innovations (Elzen *et al.* 2004). This complex and evolutionary process of energy socio-technical system changes needs to be governed systematically (Aghion *et al.* 2009) first of all by assessing the performance of the system in the current state. According to Edquist (1999), the diagnosis of a system is a preliminary step for its policy making. It then continues with policy formulation based on the system's performance. In this study, we aim to propose a framework for assessing the performance of transitions towards renewable energies (RE). We will specifically address the development of fuel cell (FC) technology in the context of Iran as the case study. The performance of the system in transition is defined in three dimensions: effectiveness, efficiency and certainty (Neely 2002). Effectiveness specifies the alignment between performed activities and the normative direction of transition. Efficiency specifies access to sufficient resources and the consistency of activities during transition. Certainty[1] identifies the missing inputs for the achievement of normative targets in transition to support comprehensiveness. The framework includes the quantitative assessment of the performance, as well as the qualitative explanation of the drivers and barriers influencing the performance. The former shows which parts of the system work improperly and need to be improved with policy interventions. The latter explains what reasons/ mechanisms have caused the system in transition to operate improperly. This twofold assessment of performance is a necessary step, which provides required inputs to formulate practical policies in transition towards RE.

Different general approaches have been developed to study transitions. Among them, four prominent approaches are: multi-level perspectives (MLP), technological innovation systems (TIS), transitions management (TM) and strategic niche management (SNM). MLP studies long-term historical transitions through the interactions of three conceptual levels namely innovation niche, existing socio-technical regime and the broader institutional landscape (Geels 2002; Geels and Schot 2007). TIS analyses the emergence of specific technologies in relation with other societal components (Carlsson and Stankiewicz 1991; Hekkert *et al.* 2007). TM governs transitions through active intervention at four levels: strategic, tactical, operational and reflexive (Rotmans *et al.* 2001; Kemp *et al.* 2006). Finally, SNM stresses deliberate creation and support of innovation niches to trigger socio-technical regimes (Schot *et al.* 1994; Hoogma 2002,

---

1 It should be noted that 'certainty' in this paper does not contradict with the basic assumption of large-scale systems theory, which is the uncertainty in structure, value of variables and behaviours of complex systems. Certainty refers to the presence of comprehensive frameworks/required inputs to support innovative actions considering the intrinsic uncertainties of complex systems.

Raven 2005). Since the aim of the study is to assess and analyse the performance of transition to RE, it should be based on a descriptive (rather than prescriptive) theoretical approach. Furthermore, this study is investigating energy transition with concentration on development of a specific technology (fuel cell) while at the same time addressing the interdependencies with societal factors. Among the reviewed approaches, TIS and MLP have been frequently used for describing transition patterns and pathways in the past research findings (Geels and Schot 2007; Bergek *et al.* 2008). We select TIS as the theoretical basis of the framework since its focus is on the emergence of new technology and the dynamic of technological change, both at the interest of our study.

Several research projects have been studying the performance of large systems transformation with TIS. They can be classified into two groups:

The first group adopts a 'functional perspective' in the assessment of performance. It defines functions as groups of activities whose fulfilment is necessary for the system success. Functions include knowledge development and diffusion, entrepreneurial activities, guidance of the system, resource mobilisation, market formation, and legitimacy creation (Hekkert *et al.* 2007; Hekkert and Negro 2009). The functional perspective enables capture of the dynamics of transitions and study of the transformation processes through time and not just in snapshots. With this functional perspective, the performance assessment usually starts with describing the transition from past to date, then continues with assessing the fulfilment of each function based on the narrative, and ends with identifying drivers and barriers pushing and hindering function fulfilment (Bergek *et al.* 2008; Alkemade *et al.* 2007; Van Alphen *et al.* 2009a, b, 2010).

The second group of studies goes further and includes the possible interactions between functions in the assessment of performance, in addition to the function fulfilment. We call the approach of this group 'transitional perspective' since it explains how a system is subject to change through the time and as the functions interact. The Motors of Innovation, constituting reinforcing interactions of system functions, are the main ideas in transitional perspectives (Suurs and Hekkert 2009; Suurs *et al.* 2009, 2010). The main focus in Motors of Innovation is to present a set of interrelated functions (called cumulative causations) which satisfy the system's requirements at each stage transition process. In this regard, the development of a TIS in formation phase can be divided into four stages including the following motors:

▶ **Science and technology push (STP)** motor which hastens research and development and reduces scientific uncertainties around the emerging system

▶ **Entrepreneurial** motor where the developed knowledge is translated into innovation and their practicality is proved by entrepreneurs

▶ **System building** motor where the performed activities become more coordinated and institutions for managing them are formed

▶ **Market** motor which opens up room for a new system in the market and tries to turn a demand push development into a market pull development (Suurs 2009)

Studies conducted by Suurs *et al.* (2009, 2010) and Negro (2007) are some renowned examples of the second group.

The rest of the paper is structured in three sections. The following section provides some background information about the development of fuel cells in Iran. There follows a discussion of the essential components and implementation steps of the framework, applied in fuel cell technology. The final section presents concluding remarks and future research.

Background of FC development in Iran

Iran, known as a developing country, is located on one of the richest oil reserves in the Middle East. The abundance of resources has affected the energy system in Iran, and oil and gas have obtained 44% and 54% of the total energy share and 90% of the electricity generation. A large part of the economy in Iran is also based on oil and gas exports (about 80%) which are led by government and public organisations. However, the Iranian Government has been trying in the past 20 years to shift from a resource-based economy to a knowledge-based economy. Youth and university graduates constitute the majority of its 75 million population. In the past 16 years, the government has emphasised its role in supporting the development of emerging technologies with innovation policies. About 10 strategic and emerging technologies were selected as top priorities in the National Science and Technology Roadmap. One of them was hydrogen and fuel cell technologies. Iran has given priority to the development of fuel cell technology based on the expected 9–10% annual growth in electricity demand up to 2025, the ability to produce energy twice as efficiently than existing fossil plants, the emphasis of government on distributed electricity generation due to inefficient transferring lines, and finally, the emergence of fuel cell motor engines (Arasti and Bagheri Moghaddam 2010).

The fuel cell is a technology that produces electricity via electrochemical reactions. To generate electricity, hydrogen and natural gas can be used as feed to the technology. Fuel cell development has been a focus of universities, industry and government as a potential option for electricity generation since the 1990s in Iran. The Iranian Government decided to formulate a comprehensive plan incorporating required strategies and policies. Consequently, a combination of governmental and public organisations formed a steering committee led by the Ministry of Energy and Iran's Centre for Innovation and Technology Cooperation (CITIC). They started to develop a national document for the development of fuel cell technology in 2002. The document was completed in 2006 and was legislated by Iran's office of presidency in 2007. This document was guiding the streams of research and production activities and prioritised working on two different fuel cell types: polymer exchange membrane fuel cell (PEMFC) and solid oxide fuel cell (SOFC) based on capability-attractive analysis.

As a result of Iran's FC National Strategic Plan, many universities, governmental institutions and industrial sectors started to get engaged in R&D activities. Table 1 shows the actors engaged, from upstream service providers, downstream service providers to intermediary organisations in the development of the fuel cell.

Table 1 Actors in Iran's fuel cell technological innovation system

Group	Actors	Upstream service providers			Downstream service providers		Intermediary organisations			
		Material suppliers	Components supplier	Manufacturers	Energy suppliers	End users	Policy making	R&D support	Financial service	Information exchange
University	Isfahan Univ., Tehran Univ., Shiraz Univ., K.N. Toosi Univ., Tabriz Univ., Ferdowsi U of Mashhad, Tarbiat Modarres Univ., Iran U of Sci. and Tech., Sharif U of Tech, Razi U of Kermanshah							*		
Gov. research institute	Renewable Energy Org. of Iran, Iran Khodro Co., Chemical Industrial Res. Ins., Ins. for Adv. Materials and new energies, Iran Polymer and Petrochemical Res. Ins., Energy and Material Res. Ins., Petroleum Industry Res. Ins., Niro Res. Ins. (RE Dep.), Scientific and Industrial Res. Org. of Iran, Joint Res. Centre of Rafsanjan Industrial Complex and Univ. of Vali-Asr, Fuel Cell Tech. Res. Center, Isfahan Eng. Res. Center							*		

Gov. org.	Iran Fuel Cell Steering Committee, Iran's electricity supply Co (Tavanir), Iran Ins. of Standards and Industrial Res., Registration of Trademarks and Intellectual Property Org., Petroleum Ministry, Ministry of Industry and Trade, Ministry of Sci., Res. and Tech., Renewable Energy Org. of Iran, Environmental Protection Org., Iran Tech. Cooperation Office	*	*	*
Private firm	Taghtiran Kashan Co., Rail Sanat Dena Co., Parsian Poya Polymer Co., Advanced Material Development Co., Iran Nasb Niro Co., Magfa, Ghods Niro, Niro Battery, Mapna, Pilar Energy Co., Perisa Energy, Mokarar Co., Hydrogen Age Tech. Co.	*	*	

These actors are involved in the development of fuel cell technology in an evolutionary process. Iran's FC system's evolution can be divided in three stages. In the first stage, diverse and disparate fuel cell research projects were conducted in order to legitimise FC development among industry and government people. In the second stage, the major emphasis was on compiling and legislating FC Strategic Plan as a guiding document. Finally, in the third stage, activities were coordinated around two options, PEMFC and SOFC, according to the FC Strategy Plan. A more in-depth discussion of the constituents of Iran's fuel cell system, including actors, institutions and their interactions can be found in Moallemi *et al.* (2014).

Although several actors are engaged and many activities have been completed, FC technology remains insufficiently developed and is not considered a successful example in Iran of a strategic emerging technology. There are still several obstacles in the development process such as lack of a strong private sector presence and difficulty in access to financial resources. Analysis of the transition process is necessary to uncover the underlying mechanisms influencing its performance.

The suggested framework

A TIS-based performance assessment needs a systemic framework in order to account for different aspects of transition. Based on the definition of performance assessment in this article's introduction, the framework comprises performance mapping and performance analysis. Performance mapping determines the fulfilment of TIS's functions in transition. It quantitatively demonstrates which aspects of the system in transition work improperly and need to be supported by policy interventions. However, function fulfilment should be linked to underlying causal inducing and blocking mechanisms (performance analysis). Performance analysis identifies existing drivers and barriers to function fulfilment and prioritises them for policy formulation.

To realise performance mapping and performance analysis, the following steps must be taken. The first step is to select a reference model for transition, against which the performance of the system is compared.

Reference model

The performance of an emerging TIS in each dimension (i.e. effectiveness, efficiency and certainty) can be assessed by comparing it with a reference model of TIS evolution in transition to RE. The reference model is developed using the concept of Motors of Innovation and functional interaction in TIS. Figure 1 illustrates the evolution of system (the reference model) in transition at different levels of aggregation. In the reference model are three hierarchical levels representing transition to RE where TIS is the main approach, Motors of Innovation are the sequential stages of transition, and functions are the constituent elements of each stage from the beginning to the end.

Figure 1 Reference model of transitions to RE

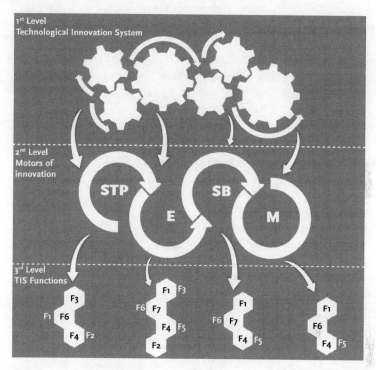

Based on the review of previous functional studies of TIS (Bergek *et al.* 2008; Hekkert and Negro 2009; Suurs *et al.* 2009), Table 2 represents the hierarchy of functions and sub-functions.

According to Suurs (2009), the importance of functions in each stage of transition can vary based on their roles in satisfying the respective motor's goal and the socio-economic context in which the study is applied (such as being a developed or developing country). The presence and significance of functions for each motor are specified using the previous empirical studies conducted by Suurs (2009). In this regard, the values of 2, 1 and 0.5 are assigned to functions based on the significance of their roles in each motor (Table 3).

Table 2 The classification of TIS functions and the outlines of questions in the proposed model

Functions and sub-functions		Outlines of questions	
Entrepreneurial activities	Informing entrepreneurs of business opportunities	Holding technology exhibition? Doing demonstrative projects?	How much success did activities realise with respect to the functions? (Effectiveness)?
	Creating innovative companies for technology commercialisation	Establishing new initiated firms? Entering incumbent firms? Creating competition among existing firms?	
	Turning innovation into commercial products	Producing technology at large-scale? Providing technology-related services such as sales, marketing, and maintenance?	
Knowledge development	Developing the knowledge of design	Working on conceptual design of process? Working on conceptual design of technologies?	
	Developing the knowledge of manufacturing (how-know)	Doing reverse engineering? Doing technology transfer?	
	Building technology prototypes	Creating product prototypes? Creating pilot manufacturing processes?	
	Developing managerial knowledge	Studying market research such as feasibility studies? Doing project management studies?	
Preservation, dissemination and exchange of knowledge	Preserving existing knowledge	Establishing regional libraries and classified databases?	How efficiently did they accomplish their missions? (Efficiency)?
	Raising awareness about the technology	Technology broadcasting? Holding conferences, seminars, workshops?	
	Improving access to the knowledge of technology	Providing up to date professional software? Coordinating training courses?	
	Improving the circulation of knowledge among actors	Initiating joint research projects? Facilitating the relationships between universities and industry?	
	Enhancing innovation capabilities of firms	Defining customised research projects? Providing industrial professional services?	
	Improving knowledge distribution	Publishing scientific journals, books, and magazines?	

Functions and sub-functions		Outlines of questions	
Guidance of the system	Shaping leaders of the system	Establishing the necessary structures for management of system?	Were sufficient resources consistently available (Certainty)?
	Guiding from cultural-cognitive perspective	Forming cognitive frameworks leading technology development? Using existing norms of society to lead technology?	
	Guiding from regulative perspective	Determining vision, mission, operational goals, and laws to manage technology? Coordinating various sectors and evaluating their performance?	
Management of resources	Managing financial resources	Financially supporting commercial and non-commercial research? Supporting technology companies with loans and trading facilities?	
	Managing human resources	Training, development and promotion of human resources? Facilitating the mobility of human resources?	
	Managing material resources	Managing materials needed for technology production? Managing supplementary materials and infrastructures?	
Market formation	Forming technical capabilities in emerging market	Providing public procurement? Protecting intellectual property? Standardisation of products and processes?	
	Forming economic capabilities in the bridge market	Providing tax exemption? Providing subsidies?	
	Forming competitive capabilities in the mass market	Balancing market supply and demand? Regulating the rate of duties?	
Legitimacy creation	Creating legitimacy in industry	Forming regional networks of entrepreneurs? Ensuring efficiency of technology development?	
	Creating legitimacy among policy makers	Creating a positive image of technology aligned with national interests? Arranging political lobbies to support technology?	
	Creating social acceptability	Shaping social supporting networks such as NGOs? Promoting use of new technologies by media?	

Table 3 Weight of functions in each motor of innovation

Source: derived from Suurs (2009)

	STP motor	Entrepreneurial motor	System building motor	Market motor
Knowledge development and diffusion (KD)	2	1	0	0
Entrepreneurial activities (EA)	0.5	2	1	1
Guidance of the system (GS)	1	1	1	1
Market formation (MF)	0	0.5	1	2
Resource mobilisation (RM)	1	1	1	1
Legitimacy (L)	0	1	2	0

Performance indicators and data collection

The intersection of performance dimensions and the proposed reference model will result in performance indicators. Based on these indicators and with the data collected from the case study, the performance of transition to RE can be systematically assessed. However, performance assessment (i.e. identifying the level of function fulfilment as well as the system's drivers and barriers) is a complicated process requiring a suitable method for data collection. Data were collected based on desktop studies (national documents and policy studies) and interviews. For interviews, the relevant outlines of questions were developed around each performance indicator. In each system function, experts were asked to comment on the degree of effectiveness, efficiency and certainty with which the activities were performed in transitions to RE. For example, in the first sub-function of entrepreneurial activities (see Table 2), questions that should be asked are:

▶ How many technology exhibitions have been held and how many demonstration projects have been done up to now?

▶ How successfully did they inform entrepreneurs of business opportunities (effectiveness)?

▶ How reasonably and efficiently could they accomplish their mission (efficiency)? Were there enough resources available to hold exhibitions and to do demonstrations, and was there a constant availability of resources (certainty)?

Table 2 presents the outlines of questions in each TIS sub-function that should be investigated for their effectiveness, efficiency and certainty from experts. These questions were asked of more than 40 experts most of them from government bodies and universities (see Table 1) with hardcopy as well as online questionnaires (depending on the availability of experts). To have well-defined questions, some scales for the responses of interviewees were defined. In the quantitative mapping of function fulfilment (performance mapping), the fulfilment level in each sub-function was represented by a seven-point scaling method (1: extremely weak/extremely little, 7: extremely strong/an extraordinary amount). In performance analysis, experts were asked for their comments in each function/sub-function and by the type of mechanisms influencing the transition process. They were told that the mechanisms could be strengths or opportunities (drivers) and weaknesses or threats (barriers). Strengths and weaknesses have internal roots in the system, but opportunities and threats are external factors, out of the system's control. Quantitative and qualitative data collected from interviews were analysed subsequently for performance mapping and analysis.

Performance mapping

Since the significance of functions is different at each stage of transition (motors), the experts' response to the level of function fulfilment should be adjusted for each stage. According to the reference model and the weight of functions in each motor (see Table 3) the function fulfilment in each stage of transitions (or equally in each motor of innovation) can be calculated.

Based on the scores given by experts according to the developed frameworks, the results of performance mapping in Iran's FC TIS are represented in the spider diagrams in Figure 2. It shows which parts of the system have been most strongly developed and which parts still need support. As shown in Figure 2, the effectiveness and certainty of three functions, knowledge development, dissemination of knowledge and guidance of the system, are relatively strong compared to others in the TIS model. As we discussed earlier, the presence of these functions is more significant for the STP motor, the first stage of transition. Therefore, it sounds reasonable if we suppose that the current transition state of TIS is in the early stages of growth with the STP motor transition stage. It is the stage when the system needs to reduce the uncertainty of technology by research and development and to obtain a long-term vision and general strategies for its development. In Iran's FC TIS, a large part of activities are devoted to research and with an aim to decrease the uncertainty of technology. At this stage, universities and governmental research institutes are taking the leading roles. They have performed several important activities in recent years such as producing the first sample of a methanol fuel cell system and fuel cell tester in Iran. Hence, learning has been the main achievement of the activities that have been accomplished in these functions up to now. There are also several actors in governmental organisations active in guiding the system. For instance, establishing a Fuel Cell Steering Committee and passing the Iran FC Strategy Plan are two turning points that have elevated the system performance of this function. These events helped to coordinate the current activities, to plan for future required tasks and to feed TIS with the necessary resources for upcoming stages.

Figure 2 Spider diagrams representing the performance level in various systems' functions

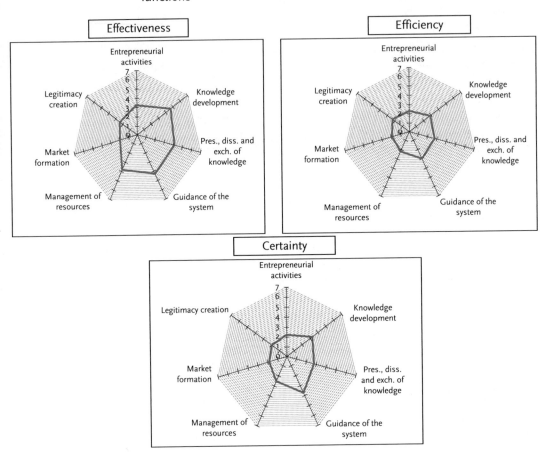

Although some functions have relatively good levels of effectiveness and certainty, the efficiency of all functions is low according to Figure 2. It means that several functions are performed without a timely and constant stream of resources. This is a major weakness in the FC TIS and many experts believe that it has affected the whole system and is one of the major factors holding the transition back. It can be attributed to internal and external reasons. As an internal reason, the governmental organisations did not clearly state financial mechanisms for the defined projects in Iran's FC Strategy Plan. It has caused difficulty in financing projects and has hampered the development of TIS. On the other hand and as an external reason, due to international sanctions, access to physical resources, namely materials and equipment, has been limited in the past couple of years. This has caused some interruptions in performing practical research and development activities. Hence, policy measures need to target the efficiency of performed activities in TIS functions, especially the three main functions engaged in the STP motor.

Performance mapping in this section gave an overview of the strengths and weaknesses of FC TIS in Iran. The reasons behind them, i.e. the drivers and barriers of transition, will be discussed in the next section.

Performance analysis

The underlying mechanisms identified by experts need to be categorised based on their influences at different stages of transition. By having inducing and blocking mechanisms categorised, the proper ways to address them in the policy making process can be subsequently identified. According to the typologies of mechanisms presented by Painuly (2001), Foxon and Pearson (2008), and Farla *et al.* (2010), six groups—technical, managerial, financial, cognitive-cultural, commercial and informational—can be used as a basis for categorisation of drivers and barriers in transition to RE.

The identified drivers and barriers should also be ranked for policy formulation. Ranking the mechanisms according to the sequence of the reference model's Motors of Innovation means identifying the most important to address in each stage of transition. Furthermore, the importance of each mechanism in each of the four transition stages should be specified in ranking. The importance of drivers and barriers in each stage of transition can be measured by experts' opinions using the Saaty nine-point comparison scale (i.e. 1 for negligible importance to 9 for extremely important; Sharma and Agrawal 2009).

A summary of drivers and barriers influencing Iran's FC TIS are presented in Tables 4 to 7. They are categorised and ranked for each stage of transition. In addition to the drivers and barriers identified for the current stage of transition in Iran's fuel cell TIS (STP motor), Tables 4 to 7 present the inducing and blocking mechanisms that should be addressed by policy measures as soon as a new stage of the transition starts.

Table 4 Classification and prioritisation of drivers and barriers identified in Iran FC TIS, STP motor

Description	Type
Barriers	
Defining small and fragmented projects which waste resources	Managerial
Lack of continuous stream of funding	Financial
Lack of regular revisions in past national documents	Managerial
Failure of timely provision of required resources (financial, technical)	Managerial
Difficulty in financial transactions for technology transfers and international collaborations	Technical
Shortage of facilities and tools for fuel cell R&D at universities	Managerial
Allocating most budgets to governmental institutions and ignoring private firms in national plans	Managerial
Disregarding the four aspects of technology transfer (hardware, software, orgaware, humanware) at the same time	Technical
Weakness in planning for mobilising human resources	Managerial

Continued

Description	Type
Drivers	
Having Iran FC Strategic Plan as a national roadmap	Managerial
The importance of fuel cell technology in enhancing the country's defence systems	Cultural-cognitive
The implementation of subsidies enforcement law and the move towards the real price for electricity	Financial
The identification of priorities for R&D, manufacturing, and implementation	Managerial
The involvement of governmental institutions in R&D which decreases the financial risk of investment	Financial
The formation of Iran FC steering committee for supervising development process	Managerial

Table 5 Classification and prioritisation of drivers and barriers identified in Iran FC TIS, relevant for entrepreneurial motor

Description	Type
Barriers	
Sanctions which lead to inaccessibility to advanced technologies and materials	Managerial
Economic depression	Managerial
Weakness in relation of university and industry	Managerial
Weakness in relation with international suppliers	Commercial
Monopoly of activities by some semi private firms supported by government	Managerial
Unwillingness of financial institutions to grant loans and other facilities to firms related to emerging technologies	Financial
Lack of some materials and equipment needed for technology development	Technical
Drivers	
The law that financially supports knowledge-oriented institutions including FC related firms	Financial
Using the output of other domestic industries like membrane industries to provide the inputs of FC development	Technical
Defining applied research by Renewable Energy Org. of Iran	Technical
Iran's success in achieving the 5 kW fuel cell CHP system which provides motivation among actors	Technical

Table 6 Classification and prioritisation of drivers and barriers identified in Iran FC TIS, relevant for system building motor

Description	Type
Barriers	
Existence of opposing macro policies that resist the development of renewable energies	Managerial
The absence of social demand and existence of fake governmental demand	Commercial
Discontinuity in presence of effective activities from policy making institutions	Managerial
The high cost of FC research and production which discourages private firms	Technical
Financial dependency of development process in early years, which if prolonged, leads to its extinction	Financial
Lack of sufficient financial resources to define commercialisation projects	Financial
Drivers	
Defining few large scale projects to improve the capabilities of internal firms	Commercial
Establishing technology management centre under supervision of Iran FC steering committee	Commercial

Table 7 Classification and prioritisation of drivers and barriers identified in Iran FC TIS, relevant for market motor

Description	Type
Barriers	
Weakness in planning frameworks for empowering competitive market	Managerial
Lack of support and cooperation from authorities in the field of technology commercialisation	Commercial
Weaknesses in doing organised research to develop economical products from FC technology	Managerial
Limited awareness of Iran FC managers with global market	Commercial
Drivers	
The mass market for FC in near future regarding the development of hybrid and electric vehicles	Commercial
Setting environmental standard in transportation which expands the usage of clean vehicles and provides niche market for FC	Commercial

Policies should aim at strengthening drivers and weakening barriers to facilitate the transition process. However, it should be noted that not all drivers and barriers but those related to the STP motor should be necessarily addressed at the first stage of transition.

Starting with the first stage, the top barriers identified in the STP motor are concerned with waste of resources, discontinuity of funding, late provision of resources, difficulty in financial transactions and shortage of required facilities; these all influence the efficiency of the performed activities. This corroborates the results of performance mapping in the previous section. There are also more managerial and financial barriers. Accordingly, the first target in policy making is to improve the efficiency of functions in the STP motor by weakening (or removing) the identified barriers and strengthening the drivers. To improve the efficiency, Iran's FC Strategic Plan should be reviewed and a specified amount of financial resources should be devoted to defined fuel cell research and projects in the National Budget Plan. The implication of fuel cell funding resources in the National Budget Plan guarantees access to the required resources as well as the continuity of resources.

In the second motor, the entrepreneurial motor, main barriers include international sanctions blocking entrepreneurs' access to advanced technologies, economic depression increasing the risk of investment, and fragmented university–industry interactions impeding the commercialisation of scientific discoveries. While addressing these barriers is not of high importance at this time, the system should be prepared to deal with them as the transition goes into this stage. Some policy recommendations for fostering transition in the second stage can be proposed. The first is to collaborate in joint ventures with other developing countries such as Turkey and India. This can provide opportunities to share experiences and also have access to the some critical technologies. Second is to grant long-term loans to entrepreneurs to decrease the risk of investment in fuel cell projects. Third is to establish science and technology parks to enhance the connection between universities and industries.

In the third motor, the system building motor, the important barriers are related to creation of legitimacy for FC as a newly introduced energy technology. NGOs can be considered as an effective tool to create legitimacy not by a top-down governmental influence, but by a bottom-up social empowerment. Finally in the market motor, the lack of a competitive market is the major barrier. Public procurements, imposing tax on imported similar products and giving subsidies to manufacturers are some measures that address this barrier.

Conclusions

Transition to renewable energies is a complex and evolutionary process transforming the large-scale systems. Transitions need to be managed by performance assessment and policy making. The performance assessment provides an understanding of inducing and blocking mechanisms which hinder or stimulate transitions to RE. The policy making phase then uses the results of this step as its targets and tries to formulate relevant measures to address them.

This research focused on proposing a framework for performance assessment of transition to RE with TIS as its main approach. The model resulted in two outputs: performance mapping and performance analysis. Performance mapping determined how well a TIS worked and performance analysis identified drivers and barriers that had influenced its performance. Applying the proposed framework in the case of Iran's FC development showed that the TIS had been working effectively and with certainty in the main functions of the STP motor although its efficiency had been weak. Various mechanisms were identified as influencing the efficiency of performed activities, including discontinuity of funding, late provision of resources, economic depression, lack of access to critical technologies, etc.

The core emphasis of this paper was on the development of a framework for the performance assessment of transition to renewable energies. However, it can also be used for performance assessment in large-scale transformation of complex-adaptive systems, such as water, food and transportation systems, towards sustainable states. As a subject for further research, the developed framework, with some adjustments, can be applied to other systems, and its practicality assessed. The topic of how to design targeted policies for improving the performance of the system is another avenue for future research. In this respect, a connection should be designed for matching various socio-economic policy tools (such as subsidies and tax) with targets derived from the performance assessment model.

References

Aghion, P., P. A. David and D. Foray (2009). 'Science, technology and innovation for economic growth: Linking policy research and practice in "STIG Systems".' *Research Policy* 38(4): 681-693.

Alkemade, F., C. Kleinschmidt and M. Hekkert (2007). 'Analysing emerging innovation systems: a functions approach to foresight.' *International Journal of Foresight and Innovation Policy* 3(2): 139-168.

Arasti, M. R. and N. Bagheri Moghaddam (2010). 'Use of technology mapping in identification of fuel cell sub-technologies.' *International Journal of Hydrogen Energy* 35(17): 9516-9525.

Bergek, A., S. Jacobsson, B. Carlsson, S. Lindmark and A. Rickne (2008). 'Analyzing the functional dynamics of technological innovation systems: A scheme of analysis.' *Research Policy* 37(3): 407-429.

Carlsson, B. and R. Stankiewicz (1991). 'On the nature, function and composition of technological systems.' *Journal of Evolutionary Economics* 1(2): 93-118.

Elzen, B., F. W. Geels and K. Green (2004). *System innovation and the transition to sustainability: theory, evidence and policy.* Massachusetts, Edward Elgar Publishing.

Farla, J., F. Alkemade and R. A. A. Suurs (2010). 'Analysis of barriers in the transition toward sustainable mobility in the Netherlands.' *Technological Forecasting and Social Change* 77(8): 1260–1269.

Foxon, T. and P. Pearson (2008). 'Overcoming barriers to innovation and diffusion of cleaner technologies: some features of a sustainable innovation policy regime.' *Journal of Cleaner Production* 16(1, Supplement 1): S148-S161.

Geels, F. W. (2002). 'Technological transitions as evolutionary reconfiguration processes: a multi-level perspective and a case-study.' *Research Policy* 31(8-9): 1257-1274.

Geels, F. W. and J. Schot (2007). 'Typology of sociotechnical transition pathways.' *Research Policy* 36(3): 399-417.

Hekkert, M. P. and S. O. Negro (2009). 'Functions of innovation systems as a framework to understand sustainable technological change: Empirical evidence for earlier claims.' *Technological Forecasting and Social Change* 76(4): 584-594.

Hekkert, M. P., R. A. A. Suurs, S. O. Negro, S. Kuhlmann and R. E. H. M. Smits (2007). 'Functions of innovation systems: A new approach for analysing technological change.' *Technological Forecasting and Social Change* 74(4): 413-432.

Hoogma, R. (2002). *Experimenting for sustainable transport: the approach of strategic niche management*, Routledge.

Kemp, R., D. Loorbach and J. Rotmans (2006). 'Transition management as a model for managing processes of co-evolution towards sustainable development.' *Perspectives on Radical Changes to Sustainable Consumption and Production (SCP)* 20: 387.

Moallemi, E. A., A. Ahamdi, A. Afrazeh and N. Bagheri Moghaddam (2014). 'Understanding systemic analysis in the governance of sustainability transition in renewable energies: The case of fuel cell technology in Iran.' *Renewable and Sustainable Energy Reviews* 33(0): 305-315.

Neely, A. D. (2002). *Business performance measurement: theory and practice*, Cambridge University Press.

Painuly, J. P. (2001). 'Barriers to renewable energy penetration; a framework for analysis.' *Renewable Energy* 24(1): 73-89.

Raven, R. P. J. M. (2005). *Strategic Niche Management for Biomass A comparative study on the experimental introduction of bioenergy technologies in the Netherlands and Denmark.*

Rotmans, J., R. Kemp and M. van Asselt (2001). 'More evolution than revolution: transition management in public policy.' *Foresight* 3(1): 15-31.

Schot, J., R. Hoogma and B. Elzen (1994). 'Strategies for shifting technological systems: The case of the automobile system.' *Futures* 26(10): 1060-1076.

Sharma, S. and N. Agrawal (2009). 'Selection of a pull production control policy under different demand situations for a manufacturing system by AHP-algorithm.' *Computers & Operations Research* 36(5): 1622-1632.

Suurs, R. A. A. (2009). *Motors of sustainable innovation: Towards a theory on the dynamics of technological innovation systems*, Utrecht University.

Suurs, R. A. A. and M. P. Hekkert (2009). 'Cumulative causation in the formation of a technological innovation system: The case of biofuels in the Netherlands.' *Technological Forecasting and Social Change* 76(8): 1003-1020.

Suurs, R. A. A., M. P. Hekkert and R. E. H. M. Smits (2009). 'Understanding the build-up of a technological innovation system around hydrogen and fuel cell technologies.' *International Journal of Hydrogen Energy* 34(24): 9639-9654.

Suurs, R. A. A., M. P. Hekkert, S. Kieboom and R. E. H. M. Smits (2010). 'Understanding the formative stage of technological innovation system development: The case of natural gas as an automotive fuel.' *Energy Policy* 38(1): 419-431.

van Alphen, K., M. P. Hekkert and W. C. Turkenburg (2009a). 'Comparing the development and deployment of carbon capture and storage technologies in Norway, the Netherlands, Australia, Canada and the United States: An innovation system perspective.' *Energy Procedia* 1(1): 4591-4599.

van Alphen, K., J. van Ruijven, S. Kasa, M. Hekkert and W. Turkenburg (2009b). 'The performance of the Norwegian carbon dioxide, capture and storage innovation system.' *Energy Policy* **37**(1): 43-55.

van Alphen, K., P. M. Noothout, M. P. Hekkert and W. C. Turkenburg (2010). 'Evaluating the development of carbon capture and storage technologies in the United States.' *Renewable and Sustainable Energy Reviews* **14**(3): 971-986.

Zahra, S., R. Sisodia and B. Matherne (1999). 'Exploiting the dynamic links between competitive and technology strategies.' *European Management Journal* **17**(2): 188-203.

Thinking the Twenty-First Century

Ideas for the New Political Economy

Malcolm McIntosh

- Radical thinking from a pioneer of the corporate responsibility and sustainability movement
- Contextual account of five global changes that will transform a new political economy
- Essential for economists, academics and engaged citizens everywhere

"McIntosh recalls Obama's comment that Nelson Mandela's leadership 'freed the prisoner and jailer'. He explains what we must do to drive the same outcome with tomorrow's economy."

John Elkington, co-founder of Volans and SustainAbility

"This is a powerful work by a man at his peak and will, in fifty years' time, be seen as a masterpiece."

Sir Tim Smit KBE, Executive Chairman, Eden Regeneration, and co-founder of the Eden Project

"This book is both timely and urgent as humanity struggles to seek solutions for a fairer and sustainable future"

Georg Kell, Executive Director, UN Global Compact

In a sophisticated and far-reaching blend of theory and reflection, *Thinking the Twenty-First Century* takes a provocative look at the changes required to build a new global political economy. McIntosh charts five system changes essential to this transition: globality and Earth awareness; the rebalancing of science and awe; peacefulness and the feminization of decision-making; the reorganization of our institutions; and evolution, adaptation and learning. That they are all connected should be obvious, but that they are written about together is less common.

McIntosh argues that these five changes are already under way and need to be accelerated. Combining science, philosophy, politics and economics, *Thinking the Twenty-First Century* questions our current model of capitalism and calls for a much-needed new order. This forceful call to action advocates a balanced political economy with trandisciplinarity, connectivity, accountability and transparency at its centre, as an alternative to a world built on the failing system of neoliberal economics.

From one of the pioneers of the global corporate sustainability and social responsibility movement, this unique book combines analysis, diary and reflection to present a radical way forward for the twenty-first century.

MALCOLM McINTOSH is former Director of the Asia Pacific Centre for Sustainable Enterprise at Griffith University and is now at Bath Spa University. He was previously Special Adviser to the UN Global Compact and is the Founding Editor of the *Journal of Corporate Citizenship*.

Published: April 2015 | **Prices:** ebook: £24.99 | €29.99 | $39.99 | pb: £24.99 | €29.99 | $39.99 | hb: £60.00 | €75.00 | $95.00

DOI: [10.9774/GLEAF.4700.2015.ju.000014]

Employee Ownership and Governance

The Carris Companies Making Change
Impacting the Whole*

Cecile G. Betit

Independent researcher, USA

Given that large scale change has to start somewhere, the image of a pebble in a pool provides a visual for the primary goal for this paper to examine employee ownership generally and selected elements within the Carris whole systems purposeful change and its ongoing wider influence. This seems particularly worthwhile given the human scale and valuing change process within Carris as a mid-size international company that brought employees into the business as owners with full voice. The Carris transition increased the economic security and quality of life for employees, in addition to encouraging their voice in decision-making and governance to create their future reality. This paper is based on a longitudinal study of the transition of the Carris Companies from a traditional shareholder-primacy orientation toward full employee ownership and shared governance to illustrate the complexities and possibilities of shifting mind-sets preoccupied with traditional efficiency and profit maximisation. William H. (Bill) Carris set a deliberate purposeful course for the whole system change that he deeply desired for his employees. The Carris transformation, innovative in its own right, provides examples of change from being traditionally owned, managed and governed to having shared ownership, participatory management and shared governance—by the whole, i.e. by all of the employees who themselves, in the process, have undergone significant transformative changes toward self, other, and system-awareness. The Carris transition can be viewed as influencing widening circles of change within whole systems and ecosystems which are aligned and share reality: locally, statewide, nationally, industry wide, and internationally.

- Whole system transformation
- Employee ownership
- Employee governance
- Employee stock ownership plan (ESOP)
- Changing core agreements
- Large scale change

* Gratefully acknowledged are: William H. Carris, Chair, Carris Board of Directors for full access; Michael Curran, CEO/President for continuing access and encouragement; Karin McGrath, retired Human Resources Director for ongoing status information; Kathy Brytowski, Human Resources Director, for knowledge and availability; David Fitz-Gerald, CFO, for information regarding financial matters, the ESOP and Carris; and Carris employee-owners for their continuing interest. Thank you to Christopher Mackin, Ownership Associates and Alexander Moss, Praxis Consulting Group for the use of their materials and the JCC reviewers for positive, constructive and helpful comments. Thank you for changes to: Joseph George Anjilvelil (Workplace Catalysts Bangaluru, India); Matthew Cropp (Vermont Employee Ownership Center); Yvonne Daley (Journalism, University of San Francisco and Vermont); Lindsey Godwin (Stiller School, Champlain College); Larry Krafft (Education, Temple University); Eleanor Miller (Sociology, University of Vermont),

With the goal of documenting a whole system transition over an extended time period, **Cecile G. Betit**, PhD, an independent researcher, began the study of the transition to employee ownership and governance at the Carris Companies at its onset. Her publications on the transition can be found in *Designing Information and Organizations with a Positive Lens; Journal of Corporate Citizenship* (Summer 2008 and Summer and Winter 2002); *Corporate Social Responsibility, Accountability and Governance: Global Perspectives* (2005); *Unfolding Stakeholder Thinking (1)— Theory, Responsibility and Engagement* (2002); *Research In Ethical Issues In Organization (3)—The Next Phase Of Business Ethics: Integrating Psychology And Ethics* (2001); and the *Journal of Organizational Excellence* (2000). A book is in process, *Making Change in the Real World: Carris Reels Transition to a 100% Employee Owned and Governed Company.*

PO Box 272, East Wallingford, VT 05742, USA

cgbetit@vermontel.net

Grace Padilla (Philippines), and Paul Wishart, (Medicine, University of Alberta). A profound thank you to Sandra Waddock (Carroll School, Boston College) for help, advice and clarity throughout the paper's submission process.

T HIS PAPER IS BASED ON a longitudinal study of the Carris Companies transition from a traditional shareholder-primacy orientation toward full employee ownership and shared governance to illustrate the complexities and possibilities of shifting mind-sets from unconsciously accepting what Ritchie-Dunham (2014) calls 'foundational agreements' based on the scarcity emphasised within traditional economics, efficiency and profit maximisation.

William H. (Bill) Carris, Owner/CEO, in speaking of the transition, often used the image of enlarging ripples from a pebble tossed into a pool to illustrate his perspective on change. Given that large scale change begins somewhere, the image provides a visual for the primary goal for this paper on the Carris transition. The company can be viewed as a system undergoing change—in the sense of a 'functioning whole[s] that cannot be divided into independent parts and be effective' (Ackoff, 1998). Carris employee ownership as applied with shared employee governance can be seen by companies and organisations as prototype for their own transformative change.

Whole systems transformation at its core means assisting people in the development of an adaptable, 'replicable and evolving enterprise-wide capability to transform the way they do things again and again in a chaotic, ever changing world' (Scherer *et al.* 2010). At company level, this means shifting what Ritchie-Dunham termed core 'agreements' that employees, management and owners typically bring to their work, e.g. about efficiency, profitability and shareholder primacy, towards a new set based on their shared new co-created reality for their emerging future. Though Carris did not know of Ritchie-Dunham's (2014) effective holistic model examining fundamental agreements, 'minding the gap' of the present to the desired future has been well-practised with good results. Such agreements seem beyond strategy and desired outcomes reflecting an approach that aims to shift an entire ecosystem to what can be considered a higher order of awareness (consciousness)—one aligned with aspirations for deeper meaning, relationship and larger impact (Scharmer 2013). These are the 'stuff' of the *Long Term Plan* (LTP), the values driven document Bill Carris wrote over a ten year period with extensive consultation and discussion. It touches what Ritchie-Dunham speaks of as 'harmonic vibrancy' (2014) and others as dynamic alignment.

This paper draws from a longitudinal study during the transition of the Carris Companies to employee ownership and governance. Action research methods included among others: interviews/conversations with managers and employees, whole organisation surveys and meeting attendance. No restrictions were placed on access to information or personnel or to materials published.

Carris Companies

Employing 452 people with US$97 million in sales, Carris, headquartered in Proctor, Vermont (US), manufactures, assembles and recycles a variety of wood, plastic and metal reels for steel and wire cable at 16 locations. Reels, known as 'spools, bobbins or wire drums' are simple products (see Figure 1). Carris has not been a highly technological company. In recent years, it invested in equipment and processes to increase employee safety and production efficiency. Some reels have a low profit margin.

Figure 1 Reels manufactured by the Carris Companies

Seven manufacturing plants are located in the US (California, Connecticut, North Carolina, Virginia and Vermont—wood, plastics and tin and bolts) and Mexico. Within a mirror plan Mexico has 100% employee ownership.

As an employee-owned company in 2008, Carris entered a financial partnership with J. Hamelin Industries, a long-term, high-quality reel manufacturer and recycler in Canada—employing 180 in Quebec and Ontario. Presently, J. Hamelin is not employee-owned.

The companies have seven reel recycling centres (three in the US, three in Canada and one in Mexico).

Carris leadership

Henry Carris founded Carris Reels in 1951. Bill Carris grew up with the company. He purchased it in 1980 with the idea of bringing employees into the business as real owners in contrast to psychological ownership (Carris, 1994).

An aspect of Bill Carris's personal legacy within the company, the LTP is widely inclusive. Respecting the management role, the LTP did not favour management (Carris 1994). 'Common good' is mentioned 12 times. Community extends outside the corporation to include the broadest possible definition. Bill Carris was comfortable everywhere in the company and employees spoke 'their truth' freely to him. His high regard and affection for employees were obvious.

At the transition's start, Michael (Mike) Curran, head of production, was promoted to Vice President. He had the special ability to give Bill Carris's vision 'feet' and 'ground'. In 2005, prior to employees owning 50% of the company, Bill Carris became Chair of the Board of Directors and Mike Currant was appointed President/CEO, the first employee-owner in that role. They didn't always agree at the start; they usually arrived at a point of agreement before implementation. They trusted their mutual commitment.

Box 1 Carris employee ownership and governance

Selected Features

→ In the *Long Term Plan*, Bill Carris wrote about the phrase taped to the bookcase, 'to improve the quality of life for our growing corporate community'. This became the mission statement for the transition and later that of the company. In reflective discussions, employees spoke about what this phrase meant to them. Over time, the mission became a motivator to those who were committed and provided reassurance to those who wavered and/or who had fear around the transition. The statement took on the role of consensus builder in discussions of how to work through the myriad details of organisation life. It provided a centring principle, touchstone for shared identity and a piece of ground within the decision-making structure of the corporation.

→ The selling price was 50% of the company's market value with the gift portion transferred to the employees first.

→ The pay range ratio from the lowest paid to the highest paid in any profit centre should not exceed 1 to 7.5.

→ The pay range company-wide should not exceed 1 to 10 (there may be higher levels of skill at corporate level).

→ The composition and work of the Carris Corporate Steering Committee (CSC) has been considered a Carris hallmark. For three days, twice a year since September 1996, corporate management, site management and elected employee representatives have gathered at headquarters. Authority and responsibility for decisions are shared equally in this future oriented group. Later, a representative from the Board of Directors by role was added. The ESOP (Employee Stock Ownership Plan) Trustees appointed by the CSC sit with voice at the CSC meetings without vote.

  → Research Group developed the CSC Charter, ways of proceeding and implementing change.

  → Developed process and procedures for selecting ESOP Trustees and for putting employees on the Board of Directors.

> → 'Open Book' was put into place with the transition. At every CSC meeting those present heard reports from sales, human resources, safety and finance. Understanding the financials was a long term focus for the CSC and employees. Leading up to the purchase of stock and the company's real estate, meetings were held to explain the dynamics and consequences of the proposed transactions. Annually, the CFO has put in place fun activities across the corporation to help build comprehension.

The Carris ESOP

Over 19 years, the Carris Companies transformed itself as a whole system, becoming 100% employee owned through an Employee Stock Ownership Plan (ESOP)—a trust, holding company shares for the deferred benefit plan established within the United States Employee Retirement Income Security Act (ERISA). In 2014, there were an estimated 7,000 ESOPs with 13.5 million participants;[1] in 2011 assets approached $950 billion.[2] Distinguishing an ESOP are: legal requirements to invest primarily in securities of the sponsoring employer; the ability to borrow money; and tax advantages.

In December 2005, Carris employees received the remaining gift stock for 50% ownership and purchased their first 15%. Following 100% employee ownership in 2008, Carris experienced its best years in productivity and profits. Research points to employee ownership being good for business and its locale (Rosen et al. 2005).

Historically, Carris has been a good employer. In response to a question, Bill Carris explained that there could be no rational reason for an employee-owned company not to pay as much as it could, within typical business constraints. Carris employees experience profitability through monthly incentives and annual profit sharing (18.6%). Profitability is recognised as important for company well-being and for the company's annual valuation.

In surveys and interviews, employees and former employees have been consistent in stating the differences company ownership made in their lives. They note that profitability increases their annual profit sharing checks and the company value increasing gives them more comfort about their retirement.

Employee ownership as transformative change

Employee ownership is purposeful, deliberate change (Waddell et al. 2014) in contrast to 'creating change that no one wants' (Scharmer 2013) within

---

1 For additional information see www.esop.org/ (accessed June 2014).
2 See www.nceo.org/articles/statistical-profile-employee-ownership (accessed June 2014).

whole systems, arguably creating greater employee awareness—best when it is systemic.

An ESOP provides plans for retirement for employees and succession for a business (with good tax advantages). Employee ownership through an ESOP can pave the way for continued 'responsible management' (Waddock and Bodwell, 2007) as it shares wealth and profits among employees; facilitates local economic security through jobs, philanthropy and community involvement; and sustains physical and social environments.

In shared ownership, workers are both stakeholders and shareholders. Carris included governance in its whole systems change, requiring a variety of approaches over many years. When Carris suffered from the dot.com bust, it engaged employees in reducing costs and increasing efficiencies. Similar processes were applied in the mid-decade recession. Corporate experience and the methodical nature of its leadership had much to do with Carris's capacity to survive those very tough times.

Most employee-owned workplaces, including Carris, describe themselves as more than a place to work and earn a living. Those are among the signs that flourishing and thriving in the context of business and work are no longer considered out of reach. Information is readily available on creating such workplaces, those that exist and the role of such workplaces in moving beyond sustainability (Carris 1994; Bakker and Schaufeli 2008; Laszlo et al. 2012).

To jump-start the changing relationship with the company, employee identity and the process toward personal and organisational awareness and change, Bill Carris proposed a *Long Term Plan* Steering Committee (LTPSC), comprising corporate and site management and employees (19 members). The committee was charged to work with the ESOP attorney, to enhance participation and understanding, to establish criteria for selecting ESOP Trustees, to advise Bill Carris as seller and the Trustees regarding 18 key legal decisions. In the first meeting, Bill Carris asked the LTPSC to consider itself and to act as if it were the corporate board of directors; at some future point that would very likely occur.

The ESOP attorney noted the Carris process as unusual. Bill Carris made two decisions: the one person/one vote provision and continuing the corporate tithe to the Carris Foundation. The LTPSC made the remaining 16 decisions and developed the allocation formulas for employee vote. The selected ESOP allocation formula was designed to be non-hierarchical and reward those who had built the value of the company. Later changed, the current formula allocates 90% based on the floor of $30,000 compensation, set at $46,329 for 2014, with 10% based on years of service.

An additional change in agreement was the consensus decision-making put in place at the beginning. That precedent continued within the company's corporate governance.

Workers share in the success of their company, create shareholder wealth, see new possibilities for themselves and often experience and influence shifts in values, norms and vision. These 'are what hold a system together and it is this core that needs to be targeted to make changes'[3] that can lead to flourishing (Laszlo *et al.* 2013).

At Carris, these changes can be considered to lead to flourishing, extending ripples beyond the company:

▶ Efforts for educational opportunities for employees

▶ Meetings, trainings, etc. at all company sites to ensure understandings of employee-ownership, safety, wellness, company performance, matters affecting employees, etc.

▶ Efforts by employees to understand the financials and the responsibility of making good decisions around company assets and wealth

▶ The creation of the local Charitable Giving Committees opened the employees to the experience of sharing corporate profits with their communities

Such changes affect wider ecosystems (Fitzduff, this issue) moving into economic development, community stability and quality of life.

The influence of the Carris ESOP

From the perspective of the ripples from a tossed pebble, as well as nesting ecosystems of individuals, families, organisations, institutions (some embedded), connecting at multiple and ever widening levels—a point to be emphasised is the relationship an employee-owned company has within its locale. Reports on ESOPs suggesting that they contribute to community stability and economic development have implications for redressing increasing economic inequality. 'Without economic development, redressing inequality will be seen as a win/lose situation, particularly for those who currently have most resources' (Fitzduff, this issue).

Employee ownership encourages active citizenship in larger political processes. As an embedded ecosystem, it can influence value expression, behaviour and change. Employee participation, ownership and governance can traverse to a variety of ecosystems found in the larger civic society (Smith 1985; Gates, 1998; Carey 2004; Blasi 2013) thus influencing diverse ecosystems.

Carris employee ownership influences and promotes a more diverse, humane, sustainable, adaptive agenda that lives in the company as an ecosystem moving outward to its larger circles—locales and industries:

▶ **Locally**. As a friend and working partner

▶ **Statewide**. Involvement in statewide initiatives. As (State) Senator, Senate Majority Leader, Bill Carris expressed Carris values. He sponsored legislation making Vermont the second state to allow corporations to focus on

---

3 For Sandra Waddock's (2014) remarks in receiving the life-time achievement award, see www.bc.edu/content/bc/publications/chronicle/FeaturesNewsTopstories/2014/news/ lifetime-achievement-honor-for-bc-s-waddock.html#.U8gqLnzmevk.email (accessed July 2014)

more than the economic bottom line (moving beyond the Friedman (1970) legacy), and to establish the Vermont Employee Ownership Center—one of two centres nationally—to encourage employee ownership

▶ **Regionally**. Bill Carris helped to establish the New England Chapter of the ESOP Association. He held several leadership positions. David Fitz-Gerald, VP/CFO has been active promoting ESOPs and was named 2011 Chapter Officer of the Year by the ESOP Association. Carris personnel are active within their locales. At meetings, they find that Carris is doing much more than other companies and is often a role model

▶ **Nationally within membership associations**. Both Bill Carris and David Fitz-Gerald have held significant elected and volunteer positions in the ESOP Association. David Fitz-Gerald will be ESOP association chair in the near future. Carris personnel are frequent speakers at meetings. Carris is called on frequently for advice at the beginning of a process and problem solving in implementation. Carris was named 2008 ESOP Association's Company of the Year. In addition to asking that the local newspaper's article be included, Vermont's Senator Patrick Leahy read the following into the *Congressional Record:*[4]

> One of the unique characteristics of Carris Reels is the company's steering committee, which goes beyond the basic functions of most ESOP committees and takes responsibility for allocations of benefits, quality of work-life issues, communications, training, and governance. Made up of both management and corporate employees, the Committee keeps alive the vision of former owner Bill Carris who moved the company toward employee ownership in 1995. Bill has said that organisations consist of three dimensions: spiritual, emotional, and physical. The strong business his family built and the employees now own is proof positive that these dimensions will remain a legacy at Carris Reels (p. 55033).

▶ **Legislative initiatives**. During the May 2014 ESOP Association Conference in Washington, DC, Carris and Gardener's Supply met with Vermont's legislators to ask for support. At that time, (national) Senator Sanders explained the upcoming legislation to support employee ownership that he would co-sponsor

▶ **Industry**. Carris employee ownership is emphasised on the website, in the corporate logo, on its stationery, trucks, etc. Carris efforts build relationships—some 30 and 40 years old—with customers and suppliers. At a recent retirement dinner in North Carolina many suppliers and customers were in attendance—some from great distances

▶ **Internationally**. Carris Mexico ploughed new legal ground in developing an employee ownership programme to mirror the one in the US. As 100% employee-owned, Carris entered a financial, working partnership—unusual in its own right—with J. Hamelin Inc. a company headquartered near Montreal, Canada

---

4 See http://thomas.loc.gov/cgi-bin/query/z?r110:S04JN8-0028 for the full entry (accessed July 2014).

Employee ownership as whole systems change may impact/influence, though not entirely address or fix, problems involving large nested systems such as economic inequality; developmental, educational, social, and economic access; sustainability; full employment; living wages; corporate governance; corporate and organisational citizenship; democracy and voice.

Systems in systems, webs of interdependence, ecosystems

As discussed above, employee-owned companies can be seen within contemporary complex interrelationships, as ecosystems within ecosystems, webs of interdependence (Senge, 2012) in living relationship (embedded, interdependent, etc.)—the connection of the larger whole—a hologram, often as ecosystem holds true. 'Each shares responsibility for the whole, not just for his piece... Each represents the whole image from a different point of view' (Senge 1990). As an example, Carris seems simply to be one company, until its many locations are considered. Each has its own set of impacts on the local employees and their communities. Carris is also part of the larger network of ESOPs, where the company has taken a leadership role in speaking and educating about shared governance and decision-making. Many companies have implemented aspects of the Carris model. In the larger 'civil conversation' involving who owns what (DeSoto 2000; Waddock and McIntosh 2011), employee ownership has a significant role to play. ESOPs are shown to reduce inequity and provide an example of a powerful alternative form of ownership.

Deliberate whole system transformative change

The Carris transition provides a relevant example of whole system change—and illustrates in many ways just how time-consuming, managerially focused and employee-participation intensive such a transition can be. While Bill Carris carried forward the family and business values in the LTP, he encouraged focus on the emerging future (Scharmer 2013). As the members of the LTPSC would wonder what to do, he would suggest they do the next right thing. He encouraged looking at change as an 'experiment' in a prototyping sense with the idea that if something didn't work, they could fix it. In language that Bill Carris might well nod to, Scharmer (this issue) offers a rationale for this practice:

> **Prototype in order to explore the future by doing.** Most current practices of action research and organisational learning are bounded by reflecting on and modifying the experience of the past. Yet, all major disruptive challenges in our systems today require us to move beyond modifying the past. They invite us to sense and actualise emerging future possibilities. This practice, learning from the emerging future, makes it possible to translate a sense of possibility into intention and intention into action by creating small living examples to explore the future by doing, and by integrating the intelligence of the head, heart, and hand.

Corporate Steering Committee

When management and employees decided to form the Corporate Steering Committee (CSC) to guide and carry the transition, they had the experience of the LTPSC as prototype. Bill Carris urged the CSC, as he had the LTPSC, to experience itself as a governance body impacting the whole company and its transitions to employee ownership and governance. The CSC was perhaps the single most important decision made about the transition.

Over time, the CSC was characterised by searching conversation and reflective discourse as management and employees worked together on their emerging future in creating identity and culture. The CSC saw itself, and was seen as, a prototype through which employee governance would evolve—it was both actor and container for the transition direction—it initiated, carried the organisational passion forward in support of the major efforts and new directions. Carris management and employees are frequently invited to speak about the CSC: its organising principles, decision-making and work.

Positive forward-looking attitudes and 'can do' language suggesting the CSC's 'noble purpose' and its understanding of abundance in its generative discussions were important transition considerations, the long term corporate strategy and goals, planned orientation for employee ownership and culture and the various reports about the state of the company and its sites.

From its beginning, the CSC, with all aspects of the organisation represented in the room, offered more forward-looking design and planning than simple problem solving (Cooperrider and McQuaid 2012). The messiness of the early days' discussions leading to agreements is often spoken of fondly. Provided with sighs and laughter may be the description of the development of the loosely defined consensus decision-making structure (in 1997 — see Figure 2) with its back-up polls and votes and ways of determining a CSC agenda item (see Figure 3). These efforts could be considered prototyping for the models that came later.

Figure 2 Original decision-making model

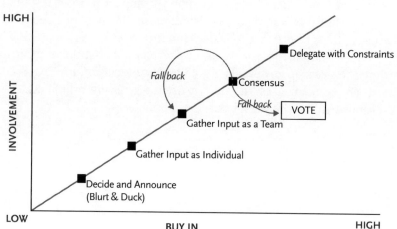

Figure 3 Way of determining CSC agenda item

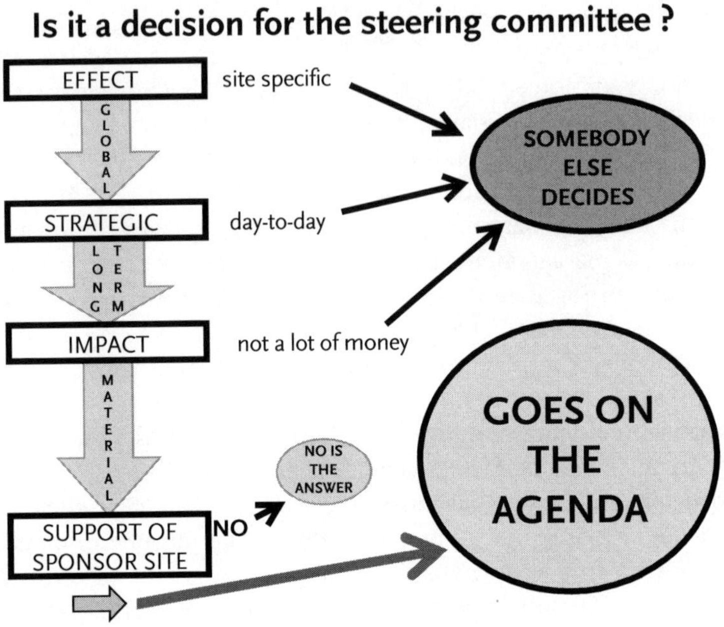

Is it a decision for the steering committee ?

Decision-making model

Ownership Associates Christopher Mackin and Loren Rodgers (currently NCEO's CEO) worked with Carris to develop an ownership culture in the context of governance, participation, voice, transparency and accountability—visible to employee owners. One major effort involved decision-making.

For each type of business decision relevant to Carris on the chart shown in Figure 4, a grid was developed showing (as roles rather than as individuals): an 'alerter' (anyone in the company could alert for a needed decision); process manager for a given decision; those consulted during the process; responsibility and accountability for making the decision; those informed of a decision; who could veto; and the time frame for a decision review. Decision reports informed each rationale and outcome for a given decision and additional information regarding the decision review. The goal to make decision-making clear was achieved. The company then began to revise the grids toward the 'ideal'—having decisions made at the most basic level possible.

Figure 4 CSC chart of basic decisions with decision maker level indicated

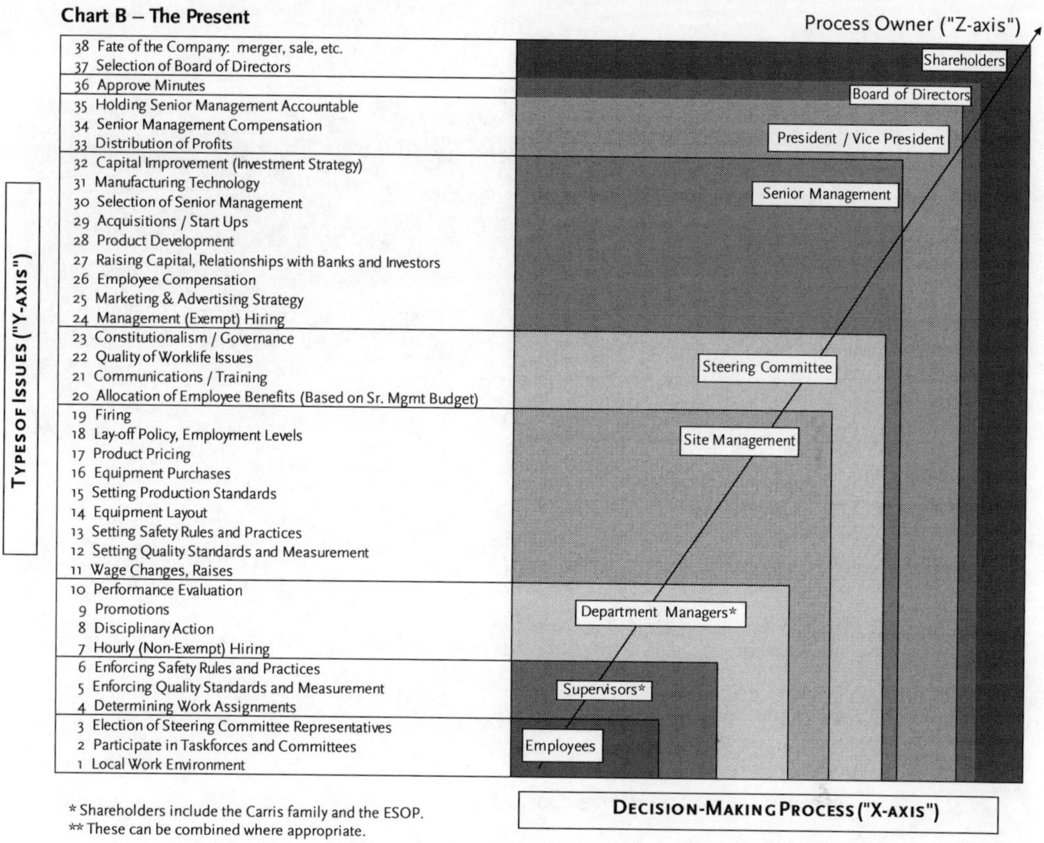

Chart B – The Present

Process Owner ("Z-axis")

TYPES OF ISSUES ("Y-AXIS")

38 Fate of the Company: merger, sale, etc.	Shareholders
37 Selection of Board of Directors	
36 Approve Minutes	Board of Directors
35 Holding Senior Management Accountable	
34 Senior Management Compensation	President / Vice President
33 Distribution of Profits	
32 Capital Improvement (Investment Strategy)	Senior Management
31 Manufacturing Technology	
30 Selection of Senior Management	
29 Acquisitions / Start Ups	
28 Product Development	
27 Raising Capital, Relationships with Banks and Investors	
26 Employee Compensation	
25 Marketing & Advertising Strategy	
24 Management (Exempt) Hiring	
23 Constitutionalism / Governance	Steering Committee
22 Quality of Worklife Issues	
21 Communications / Training	
20 Allocation of Employee Benefits (Based on Sr. Mgmt Budget)	
19 Firing	Site Management
18 Lay-off Policy, Employment Levels	
17 Product Pricing	
16 Equipment Purchases	
15 Setting Production Standards	
14 Equipment Layout	
13 Setting Safety Rules and Practices	
12 Setting Quality Standards and Measurement	
11 Wage Changes, Raises	
10 Performance Evaluation	Department Managers*
9 Promotions	
8 Disciplinary Action	
7 Hourly (Non-Exempt) Hiring	
6 Enforcing Safety Rules and Practices	Supervisors*
5 Enforcing Quality Standards and Measurement	
4 Determining Work Assignments	
3 Election of Steering Committee Representatives	Employees
2 Participate in Taskforces and Committees	
1 Local Work Environment	

* Shareholders include the Carris family and the ESOP.
** These can be combined where appropriate.

DECISION-MAKING PROCESS ("X-AXIS")

CSC Research Group

Beginning in 2008, Alexander (Alex) P. Moss, Founding Partner of the Praxis Consulting Group worked with the CSC to bring shared governance to life. Drawing from experience in employee ownership and governance, he worked with the Research Group to methodically develop a charter and answer the questions that Mike Curran, CEO, had developed:

> What role do we want the CSC to play? What is the CSC responsibility to Carris employee-owners? …What role should CSC play in helping the CEO frame his vision? Years from now, do we want the CSC to act more like a Board of Directors? Should the decision live with the CSC instead of the Board of Directors in setting the standards for the CEO or the boundaries for the company? …What is the Future Role of the CSC: As advisory body: to who, for what and when? As representatives: of whom, for what and when? …In relationship to the four decisions on the chart: should there be others?

As seen in Figures 5 and 6, the CSC is the key difference in Carris governance structure.

Figure 5 Typical governance structure

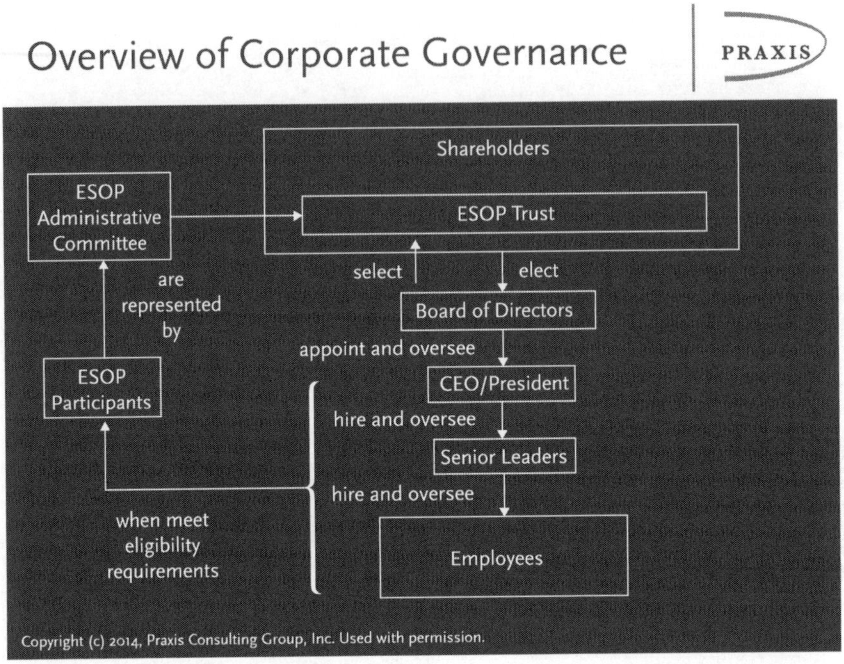

Overview of Corporate Governance

PRAXIS

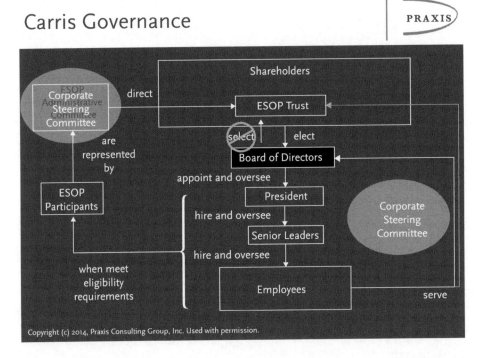

Figure 6 Carris governance structure

Carris Governance

PRAXIS

With Alex Moss, the Research Group answered Mike Curran's questions and framed its work in ways useful to the CSC and corporation for many years. That effort was instrumental in the discussions on formalisation of role and selection process for the ESOP Trustees and Board of Directors. Those who study human and organisation development addressing system change in the context of transformation, contrast the incremental emphases of reform and growth to deliberate and purposeful new vision directed toward high effectiveness with inclusive and encompassing objectives, increasing capacity and competence, and values driven emergence (Ackoff 2004; Cooperrider 2012; Kegan 1982; M. McIntosh 2007; S. McIntosh 2007; McKibben 2010; Waddell et al., 2014; Waddock and McIntosh 2011). Deliberate transformation (Kegan et al., 2014) such as employee ownership often includes within its infrastructure greater awareness in the present (Snowden, this issue) of relationship and attention to consequences for the quality of life. The Carris transformation in its deliberateness provides an illustration of these principles as well as shifts in relationships such as those in the CSC that no one foresaw in terms of their overall effect within and outside the company. How we, as humans, live; how we relate to one another and the environment; what we value; how we set our purposes and goals, i.e. the fundamental 'agreements' entered into in an employment situation can be deliberately altered towards more constructive and appreciative agreements rooted in abundance as Ritchie-Dunham (2014) notes as change producing. The Carris discussion to continue with internal ESOP Trustees was pivotal. Following examination of the US Department of Labor's fiduciary accountability requirement, Carris instituted a strong programme to educate internal ESOP Trustees rather than hiring externally.

Another insight into the Carris transformation arises with Peter Drucker's (2006) distinction between 'right things' (effectiveness) versus doing 'things right' (efficiency); and Ackoff's (2004) reference to effectiveness as an intent of transformation.[5] With efficiency being value-free, 'Effectiveness is efficiency weighted by the values of the ends achieved; it is value-full' (Ackoff, 1998). Similarly, Ken Wilber puts simple change in the lateral/horizontal sense as 'translation' while transformation offers a vertical dimension (a higher and deeper order) of change (1997). Carris brought all facets of the corporation together in the same room to work on the transition effectively. This fostered the shift of Carris identity from a family-owned company to a 100% employee-owned and governed company. Carris's efforts have been well supported beginning with Bill Carris's understanding of the role of social actions in creating transformation that is sustainable and flourishing. In the main, Carris employees know what they have accomplished over the years in the transition. From the beginning they knew the end game of the transition would be 'employees on the Board of Directors'.

Understanding change in the context of developmental change

Transformative, whole system and large scale change suggests evolution of self-awareness and human consciousness specifically in relationship to identity, values, norms and vision (S. McIntosh, 2007; Wilber 1997; Beck and Cowan

---

5 See Ackoff (2004) reissued 31 March 2014 as a blog http://ackoffcenter.blogs.com/ackoff_center_weblog/2014/04/transforming-the-systems-movement.html

1996; Laloux 2014). In spite of different labels, there is general agreement that individuals move from pre-conventional stages of reasoning (where there is little understanding of the broader system) to conventional reasoning (where the system is generally accepted as it is), toward post-conventional reasoning (which questions the system as it currently exists and encompasses numerous perspectives) (Wilber 2000).

Each advancing stage of development involves 'transcend and include', where earlier stages are encompassed and surpassed by later stages in a nested way (Wilber 1997). In the developmental cycle, former stages continue to exist to be reactivated as conditions arise.

Those working in Spiral Dynamics (Graves, 1970; Beck and Cowan, 1996; Wilber, 1997) note Tier I and Tier II characteristics. Within Tier I, at each developmental level, even as self-awareness grows, people think that their worldview is the correct, best perspective without really understanding more advanced levels. Theoreticians consistently make the point that when stages are healthy, they all contribute to the common good (Beck, nd; Wilber, 2000). Within Tier II thinking, there is awareness (often inarticulate) of the interior stages of development, of relationship, pattern and interdependence; and the big picture in a more universalistic and inclusive ecosystemic sense (Wilber 1995, 1997; Beck and Cowan 1996; Laloux 2014).

Returning to efficiency and effectiveness, Tier I logic stands out within the attraction for efficiency (ubiquitous in our time). At Carris, early in the transition, concern was expressed that meetings took away from 'getting wood out the door'. The logic of efficiency is pervasive in many companies, and in the economic system as a whole.

Alternatively, holding awareness and working toward 'doing the right thing' in a given circumstance is not always a clear path (Beck, nd; Graves, 1970; Wilber, 2000). The question arises as to how to activate higher order values. The inquiry becomes more serious as the desire for a Tier II response is factored in.

The primary ways that Carris built its framework toward a Tier II response were three foci that Bill Carris included within the LTP. The first was the mission involving 'improving the quality of life for our growing corporate community' as a shared purpose (Laloux 2014); the second was the emphasis on the common good; and the third was the emphasis on inclusion. In the LTPSC, CSC and other meetings, Bill Carris asked questions to keep these elements among others in the foreground, often in the context of values. Gradually over time, the baton was passed. Whether Bill Carris was present or not, employees or managers would ask the questions that moved the group towards a broader set of values, related to trust, personal awareness, system effectiveness, such as doing the next right thing. Good listening and paying attention seemed basic to the process.

Reflective practice

Shifts in individual and organisational consciousness and transformation grow out of reflective practices such as discourse, meditation, mindfulness, journaling, walking, storytelling, art, periods of quiet and silence, and ways of checking in at the beginning of meetings (Kegan *et al.* 2014; Scharmer 2013; Torbert 2004). Opportunities for reflection promote changes in consciousness as well as inquiry and creativity (Waddock 2001; S. McIntosh 2007; Cooperrider, 2012; Laszlo *et al.* 2012; Laloux 2014). The Carris transformation encouraged being mindful, of checking in, looking at how things were working and how people were being affected, what they understood, what they needed to be able to understand more fully. In terms of Ritchie-Dunham's ecosynomics framework (2014), the Carris transformation can be characterised as a movement from scarcity-based to abundance-based employee agreements where the core question about resources shifts from 'what is available capacity' to 'what is potential capacity'.

Employee owners share experience, identity and purpose. Carris's promotional literature states 'Ownership in everything we do' in a similar way as Ritchie-Dunham's example at Thorlo (2014) and what Laloux speaks of as shared purpose. Carris employees on the CSC, local safety and charitable gift committees and other groups have the opportunity for discourse and relationship, collaboration and common fate putting their efforts together for the success of their company. They experience the economy directly (through profit sharing and their shares) and learn well what makes it work, interrelating with other ecosystems (though perhaps unable to articulate this knowledge) at conferences, workshops, and other external events. These experiences encourage them to reflect and grow.

An element which should not be underestimated involves the relationship of shifts in consciousness and changes in self-awareness: how one thinks affects what one sees, what one thinks about and does (Beck and Cowan, 1996; Wilber, 2000; Laloux 2014). Employees changed what they paid attention to at the start and end of the transition. Questions changed from how ownership would affect personal finances to a larger context such as retirement. Participation, future goals and a kind of 'sharing in the enterprise' and fun seem to be present. Employees and management's sense of the core 'agreements' shifted, from 'efficiency' and cynicism, towards greater trust, participation, ownership, inclusivity and effectiveness (in Drucker's sense of the right thing to do).

Chris Laszlo *et al.* (2012) stress that in shifting consciousness toward connection, reflective practices facilitate embedding of sustainability. Connection and the common good seem necessary for shared employee ownership. Employee owners can call into question and promote reflective discourse regarding many areas of the shared experience such as values, information, decision-making, as well as their meaning in the larger company picture and in the lives of its many owners at home and in their communities. At Carris one can see this clearly in the number of ongoing group efforts moving forward for improvement whether in safety, production, social activities, or community service.

'Reflective discourse', occurs in many of these activities as 'the progressive taking in, digesting and reconstructing of perspectives different from our own. (It is a) primary form through which transformative learning takes place' (Daloz 2000). Carris efforts to build an ownership culture involved steps toward creating the emerging future. Groups may well be seen as promoting transformative learning within 'communities of practice' (Torbert, 2004). Encouraging each other's' growth, moving into discussions with implications for shared ownership can open doors to self-awareness of values, connectedness and the importance of personal responsibility and efforts to serve the common good. These may be avenues toward embedding sustainability, increasing consciousness and flourishing.

Shared ownership

Employee owners have wide differences in skill and education. This means that development of understanding of the intricacies of the ESOP itself and the personal implications is no small feat for them and their companies. Years of effort went into teaching Carris employees the business, communication, decision-making, the ESOP, the complex financial transactions for ownership and governance (establishing requirements, terms etc. with full selection process for ESOP Trustees and employees on the Board of Directors). The Carris experience provides a perspective of the whole (Talbot, 1992). Its forward-looking views on governance and policies have 'nudged' (Thaler, 2009) other employee-owned companies and changed the conversation at many national forums where it is considered 'a poster child for innovation'.

As an example of a whole systems approach, Carris as an ecosystem became more self-aware and aligned with its aspirations for deeper meaning, real relationship and larger impact. The Carris transformation set in motion a set of dialogic and generative circumstances including reflective discourse and relationship building that fostered its self-awareness, its development and making change in the larger ecosystem. Its opening to Tier II consciousness holds the potential for embedding sustainable change not only for itself but for the systems and ecosystems that contribute to it, those that Carris influences directly and indirectly and those that find Carris an exemplar.

Conclusion

Carris began and ended the transition looking at creating its desired future with emerging possibilities. Carris has typically made its agreements through consensus and shared purpose from a place of shared reality. With new efforts going forward in strategic planning and leadership development, that work continues. It can be anticipated that change will occur higher in the spiral in the evolutionary sense leading to another expression of harmonic vibrancy that can be shared. As a 100% employee-owned and governed company, it is living and contributing to Bill Carris's legacy. Using the image of the enlarging ripples of the pebble tossed in the pond, it has changed the lives of its own employee owners who are now sharing the wealth of the company, their own experiences of transformative learning, shifts in consciousness and more possibilities for their own lives. Their awareness of choice increases. As Carris employee owners travel to ESOP-related meetings or other meetings in their locale, they return to their site saying that they feel like 'poster children'. They tell their colleagues that what they took for granted as the way 'we do things' shows up outside as very special.

In the larger picture, using a positive change lens, employee-ownership can be seen as offering an effective way of making change. It can lead to 'doing the right thing' with and for people, in the values and economic senses as well as taking good care of the environment—all as systems and ecosystems. With reflective discourse and other practices it is more likely that higher order behaviours such as embedding sustainability and flourishing can take hold for the common good.

References

Ackoff, R. (1998), A systemic view of transformational leadership, Systemic Practice and Action Research, 11, 1, 23-36.

Ackoff, R. (2004), Transforming the systems movement www.acasa.upenn.edu/RLAConf Paper.pdf (accessed June 2014).

Bakker, A. B. and Schaufel, W.B. (2008), 'Positive organizational behavior: Engaged employees in flourishing organizations', Journal of Organizational Behavior, 29, 147–154.

Beck, D. E. (nd) 'How value systems shape organizational productivity', National and Global Transformation http://spiraldynamics.net/DrDonBeck/essays/human_capacities.htm (accessed June 2014).

Beck, D. E. and Cowan, C.C. (1996), Spiral dynamics: Mastering values leadership, and change. Blackwell Publishing, Malden, MA.

Blasi, J., Freeman, R.B., Kruse, D. L. (2013), The citizen's share: Putting ownership back into democracy. Yale University Press, New Haven, CT.

Carey, R. (2004). Democratic capitalism: The way to a world of peace and plenty, Author-House, Bloomington, IN.

Carris, W. H. (1994). The Long Term Plan for the Carris Community of Companies. Rutland, Vermont: Carris Companies.

Cooperrider, D. L. (2012), 'The concentration effect of strengths: How the whole system "AI" summit brings out the best in human enterprise', Organizational Dynamics, 41, 2, 106-117.

Cooperrider, D. L. and McQuaid, M. (2012), 'The positive arc of systemic strengths: How appreciative inquiry and sustainable designing can bring out the best in human systems', Journal of Corporate Citizenship 46, 1-32.

Daloz, L. A. P. (2000). 'Transformative learning for the common good', in Mezirow, J. (Ed), Learning as transformation: Critical perspectives on a theory in progress, Jossey Bass, San Francisco: 103-123.

DeSoto, H. 2000. The mystery of capital: Why capitalism triumphs in the West and fails everywhere else. Basic Books, New York.

Drucker, P. J. (2001), The essential Drucker, Harper and Row, New York.

Drucker, P. J. (2006), The effective executive: The definitive guide to getting the right things done. Harper and Row, New York (first published 1967).

Friedman, M. (1970). 'The social responsibility of business is to increase its profits', New York Times Magazine, September 13: 32-33, 122-124.

Gates, J. (1998), The ownership solution: Toward a shared capitalism for the twenty-first century. Addison-Wesley, Reading, MA.

Graves, C. (1970) 'Levels of existence: An open system theory of values', Journal of Humanistic Psychology, 10-2, 131-155.

Hennessey, S. (2014) Lifetime achievement honor for BC's Waddock. www.bc.edu/content/bc/publications/chronicle/FeaturesNewsTopstories/2014/news/lifetime-achievement-honor-for-bc-swaddock.html#.U8gqLnzmevk.email (accessed July 2014).

Kegan, R. (1982), The evolving self: Problem and process in human development, Harvard University Press Cambridge, MA.

Kegan, R. Lahey, L., Fleming, A., Miller, M., and Markus, I. (2014) 'Making business personal: companies that turn employees' struggles into growth opportunities are discovering a new kind of competitive advantage', Harvard Business Review: 92.4; 44.

Laloux, F. (2014), Reinventing organizations: A guide to creating organizations for the next state of human consciousness, Digital edition.

Laszlo, C., Brown, J.S., Sherman, D, Barros, I., Boland, B., Ehrenfeld, J., Gorham, M., Robson, L., Saillant, and Werder, P. (2012), 'Flourishing: A vision for business and the world', Journal of Corporate Citizenship, 46, 31-51.

McIntosh, M. (2007). A conversation about the future: Sustainable Enterprise. Background paper from the Applied Research Centre in Human Security (ARCHS).

McIntosh, S. (2007), Integral consciousness and the future of evolution, Paragon House, St Paul, MN.

McKibben, B. (2010), Eaarth: Making a life on a tough new planet, St. Martin's Griffin, New York.

Ritchie-Dunham, J. (2014). Ecosynomics: The science of abundance, Belchertown, MA: Vibrancy Publishing.

Rosen, C., Case, J. and Staubus, M. (2005) Equity: Why employee ownership is good for business, Harvard Business School Press, Boston, MA.

Scharmer, O. (2013) Leading from the emerging future: From ego-system to eco-system economies. Berrett Koehler, San-Francisco, CA.

Scherer, J. J., Lavery, G., Sullivan, R., Whitson, G., and Vales, E. (2010), 'Whole system transformation: The consultant's role in creating sustainable results', In Buono, A. F. and Jamieson, D. W. (Eds), Consultation for organizational change. Information Age Publishing, Charlotte, NC: 57-78.

Senge, P. (1990). The fifth discipline: The art and practice of the learning organization. New York: Doubleday.

Senge P. (2012), 'What is systems thinking? – Peter Senge explains systems thinking approach and principles' Posted on October 5, 2012 in Featured Science (accessed May 2014).

Smith, S. (1985), 'Political behavior as an economic externality: Econometric evidence on the relationship between ownership and decision making participation in US firms and participation in community affairs', in Jones, D. C. and Svejnar, J. (Eds.), Advances in the Economic Analysis of Participatory and Labor-Managed Firms, JAI Press, Greenwich, CT 123-136.

Talbot, M. (1992), The holographic universe. Harper Collins, New York.

Thaler, R. H. (2009), Nudge: Improving Decisions about Health, Wealth, and Happiness, Penguin Books, NY.

Torbert, B. and Associates (2004) Action inquiry: The secret of timely and transforming leadership, San Francisco, Berrett-Koehler.

Waddell, S., Hsueh, J., Birney, A., Khorsani, A. and Feng, W. (2014), 'Turning point: Large systems change: producing the change we want', Journal of Corporate Citizenship, 53, 5-8.

Waddock, S. (2001), 'Integrity and mindfulness', Journal of Corporate Citizenship, 1, 25-37.

Waddock, S. and. Bodwell, C. (2007), Total responsibility management: The manual. Greenleaf Publishing, Sheffield, UK.

Waddock, S. and McIntosh, M. (2011), SEE CHANGE: Making the transition to a Sustainable Enterprise Economy, Greenleaf Publishing, Sheffield, UK.

Wilber, K. (1995). Sex, ecology, spirituality: The spirit of evolution. Shambala Publications, Boston, MA.

Wilber, K. (1997), The eye of spirit: An integral vision for a world gone slightly mad. Shambala Publications, Inc, Boston, MA.

Wilber K. (2000), A theory of everything: An integral vision for business, politics, science and spirituality, Shambala Publications, Boston, MA.

About the Journal of Corporate Citizenship

THE JOURNAL OF CORPORATE CITIZENSHIP (*JCC*) is a multidisciplinary peer-reviewed journal that focuses on integrating theory about corporate citizenship with management practice. It provides a forum in which the tensions and practical realities of making corporate citizenship real can be addressed in a reader-friendly, yet conceptually and empirically rigorous format.

JCC aims to publish *the best ideas integrating the theory and practice of corporate citizenship in a format that is readable, accessible, engaging, interesting and useful* for readers in its already wide audience in business, consultancy, government, NGOs and academia. It encourages practical, theoretically sound, and (when relevant) empirically rigorous manuscripts that address real-world implications of corporate citizenship in global and local contexts. Topics related to corporate citizenship can include (but are not limited to): corporate responsibility, stakeholder relationships, public policy, sustainability and environment, human and labour rights/issues, governance, accountability and transparency, globalisation, small and medium-sized enterprises (SMEs) as well as multinational firms, ethics, measurement, and specific issues related to corporate citizenship, such as diversity, poverty, education, information, trust, supply chain management, and problematic or constructive corporate/human behaviours and practices.

In addition to articles linking the theory and practice of corporate citizenship, *JCC* also encourages innovative or creative submissions (for peer review). Innovative submissions can highlight issues of corporate citizenship from a critical perspective, enhance practical or conceptual understanding of corporate citizenship, or provide new insights or alternative perspectives on the realities of corporate citizenship in today's world. Innovative submissions might include: critical perspectives and controversies, photography, essays, poetry, drama, reflections, and other innovations that help bring corporate citizenship to life for management practitioners and academics alike.

JCC welcomes contributions from researchers and practitioners involved in any of the areas mentioned above. Manuscripts should be written so that they are comprehensible to an intelligent reader, avoiding jargon, formulas and extensive methodological treatises wherever possible. They should use examples and illustrations to highlight the ideas, concepts and practical implications of the ideas being presented. Theory is important and necessary; but theory—with the empirical research and conceptual work that supports theory—needs to be balanced by integration into practices to stand the tests of time and usefulness. *JCC* aims to be the premier journal to publish articles on corporate citizenship that accomplish this integration of theory and practice. We want the journal to be read as much by executives leading corporate citizenship as it is by academics seeking sound research and scholarship.

JCC appears quarterly and includes peer-reviewed papers by leading writers, with occasional reviews, case studies and think-pieces. A key feature is the 'Turning Points' section. Turning Points are commentaries, controversies, new ideas, essays and insights that aim to be provocative and engaging, raise the important issues of the day and provide observations on what is too new yet to be the subject of empirical and theoretical studies. *JCC* continues to produce occasional issues dedicated to a single theme. These have included 'Story Telling: Beyond the Academic Article—Using Fiction, Art and Literary Techniques to Communicate', 'Sustainable Luxury', 'Business–NGO Partnerships', 'Creating Global Citizens and Responsible Leadership', 'Responsible Investment in Emerging Markets', 'The Positive Psychology of Sustainable Enterprise', 'Textiles, Fashion and Sustainability', 'Designing Management Education', 'Managing by Design' and 'Innovative Stakeholder.

EDITORS

General Editor:

Professor Malcolm McIntosh; email: jcc@greenleaf-publishing.com

Regional Editor:

North American Editor: Sandra Waddock, Professor of Management, Boston College, Carroll School of Management, Senior Research Fellow, Center for Corporate Citizenship, Chestnut Hill, MA 02467 USA; tel: +1 617 552 0477; fax: +1 617 552 0433; email: waddock@bc.edu

Notes for Contributors

SUBMISSIONS

All content should be submitted via online submission. For more information see the journal homepage at www.greenleaf-publishing.com/jcc.

The form gives prompts for the required information and asks authors to submit the full text of the paper, including the title, author name and author affiliation, as a Word attachment. **Abstract and keywords will be completed via the online submission and are not necessary on the attachment.**

As part of the online submission authors will be asked to tick a box to state they have read and adhere to the Greenleaf–GSE Copyright Guidelines and have permission to publish the paper, including all figures, images, etc. which have been taken from other sources. It is the author's responsibility to ensure this is correct.

In order to be able to distribute papers published in Greenleaf journals, we need signed transfer of copyright from the authors. We are committed to a liberal and fair approach to copyright and accessibility, and do not restrict authors' rights to reuse their own work for personal use or in an institutional repository.

A brief autobiographical note should be supplied at the end of the paper including:

- Full name
- Affiliation
- Email address
- Full international contact details

Please supply (via online submission) an **abstract outlining the title, purpose, methodology and main findings**. It's worth considering that, as your paper will be located and read online, the quality of your abstract will determine whether readers go on to access your full paper. We recommend you place particular focus on the impact of your research on further research, practice or society. What does your paper contribute?

In addition, please provide up to **six descriptive keywords**.

Please address all new manuscripts via the online submission system to the incoming Editor for 2016-2018, David Murphy.

FORMATTING YOUR PAPER

Headings should be short and in bold text, with a clear and consistent hierarchy.

Please identify **Notes or Endnotes** with consecutive numbers, enclosed in square brackets and listed at the end of the article.

Figures and other images should be submitted as .jpeg (.jpg) or .tif files and be of a high quality. Please number consecutively with Arabic numerals and mark clearly within the body of the text where they should be placed.

If images are not the original work of the author, it is the author's responsibility to obtain written consent from the copyright holder to them being used. Authors will be asked to confirm this is the case by ticking the box on the online submission to say they have read and understood the Greenleaf–GSE copyright policy. Images which are neither the authors' own work, nor are accompanied by such permission will not be published.

Tables should be included as part of the manuscript, with relevant captions.

Supplementary data can be appended to the article, using the form and should follow the same formatting rules as the main text.

References to other publications should be complete and in Harvard style, e.g. (Jones, 2011) for one author, (Jones and Smith, 2011) for two authors and (Jones *et al.*, 2011) for more than two authors. A full reference list should appear at the end of the paper.

- For **books**: Surname, Initials (year), *Title of Book*, Publisher, Place of publication.
  e.g. Author, J. (2011), *This is my book*, Publisher, New York, NY.
- For **book chapters**: Surname, Initials (year), "Chapter title", Editor's Surname, Initials, *Title of Book*, Publisher, Place of publication, pages (if known).
- For **journals**: Surname, Initials (year), "Title of article", *Title of Journal*, volume, number, pages.
- For **conference proceedings**: Surname, Initials (year), "Title of paper", in Surname, Initials (Ed.), Title of published proceeding which may include place and date(s) held, Publisher, Place of publication, Page numbers.
- For **newspaper articles**: Surname, Initials (year) (if an author is named), "Article title", *Newspaper*, date, pages.
- For **images**:
  Where image is from a printed source—as for books but with the page number on which the image appears.
  Where image is from an online source—Surname, Initials (year), Title, Available at, Date accessed.
  Other images—Surname, Initials (year), Title, Name of owner (person or institution) and location for viewing.

▶ **To discuss ideas for contributions**, please contact the General Editor: Professor Malcolm McIntosh; email: jcc@greenleaf-publishing.com.

For Product Safety Concerns and Information please contact our EU
representative GPSR@taylorandfrancis.com Taylor & Francis Verlag GmbH,
Kaufingerstraße 24, 80331 München, Germany

Printed and bound by CPI Group (UK) Ltd, Croydon, CR0 4YY
10/05/2025
01866286-0001